BEGINNING TEACHING
WITH DIGITAL TECHNOLOGY

Sara Miller McCune founded SAGE Publishing in 1965 to support the dissemination of usable knowledge and educate a global community. SAGE publishes more than 1000 journals and over 800 new books each year, spanning a wide range of subject areas. Our growing selection of library products includes archives, data, case studies and video. SAGE remains majority owned by our founder and after her lifetime will become owned by a charitable trust that secures the company's continued independence

Los Angeles | London | New Delhi | Singapore | Washington DC | Melbourne

BEGINNING TEACHING
WITH *DIGITAL*
TECHNOLOGY

JOANNE BLANNIN

Los Angeles | London | New Delhi
Singapore | Washington DC | Melbourne

Los Angeles | London | New Delhi
Singapore | Washington DC | Melbourne

SAGE Publications Ltd
1 Oliver's Yard
55 City Road
London EC1Y 1SP

SAGE Publications Inc.
2455 Teller Road
Thousand Oaks, California 91320

SAGE Publications India Pvt Ltd
B 1/I 1 Mohan Cooperative Industrial Area
Mathura Road
New Delhi 110 044

SAGE Publications Asia-Pacific Pte Ltd
3 Church Street
#10-04 Samsung Hub
Singapore 049483

Editor: James Clark
Senior assistant editor: Diana Alves
Assistant editor, digital: Mandy Gao
Production editor: Katherine Haw
Copyeditor: Chris Bitten
Proofreader: Neil Dowden
Indexer: Martin Hargreaves
Cover design: Naomi Robinson
Typeset by: C&M Digitals (P) Ltd, Chennai, India
Printed in the UK

Library of Congress Control Number: 2021940384

British Library Cataloguing in Publication data

A catalogue record for this book is available from the British Library

ISBN 978-1-5264-8868-8
ISBN 978-1-5264-8869-5 (pbk)

At SAGE we take sustainability seriously. Most of our products are printed in the UK using responsibly sourced papers and boards. When we print overseas we ensure sustainable papers are used as measured by the PREPS grading system. We undertake an annual audit to monitor our sustainability.

CONTENTS

ABOUT THE AUTHOR

Dr Joanne Blannin has taught in four countries, in three languages and has an in-depth understanding of learning and teaching across a range of contexts. Her many education roles previously include language and bilingual teacher, curriculum leader, leading teacher, teacher trainer, Department of Education project officer and school leadership coach. In the past five years, Dr Blannin has supported more than 400 Australian schools to engage effectively with technologies for their own and their students' learning. She continues to research effective digital pedagogies and change leadership through international and national collaborations. Dr Blannin is currently Senior Lecturer in Digital Transformations at Monash University.

ACKNOWLEDGEMENTS

I owe a debt of gratitude to my academic colleagues at Monash University, in particular the members of the Digital Transformation Lab who allowed me to use the group as my personal space to test ideas. I would also like to thank my colleague and friend Dr Kerry Elliott who has maintained an interest in this project and often listened and given feedback as I expounded on some theory or another. Without their support, this book would not be possible. I am also immensely grateful to my family and friends for their ongoing encouragement and acceptance of my lack of availability as I spent evenings and weekends writing.

Additionally, my special thanks to Diana Alves – it has been a wonderful experience to work with you as my editor. Your feedback was always so very useful, thank you.

Finally, I would like to thank the many people who have helped me learn and practise the art and science of teaching with technology. Every success and failure meant I learnt more about what does and doesn't work at the classroom level. Thank you to the school leaders who, over many years, encouraged my transition to an academic career and supported me to explore, discover and understand how technology can improve teaching and learning for today's learners.

ONLINE RESOURCES

This book is supported by a range of online and downloadable resources available at:
https://study.sagepub.com/blannin

Resources include:

- Lecturer PowerPoint slides
- Selected SAGE journal articles

1

INTRODUCTION

IN WHAT WAYS HAVE YOUR USED TECHNOLOGY SO FAR TODAY?

Perhaps you watched a streaming TV show, read and replied to emails, texted friends or downloaded a new playlist. Around the world, technology continues to change how we live and work. There is hardly an industry that remains untouched by technology, from meetings based online (Hecht, 2018) to collaborative international artworks. How then are these changes represented and embedded in our classrooms and education systems?

From early childhood to high school leavers, many countries now expect teachers to provide technologically enabled learning experiences. It could be argued that until recently, technology was not used by many teachers. However, the pace of global technological change has continued to exceed predictions (Dorr, 2017) and presents an ongoing challenge to education systems to maintain currency (Schleicher, 2015).

AN EDUCATIONAL TECHNOLOGY IMPERATIVE

In 2020, the world stopped as the Covid-19 virus raced around the planet. International organisation UNESCO (2020) mapped the disruption to education following the pandemic, as those in the teaching profession felt the full impact of lockdowns and school closures (Vlies, 2020). Fifty-five countries closed down their education systems entirely.

As I write this book in the middle of 2021, we continue to experience massive interruptions to learning. 'One year into the COVID-19 pandemic, close to half the world's students are still affected by partial or full school closures, and over 100 million additional children will fall below the minimum proficiency level in reading as a result of the health crisis' (UNESCO, 2020).

The World Economic Forum further elaborates that the challenges of missing several months of schooling are minor compared to the number of children who may, for economic, social and family reasons, never return to education. They claim that 'At the peak of the global lockdowns imposed to counter the spread of COVID-19, 1.6 billion children were out of school. A staggering number, but if they all return to school as society begins to adjust to a new normal, then it's just a few months of lost learning ... Only not all of them will [return to learning]. Even before this crisis, 250 million children were already out of school, and now many more are unlikely to return' (Karboul, 2020).

As the Covid-19 crisis spread worldwide, technology became increasingly used by teachers to connect with their learners. Digital classrooms were set up, online video conferencing software was purchased, and new teaching methods were tested and embedded. Early childhood teachers were seen reading picture storybooks over video. High school teachers led 'kitchen chemistry' sessions from their homes, and primary school teachers developed creative games and virtual worlds for learning.

Teachers in today's schools are located at a point in educational history where their day-to-day actions are increasingly mediated by and through technology, regardless of whether they are quarantined at home, teaching remotely or returned to the classroom. The experiences we gained from Covid-19 can inform how we can learn and teach online and are undoubtedly a platform to grow our understanding and skills with technology.

While the pandemic forced many of those in the teaching profession to reconsider their practices (Ferdig et al., 2020), the challenges and expectations of those beginning their teaching career seem to be higher than before. As more educational technology companies experience growth in demand for their products, the pressure on teachers to learn new skills in technology and pedagogy grows (Teräs et al., 2020). This dynamic learning space asks teachers to continue to add to their pedagogical repertoire. For graduate teachers in their first years of teaching, this is a significant demand on their time and abilities. This book offers you insight into how technology can be used in the classroom. We explore several theories to help make sense of how technology can support and enhance learning. We provide examples of what technology use can look like in the classroom or early childhood centre.

Covid-19 may have provided us with opportunities to explore new technologies and conquer our fears of how and when to use digital resources or engage in student-centred learning. How we capitalise on these experiences, however, is up to us. During the pandemic lockdowns of 2020, some teachers moved their entire offline classroom to an online space without altering their approach to teaching. Other teachers re-invented themselves and their teaching practices to meet the needs of their learners. Neither of these examples should be considered either negative or positive. Every teacher has a unique perspective on their learners and an understanding of their teaching context. The role of the teacher, however, does appear to be shifting. The traditional roles of teaching, planning and administrative tasks appear to be changing to include more 'flexibility and more time for student–teacher interactions' (Barron et al., 2021). Technology is one way to support these changes. Technology can enable learners to progress at their own pace, engage in ways that meet their needs or create and make new and exciting media.

Returning to the dire predictions of lower school enrolment after the pandemic (Karboul, 2020), is there a way that increased and effective use of technology for learning might support those learners to re-engage with education? This is, of course, a complex problem and one that will not be solved in one year or one book. What we have presented here, however, are ways that research-informed technology use can enhance learning, how today's children are positioned as digitally enabled learners within an increasingly sophisticated digital society. As we reflect on the Covid-19 pandemic and education's frantic move to online learning, we need to ask, as a teacher isn't it up to me to learn, grow and develop myself? In so doing, we give our learners the best chance for a happy, successful and inclusive life. And don't those changes in practice need to start with me?

CHANGES TO OUR LEARNERS

The need for teacher practice to change to include effective technologies is one aspect of twenty-first-century learning. Another driver for change in educational technology use is the daily lives of our young people. We are now into our third decade of the twenty-first century. The typical school system begins at ages 4–7 and continues until age 18. This means every child in every school and early childhood setting in every country worldwide was born in the twenty-first century. Why is this relevant? Today's learners are different. Many, if not most, have never experienced a world without wireless Internet (remember dial-up connections?), smartphones (remember home phones used by one person at a time?) or Google (remember library index cards?). While we should avoid dividing learners by age group, as many of us fall outside this binary description of users or non-users of technology, there are drivers inherent in the world in which today's learners are growing up.

For today's students, the world we grew up in, 10, 20 or 30 years ago, is now largely unrecognisable (Project Tomorrow, 2013). We might speak of our schooling and describe practices that are wholly unfamiliar such as wheeling the television into the classroom, heading to the computer lab to practise calculating basic maths sums or having to beg a parent for a lift to the library at the weekend.

This presents a growing challenge for teachers. As technology frames so much of our daily lives and our students' lives, education needs teachers prepared to engage effectively with digital technologies (Care and Griffin, 2017). The alternative is worrying: a future where teachers do not see technology as part of teaching may see nations with underprepared and disadvantaged citizens entering the workforce in the next 10 to 20 years.

Despite the rapid pace of change, we encourage you to note the pedagogical strategies proposed in this book as one way to respond to ever-changing devices and software. Despite new devices and software, teachers are increasingly crucial for learning as students enter digital adulthood. We will not be replaced by online courses or social robots anytime soon. We cannot, however, afford to rest on our laurels. We can no longer teach today's learners in the same way that we were taught. Society, both locally and globally, has changed too much to repeat the past. As Dewey (1994, p. 167) presciently noted, decades before the technology boom of this century, 'If we teach today as we taught yesterday, we rob our children of tomorrow'.

USING THIS BOOK

This book offers you the opportunity to explore how technology can be used in your classroom to support your students' learning. Each chapter can be read alone or in sequence and you are welcome to engage with the chapters you find most relevant and return to others at a later date. To enable you to engage more easily with the text, this next section offers you an overview of each chapter.

The first five chapters provide you with a theoretical underpinning of educational technology. We explore what we mean by effective technology use (Chapter 2), then consider the lives of our students in today's technology-enabled world (Chapter 3). As teachers we need to make informed decisions about whether a technology device or resource has the potential to enhance students' learning. We explore how to make these decisions in Chapter 4.

In Chapter 5, we delve into theoretical understandings of technology use, asking questions such as where knowledge exists in a digitally enabled classroom. We then consider Papert's (1980) theory of constructionism as a way for learners to explore abstract concepts in a digital space. This exploration of theory can inform your understanding of how and why we use technology as a tool for learning.

Chapters 6 to 9 focus on technology use in certain learning areas: literacy, mathematics, STEM and the arts. These chapters provide you with ideas, concepts and practical examples of technology use. Each chapter begins with a scenario from a classroom and presents common challenges faced by teachers. Reading through the chapter you will learn how to address these potential problems, explore key theories and concepts, and review examples of practice in early childhood, primary and secondary classrooms. Each chapter concludes with a return to the initial scenario to resolve those initial challenges.

In Chapter 10, you will learn what we mean by 'coding in the classroom'. We study types of computer coding and their application in learning and ask you to consider whether your planned lessons are asking students to learn to code, or code to learn.

Chapter 11 investigates a growing phenomenon in today's schools: bring-your-own-device programmes. Faced with a classroom full of technology devices we ask, what do you need to know, learn and consider? You will reflect on how we can ensure equitable learning experiences for every child and how you can support a bring-your-own-device programme at your school.

To conclude the book, we complete our exploration of technology for today's learner with a discussion of how you, as a teacher, can lead change and improve learning. Finally, we present a futuristic scenario of a classroom in 2040. Here you will learn about the possible future of technology and what changes you might anticipate during your career. Every technology in this scenario is currently available for use and, as we conclude this book, we ask you to consider what new technologies might emerge during your teaching career. No matter what new technology is developed, this book seeks to offer you theoretical and decision-making resources to enable you to teach today's and tomorrow's learners in ways that inspire and engage them.

REFERENCES

Barron, M., Cobo, C., Munoz-Najar, A. & Ciarrusta, I. S. (2021). *The Changing Role of Teachers and Technologies amidst the COVID 19 Pandemic: Key Findings from a Cross-country Study*. Retrieved from https://blogs.worldbank.org/education/changing-role-teachers-and-technologies-amidst-covid-19-pandemic-key-findings-cross (accessed 30 June 2021).

Care, E. & Griffin, P. (2017). Assessment of collaborative problem-solving processes. In B. Csapó and J. Funke (eds), *The Nature of Problem Solving. Using Research to Inspire 21st Century Learning* (pp. 227–243). Paris: OECD.

Dewey, J. (1994). *Democracy and Education*. New York: Macmillan Company.

Dorr, A. (2017). Common errors in reasoning about the future: Three informal fallacies. *Technological Forecasting and Social Change, 116*, 322–330.

Ferdig, R. E., Baumgartner, E., Hartshorne, R., Kaplan-Rakowski, R. & Mouza, C. (2020). Teaching, technology, and teacher education during the COVID-19 pandemic: Stories from the field. Association for the Advancement of Computing in Education. Retrieved from www.learntechlib.org/p/216903/ (accessed 30 June 2021).

Hecht, J. (2018). How technology is driving change in almost every major industry. *Forbes*, 30 November. Retrieved from www.forbes.com/sites/jaredhecht/2018/11/30/how-technology-is-driving-change-in-almost-every-major-industry/ (accessed 30 June 2021).

Karboul, A. (2020). COVID-19 put 1.6 billion children out of school. Here's how to upgrade education post-pandemic. *World Economic Forum*, 4 December. Retrieved from www.weforum.org/agenda/2020/12/covid19-education-innovation-outcomes/ (accessed 30 June 2021).

Papert, S. (1980). *Mindstorms: Children, Computers, and Powerful Ideas*. New York: Basic Books.

Project Tomorrow (2013). *2013 Trends in Online Learning: Virtual, Blended and Flipped Classrooms*. Retrieved from https://tomorrow.org/speakup/2013_OnlineLearningReport.html (accessed 30 June 2021).

Schleicher, A. (2015). *Education in an Uncertain World*. Retrieved from www.project-syndicate.org/commentary/education-technological-skills-more-important-by-andreas-schleicher-2015-12 (accessed 10 November 2016).

Teräs, M., Suoranta, J., Teräs, H. & Curcher, M. (2020). Post-Covid-19 education and education technology 'solutionism': A seller's market. *Postdigital Science and Education, 2*(3), 863–878.

UNESCO (2020). *Education: From Disruption to Recovery*. Global Education Coalition, UNESCO, 4 March. Retrieved from https://en.unesco.org/covid19/educationresponse (accessed 30 June 2021).

Vlies, P. (2020, July 12). How teaching online during COVID-19 lockdown made me think deeply about how physical presence matters. *EduResearch Matters*, 13 July. Retrieved from www.aare.edu.au/blog/?p=6919 (accessed 30 June 2021).

2

WHAT IS EFFECTIVE TECHNOLOGY USE FOR LEARNING?

IN THIS CHAPTER YOU WILL LEARN:

- How technology's use can be categorised
- Frameworks for understanding technology use
- Strategies for making decisions about your technology use
- Why not all technology use in classrooms is effective technology use.

INTRODUCTION

Teachers in today's schools are located at a point in educational history where their day-to-day actions are increasingly mediated by and through technology. Using technology has become the norm for interacting, playing, shopping and buying. Consider the last time you bought anything substantial, either in a brick-and-mortar shop or online. Many of us now use the Internet to research the item, find the best price and compare models and makes. The simple act of buying a new refrigerator is now facilitated in the online world, even if we end up in a physical store to make the final purchase.

In many medical and scientific fields technology has also revolutionised the ways that data are gathered and understood. We now know more about cancer, climate change and global health, for example, than ever before, primarily because of the advances in computers and computing power. As technology becomes smarter, smaller and faster, we can do more, connect more and learn more. However, what about technology in the classroom? This is a crucial question for teachers in today's schools: Is technology helping our students learn, and our teachers teach?

The first, and foundational, premise for this book is that technology, in and of itself, cannot help us learn or teach. The teacher must remain integral to learning in school classrooms, and the teacher's role in student learning should not be diminished nor discounted as classroom technology resources increase. We must remember that technology is inanimate, and has been created, programmed, designed and marketed to us by other humans. While some of these processes may be replaced by technology in the future, human interaction will continue to be necessary to make critical decisions about what is imagined, designed and ultimately built in the world of technology.

One example of the limitations of technology can be seen in the field of artificial intelligence (AI). AI is booming in industry and higher education, but we are yet to envisage a future where computers replace teachers entirely. Indeed, a future of robot-led classrooms may never be possible or desirable simply because humans can be seen to require social interactions with other humans in order to learn (read more here: https://eric.ed.gov/?id=EJ570956).

Despite the best efforts of engineers and programmers around the world, we have yet to see a robot or computer program that can effectively analyse, plan, implement or evaluate learning for each student in your classroom. Created in Japan, Pepper is an example of AI that is beginning to push the boundaries of what is possible for human/robot interactions. Pepper is a humanoid-shaped robot that stands at 1.2 metres. Pepper has been programmed to read your facial expressions and to respond appropriately to your mood (read about Pepper here: www.softbankrobotics.com/emea/en/pepper). While undoubtedly impressive and indicative of the significant advances being made, Pepper is not, however, a replacement for a professionally trained teacher. Pepper cannot notice Sami in the corner of the classroom and note that today is Friday and she will be collected by her grandma after school, while her mum is at work overnight. Pepper will not be able to understand that Sami's sullenness is linked to the recent break-up of her family unit or the death of a beloved pet. As teachers, we know that these emotional needs impact strongly on how and when a student is ready to learn. So, be reassured that the complexities and nuances of learning and teaching will not soon be replaced by AI or robots. If the technology to do this does emerge in the future, the skills, knowledge and understanding of effective teachers will remain vital for learning.

To make judgments about the technology we use in our classrooms, we must first understand our students and their learning needs. Some technology use might not be useful for a particular student at a particular time and more traditional, pen-and-paper activities might better support the learning of a new concept.

IN THE CLASSROOM TODAY

Consider a group of Year 8 (14-year-old) students in a high school mathematics classroom. The focus for the week is understanding the connection between fractional numbers and decimal numbers. The teacher moves around the room noticing the answers that students are providing to three questions that she has set. These will help her plan for the next steps. The teacher sees that a group of four students are struggling with basic fraction concepts. The teacher considers that she could send them to a website that offers multiple, self-correcting questions that would enable them to rehearse the fraction concepts many times.

However, she notes that these students seem to be missing some critical conceptual knowledge about the connection between fractions and decimals. The teacher has considered the technological options, but her professional understanding of *how* this concept can best be learned informs her decision. She pulls out a box of plastic blocks and connects ten together. Working with the students she first models, then supports, them to identify that 0.2 is the same as 2 out of the ten blocks: 2/10 and 0.2 represent the same amount of the whole set of blocks. In this case, the physical handling of materials helps the students to make conceptual connections which can then be built upon using technology. In the next lesson, the teacher plans to have these same students work on the fraction website, using the physical blocks at the same time.

This short snapshot of a classroom helps us understand that not all technology use is effective technology use. The teacher must bring their professional knowledge and understanding to the learning experience and make informed decisions about when and how technology will be effective. Later in this chapter, we will explore several frameworks that can help you as you use technology in the classroom.

WHAT DO WE KNOW ABOUT THE EDUCATIONAL USE OF TECHNOLOGY?

It would be hard to deny that technology has changed the way that we work and live. In education, however, we have not yet seen a similarly significant shift towards technology-enabled learning and teaching. There is ongoing concern that students are not yet learning about or accessing the digital resources and tools that may improve their learning and their workforce readiness (Regional Australia Institute, 2016). The most recent Australian National Assessment Program for Information and Communication Technology Literacy (ICT Literacy) demonstrated that Australian students' digital literacy had, 'decreased … significantly by 22 scale points between 2011 and 2014' (Australian Curriculum, Assessment and Reporting Authority, 2015, p. xxii).

Of concern is that these national results are regressing despite numerous injections of funds and resources into Australian schools. Two major Australian government initiatives were the Digital Education Revolution (DER) (Digital Education Advisory Group, 2013) that saw all Australian 15-year-old students receive a laptop and the Building Education Revolution (BER) (Australian National Audit Office, 2011) that provided new buildings and Internet connectivity to schools in a $16.2 billion project across the country. The BER and DER projects focused on devices and infrastructure, not on teachers or pedagogical strategies. Perhaps this is the reason why teachers' practices and students' learning experiences have not significantly changed in the years following these large financial investments (Crook et al., 2013). In addition, some educational researchers continue to question whether teaching and learning have improved with the introduction of technology into schools (Crook et al., 2013; Lee et al., 2011).

We do know, however, that some technology is more effective than others for improving learning outcomes. One area that has been more intensively researched is the field of technology sometimes called 'Web 2.0' or 'interactive technologies'. These technologies have been defined in a number of ways (Allen, 2009; Kamel Boulos & Wheeler, 2007; Murugesan, 2007); however, the definitions have similar meanings. The commonality appears to be the concepts of:

Collaboration

Creativity

Communication

What can be considered lower-level use of technology, such as creating a digital presentation or using email, does not have a research base to confirm a positive impact on student outcomes. Interactive technologies, such as blogging, virtual reality, augmented reality, voice recognition, AI, co-created online resources or real-time, multi-media communications, do, however, have an emerging research base that suggests a positive impact on student learning (Ang and Wang, 2006; Doherty, 2011; Gregory and Lloyd, 2010; Passey et al., 2004; Selwyn and OECD, 2010; Zylka et al., 2015). It is these interactive technologies that this book explores and promotes.

Making decisions based on evidence, rather than on your personal preferences or school-wide resources, is a core principle in understanding how technology might impact on your students' learning. Hattie (2009) has famously explored the use of evidence to make decisions about the way in which we teach and evaluate our students. Underpinning his well-known text *Visible Learning for Teachers* (Hattie, 2009) is the understanding that expert teachers do not have a set approach to teaching. Rather, they use a range of strategies in the classroom to understand what their students know and are ready to learn. Using this information, expert teachers then make informed choices. Both the evidence of their students' knowledge and their knowledge of effective teaching strategies are used to plan for learning in the classroom. When thinking about using technology for learning and teaching, we need to apply the same level of rigour as we would to any other decision we make about student learning. We need to ask questions, consider alternatives and be flexible based on what our students need to learn effectively, whether that is online or offline.

Research continues into the use of technologies for learning. However, we should note that research findings also continue to confirm that interactive technologies, like those listed above, are shown to have a more positive impact on student outcomes than basic skills such as emailing, word processing or designing PowerPoint presentations.

SOCIAL CHANGES

In Australia, we have seen exponential growth in the personal use of digital technologies (Australian Bureau of Statistics, 2011). It is now reported that Australia's relatively small population has embraced wireless Internet and mobile technologies, with 86 per cent of Australians using the Internet in their homes.

These statistics also give us insight into how technology is used outside of school. The 2014–2015 *Household Use of Information Technology* tells us that, on average, each Australian household has six Internet devices; this number increases to seven devices if there are children under 15 living in the home (Australian Bureau of Statistics, 2016). The younger the children in the home, the more devices they will have. These statistics are important to us as teachers. As our students continue to engage with technology at increasingly younger ages and across a growing range of devices, we need to better understand the impact of these out-of-school experiences on students' desires to learn at school.

Before we begin to consider what this means for us, in our schools and educational setting, we will pause a moment to consider this quote, written in 2001 by a futurist about the rate of development of technology:

> We will not experience 100 years of progress in the 21st century – it will be more like 20,000 years of progress (at today's rate). (Kurzweil, 2001, as quoted on The Artificial Intelligence Channel, 2017)

As we approach the third decade of the twenty-first century, this quote suggests that we have already experienced, in the first 20 years of this century, the amount of technological change that our ancestors experienced in 1000 years. To put this into context, the entirety of the technological change that Britain experienced from the invasion of the Roman Empire in 43 CE to the Norman Conquest in 1066 CE has been experienced in 20 years of our lives – and it continues to change exponentially.

Kurzweil's predictions are considered highly accurate, based on past predictions, 'In fact, of the 147 predictions that Kurzweil has made since the 1990s, fully 115 of them have turned out to be correct, and another 12 have turned out to be "essentially correct" (off by a year or two), giving his predictions a stunning 86% accuracy rate' (Basulto, 2012).

Before moving away from these startling facts, however, consider for a moment that the above Kurzweil quote was written in 2001. This means it was written before the existence of:

- Smartphones (or even camera phones)
- Tablet computers
- Shared online software
- Personal GPS systems
- Social media: YouTube, Facebook, Twitter, Instagram
- Digital book readers (such as Kindle)
- Bitcoin
- BitTorrent
- Personal gaming consoles (such as Xbox and Nintendo)
- 3D printing
- Virtual/augmented reality
- Coding in schools
- Consumer accessible facial and fingerprint recognition
- 360-degree cameras and movies

Kurzweil may not be 100 per cent accurate in his predictions, but considering the items on the list above, most of us could identify massive changes to our daily lives in the past 20 years. With this 2001 prediction in mind, how might the world change again in the next 20 years? What will society and education look like with another 1000 years of technological progress?

Many of our students will spend a large part of the next decades in our classrooms. As you consider how to use technology in the classroom, keep in mind that your students remain the focus of your work as a teacher, despite the changes in the world around you. You will need to become a lifelong learner, bringing your professional knowledge and experience to the classroom as technology evolves, grows and makes it possible to learn in ways that are not even dreamt of yet.

MAKING DECISIONS ABOUT TECHNOLOGY USE

In 2018, every minute on the Internet represents 4.3 million videos viewed on YouTube, 3.7 million searches on Google and 18 million text messages sent (Desjardins, 2018). Each of these activities represents humans interacting with technology and with other humans. With such a large amount of information shared in the online world, it is easy to feel overwhelmed. When we reflect on how we might use that information for teaching and learning, the task becomes more complicated. We must ask ourselves:

- How do we know what technology resources or tools are reliable, safe and effective for my students in my educational setting?
- How do I make sense of what each technology resource or tool is offering?

To answer these questions we can consider several frameworks that help unpack the technology, its potential uses and our professional knowledge as teachers. In the following sections, we will explore three frameworks that have been shown to be particularly useful. They are called the TPCK model (Mishra and Koehler, 2006), Bloom's Digital Taxonomy (Krathwohl et al., 2001) and the Social Constructivist Digital Literacy framework (Reynolds, 2016).

TPCK

The Technological, Pedagogical and Content Knowledge (TPCK) framework was developed relatively recently in 2006 by two researchers seeking to acknowledge the specific types of knowledge a teacher needs to be effective in today's technology-enabled world (Mishra and Koehler, 2006). To understand the purpose and usefulness of the TPCK model, we need to briefly explore the history of the original model, developed two decades earlier (Gudmundsdottir and Shulman, 1987). This model was called the Pedagogical Content Knowledge (PCK) framework.

Gudmundsdottir and Shulman (1987, p. 69) wrote about the specific types of knowledge that teachers needed to become 'master teachers'. Their work described an overlap between pedagogical knowledge and content knowledge that they called Pedagogical Content Knowledge (PCK). PCK built on Shulman's previous writing (1981) that identified, and separated, the types of learning and skills a person needs to become an effective teacher. He argued that content knowledge was, of course, necessary for a person to be an effective teacher, but that the ability to *apply pedagogical knowledge* to content distinguished teachers from non-teachers.

Using Gudmundsdottir and Shulman's (1987) reasoning, an architect may be considered an expert in the field of architecture. A *teacher* of architecture, however, must be an expert in both pedagogy and architecture. This, Shulman argues, is what separates teachers from content experts. He called this Pedagogical Content Knowledge (PCK):

> We demonstrate that the important difference between the novice and the expert is manifested in a special kind of knowledge that is neither content nor pedagogy per se. It rests instead in pedagogical content knowledge, a form of teacher understanding that combines content, pedagogy and learner characteristics in a unique way. (Gudmundsdottir and Shulman, 1987, p. 59)

The PCK model showed that teachers need both pedagogical knowledge and content knowledge that are brought to gather in a new type of knowledge.

PCK describes how a teacher's understanding of subject matter is transformed to make it 'teachable'. It is this way of knowing and understanding the subject matter that distinguishes the teacher from the subject-matter specialist (Shulman, 1987, p. 60). In the 1990s and into the 2000s, technology increasingly became seen as a potential learning and teaching tool, and teachers and researchers identified another type of knowledge that was necessary for effective, contemporary teaching.

Following the increase in technology in schools, Mishra and Koehler (2006) reviewed the concepts laid out by Shulman and Gudmundsdottir and argued for the addition of Technological Knowledge to the PCK framework. This has become known as Technological, Pedagogical and Content Knowledge (TPCK, sometimes referred to as TPACK) model.

Mishra and Koehler (2006) saw a challenge with the use of technology in the classroom, namely that Shulman's PCK model did not acknowledge the changes in pedagogy and content knowledge that technology use required. Teachers, they argued, required more than knowledge of the capabilities of technology: 'Part of the problem, we argue, has been a tendency to only look at the technology and not how it is used' (Mishra and Koehler, 2006, p. 1018). The TPCK model was seen as a tool to make sense of how teachers were engaging with technology.

In developing the TPCK model, Mishra and Koehler (2006) also sought to address the needs of teachers in the classroom: 'Having a framework goes beyond merely identifying problems with current approaches; it offers new ways of looking at and perceiving phenomena and offers information on which to base sound, pragmatic decision making' (Mishra and Koehler, 2006, p. 1019). As we discussed previously in this chapter, using evidence to make decisions about our teaching is crucial to effective learning for our students, and our use of technology in the classroom. TPCK seeks to provide a framework through which we can make sense of our technology use in the classroom.

Of importance in this diagram are the overlapping types of knowledge that TPCK represents. These are:

- Pedagogical Content Knowledge (PCK)
- Technological Content Knowledge (TCK)
- Technological Pedagogical Knowledge (TPK).

As in the PCK model presented by Gudmundsdottir and Shulman (1987), this redesigned model presents some specific types of knowledge that a teacher requires to engage effectively with technology for learning.

TPCK (Mishra and Koehler, 2006) sought to support teachers and leaders to understand the complex nature of using digital technologies in teaching and learning. The TPCK model presents the perceived intersections between three types of knowledge: pedagogical (how to teach), technological (how to use technology) and content (about the topic).

The original TPCK diagram represented an equal balance between these three key aspects of the model. Each circle in the Venn diagram is the same size and overlaps equally with the others. Mishra and Koehler (2006) did not offer the TPCK model as a full and all-encompassing theoretical framework for teachers. They acknowledged that one model could not provide teachers with everything they need:

> We are sensitive to the fact that in a complex, multifaceted, and ill-structured domain such as integration of technology in education, no single framework tells the 'complete story'; no single framework can provide all the answers. The TPCK framework is no exception. However, we do believe that any framework, however impoverished, is better than no framework at all. (Mishra and Koehler, 2006, p. 1047)

In acknowledging the complexity of teachers' uses of technology, Mishra and Koehler shared their belief that the contextual factors surrounding their research are significant yet challenging. Teachers, it is claimed, must:

> integrate knowledge of student thinking and learning, knowledge of the subject matter, and increasingly, knowledge of technology. At the intersection of pedagogy, content, and technology, is the very specialised brand of teacher knowledge represented by TPCK. (Mishra et al., 2010, p. 24)

This model of technology integration might be useful for some teachers in some settings, and our setting will impact on how we choose, interact with and evaluate technology. As Beeson et al. (2014, p. 119) have explained, the 'teacher's role is crucial' for classroom technology use, and yet the teacher is not included in the TPCK model. While this is a challenge, the TPCK model can offer us a way of reflecting on our teaching that can help us make informed, effective choices with technology.

Using TPCK to evaluate our learning requires experience in identifying the types of knowledge that are used to make decisions. In Chapter 4, we will delve deeper into this and explore how TPCK can support our work.

Before we can make use of TPCK for our learning, we need to ensure we fully understand the TPCK model. To do this, you will next read two short snapshots of technology use in a classroom and answer several questions. It is worth noting that these brief classroom snapshots are not necessarily examples of excellent, effective teaching with technology. Instead, they offer you the opportunity to reflect further with the TPCK model.

IN THE PRIMARY CLASSROOM

In Year 2, Rami is learning about story writing. Everyone in the class has to write a short story, based on a photo that the teacher has provided them. Rami's picture shows a man standing at a window looking out to a snow-covered mountain. By his side is a large fluffy dog who is also staring out the window. The weather outside looks cold and windy, and there is snow on the windowsill. It is a beautiful picture, but Rami is confused – he has never seen snow! What does it feel like, what might the man or dog want to do outside in the snow?

Rami's teacher, David, comes over and they sit together at the classroom computer. Rami asks questions, and David types them into a search engine. A list of websites appears, and

Rami chooses one with the word 'snow' in the title. David says, 'Ok, read that and you'll be fine', and moves away to help another student.

1. What do you think about David's *Technological Pedagogical Knowledge* in this snapshot?
2. How has David connected *pedagogy and content* and *technology and content*?
3. How might David improve his *TPCK* to support Rami further?

IN THE SECONDARY CLASSROOM

Jaylin is working in a Year 7 media studies classroom. Today, Jan, the teacher, is helping the students identify design elements in three logos from well-known fast-food restaurants. The students are working in small groups and have been given printed copies of the logos. They need to cut the logos up and categorise the design elements from the three logos. Finally, they must photograph their categories and write a blog post about their work on the class blog. Jan explains that the blog post must include their images, clear descriptions and justifications for their categories. They also need to identify one question they still have that their classmates may be able to answer.

1. *What kind of knowledge* do you think Jan is using when she asks the students to make categories of the design elements?
2. What *knowledge is Jan drawing on* by asking students to write questions online in a blog format?
3. How has Jan connected *technology and content knowledge* in this activity?

BLOOM'S DIGITAL TAXONOMY

A second framework, or model, that you might already be familiar with is Bloom's Taxonomy (Bloom, 1956). This taxonomy was created in the 1950s and sought to represent the hierarchical nature of knowledge acquisition through six, levelled, cognitive domains. Each domain builds upon the previous and represents increasing levels of abstraction through a cumulative learning pathway. This means that a student demonstrating a higher-level domain must also have already accumulated knowledge and understanding of the lower domains.

Following is a brief explanation of each of the six levels in the taxonomy. The language below reflects revisions to the original taxonomy, made in 2001 by Krathwohl et al. (2001).

Remembering

You can be seen to have achieved this domain when you can draw on your memory to recite facts or provide a definition of something. In remembering something, you can repeat learned facts or information.

Understanding

Building on your remembered knowledge (remembering), you next take what you remember and use that knowledge to make a summary of the facts. Achieving in this domain means we can take what we remember and explain it to someone else.

Applying

Once you can explain knowledge to another person (understanding), this next domain sees you use this knowledge to share it in a new way. This might be through a presentation or an artwork. You might show or exhibit your understanding in a way that makes sense to you and other observers.

Analysing

Having applied your knowledge and made a representation of it (applying), this next domain leads you to develop a deeper understanding of the knowledge. You will pull apart your knowledge or understanding and make sense of the connections between parts of the whole. You might analyse, compare or organise your knowledge in ways that express complexity.

Evaluating

With a deeper understanding of how the information has been drawn together, you next begin to consider the way that knowledge is organised and relates to each other (analysing). You use this to make judgments about the knowledge itself. You are more critical of what you have learned and seek to check facts and explanations against other works or a set of criteria. You hypothesise about what you have learned and make decisions about its quality.

Creating

At the highest level of Bloom's taxonomy is the ability to create new information in new forms. This might include re-analysing what you have learned to create a new structure that represents key points in new ways or with new connections, inventing a new way of presenting it or designing or creating new meaning.

MAKING LEARNING DIGITAL

With an awareness of the growing role of technology in today's digital world, this taxonomy has been refined numerous times to reflect the digital resources, tools and thinking strategies that our curriculum and students now use.

The original publisher of this digital version of Bloom's Taxonomy is Andrew Churches (2008). There are several variations of this that you can find through an Internet search. You will note that the original stages or levels of Bloom's Taxonomy remain. The difference is in the verbs used to describe the actions a learner might take at each level. These now refer to online, digital activities.

Some of these verbs remain the same (designing, checking, comparing) and others have been added to reflect similar activities in the digital domain (animating, moderating, mashing).

The following is a useful rationale to understand the development of Churches' digital version of Bloom's work:

> This is an update to Bloom's Revised Taxonomy which attempts to account for the new behaviours and actions emerging as technology advances and becomes more ubiquitous. Bloom's Revised Taxonomy describes many traditional classroom practices, behaviours and actions, but does not account for the new processes and actions associated with Web 2.0 technologies, infowhelm (the exponential growth in information), increasing ubiquitous personal technologies or cloud computing or Web 3.0 Collective & ubiquitous intelligence. (Churches, 2008, p. 2)

Bloom's Digital Taxonomy does not focus on digital tools or technologies; rather it is concerned with how the six domains support student learning. Churches recommends that learning rubrics are designed when using Bloom's Digital Taxonomy: 'Like the previous taxonomies, it is the quality of the action or process that defines the cognitive level, rather than the action or process alone' (Churches, 2008, p. 2).

A rubric provides levels of sophistication within a specific area of the Taxonomy. For example, if a student is annotating a resource for future use, we might consider that the student is working in the 'Understanding' domain of the Digital Taxonomy. You can find examples of this type of rubric in Churches' (2008) work. Rubrics, then, are used within Bloom's Digital Taxonomy to measure the competence and quality of the students' learning.

Bloom's Digital Taxonomy lends itself to problem- and project-based learning design where our students work through an entire development process and then evaluate their work. While individual learning experiences may offer small insights into students' cognitive levels and successful learning, planning units of work that thread the Digital Taxonomy through a learning sequence will provide more opportunities for students to learn and demonstrate their skills and knowledge.

IN THE PRIMARY CLASSROOM

Gabi is a teacher in a foundation classroom of 5-year-olds. Today the class is completing a unit of work in mathematics. The students are using iPad cameras to take photos of shapes around the school. When they return to the classroom, they work in pairs to categorise the shapes they found into a collage using a photo app on their iPad. Gabi observes each pair and is making notes on the type of learning that is occurring for each child. Gabi realises this is only a snapshot of the students' work and plans to observe them over several days to develop more detailed notes. Gabi moves to watch Tai. Tai is working with a friend, and they have collected 17 photos. Tai notices that lots of the photos contain rectangles. He uses the correct language to describe what he sees: 'there are four sides and four corners, so it's like a square only it's a bit longer, so that's a rectangle'. Tai's partner seems confused and says, 'but it doesn't look like that picture … ', pointing to the shape poster on the wall. Tai tries again: 'But this photo of our window has four sides and four corners [*counting them out*] and this door has the same, so they are both rectangles.'. Tai's partner is still confused so Tai tries one more time: 'So this photo of the frisbee, see, it doesn't have any corners at all [*tracing his finger around the circle*], so it's a circle I think … but it's definitely not a rectangle. Let's put all the circles together and then see what's left over …'. The pair start searching for more circles in their photos; Tai's partner keeps looking up at the poster of shapes on the wall.

1. What should Gabi write in her notes about Tai's understanding of shapes?
2. Which skills from Bloom's Digital Taxonomy do you think Tai has demonstrated here?
3. Which skills has Tai's partner demonstrated?
4. What skills might Tai's partner need to be supported to learn next? How can the Digital Taxonomy help?

IN THE SECONDARY CLASSROOM

In chemistry class, Anh is working on a blog post about her findings from an online simulation. In Year 11, Anh knows that she is expected to make informed judgments about her work and wants to do well. Her teacher, Yoshi, explains that the blog post needs to share the question they were trying to answer, the simulation they used and their explanation of what they found. Once they share their blog post, they will need to answer questions from their peers.

Anh clicks 'post' and her work goes live on the class blog. Two of her classmates have already finished their posts, so she opens one of them up and reads it, twice. Anh notices that her classmate has shared the simulation she used, but it does not make sense with what they have written. The simulation shows different data to their explanation. Anh copies the data into a simulation on her computer and reruns it. Same result. How did her classmate get that answer? She runs it one more time. Same again. Finally, Anh asks her classmate to send her the raw input data to check her work. Running the simulation a final time, Anh finds the answer! There is a typo in the initial data. Her classmate knew what she wanted to find out so just wrote about it without checking the actual data, so her findings are right, but the data in the simulation is wrong. Anh takes screenshots of the accurate simulation and writes up the error she found. She posts it as a comment on her classmate's post. Then she heads to her post to answer the four questions she now has about her simulation and findings.

1. When Yoshi reads Anh's comments on her classmate's post, what skills from Bloom's Digital Taxonomy might she identify?
2. What about Ahn's classmate? What skills has she demonstrated?

3. Consider the planning that Yoshi, as the teacher, has done for this lesson. Has it offered the students the opportunity to express their learning within the six domains of Bloom's Digital Taxonomy?

4. If yes, explain how. If no, what might Yoshi do next lesson to improve this?

SOCIAL CONSTRUCTIVIST DIGITAL LITERACY

A relatively new way to make sense of technology use has been framed around the digital literacy skills of learners. As teachers, we are, of course, already concerned with several literacies including language and mathematics.

Digital literacy (DL), however, is harder to conceptualise and define, although many have tried (Livingstone and Helsper, 2007; Jenkins, 2009). An often-used definition that suits our purposes here is provided by Martin et al. (2008):

> DL is the awareness, attitude and ability of individuals to appropriately use digital tools and facilities to identify, access, manage, integrate, evaluate, analyse and synthesize digital resources, construct new knowledge, create media expressions, and communicate with others, in the context of specific life situations, in order to enable constructive social action, and to reflect upon this process. (Martin et al., 2008, pp. 166–167)

Digital literacy, then, is the ability to make informed choices and use technology effectively to meet your learning needs and solve problems. You might notice that the verbs used in the above quote have similarities to those used in Bloom's Digital Taxonomy (Churches, 2008). They suggest a hierarchy of digital technology capabilities (literacies) from 'identify' to 'synthesise' across a range of digital resources such as multi-media and communication tools.

Digital literacy, or fluency, is increasingly a skill that teachers are required to teach. In Australia, a curriculum domain called 'Digital Technologies' focuses on skills for student technology use, and a further interdisciplinary stream, called Information and Communications Technologies (ICT), is embedded across all curriculum areas and stages of learning, from ages 5 to 16 (Education Services Australia, 2016). These two curriculum demands place the teacher at the centre of digital literacy development; students are required to have both specific skills in the technology itself and the use of technology as a learning tool. These are two different outcomes that teachers will need to teach, and students need to learn.

Traditionally, computer science teachers have taught technology skills only to those students who sought to work in the field of technology. An increasing number of today's industries require a deep understanding of technology skills and concepts. While some schools continue to offer specialised 'Digital Technologies' courses in secondary schools, all students are now expected to meet DT curriculum outcomes from ages 5 to 16.

An example of the shift from teaching technology skills as a specialisation to teaching more general technology competencies is seen in the role of a traditional computer science teacher, who teaches students how to code simple programs using a specific coding language. Compare this to a humanities teacher who teaches students to code so that they can create visualisations of the data they collected during a geography field trip. The first teacher sees the coding itself as a learning outcome; the second teacher positions coding as a skill that enhances her students' learning of geography concepts.

The challenge in today's schools is understanding the levels of digital literacy and technology skills that our students bring with them to school and what we as teachers should develop to meet these changing curriculum demands.

To address this ongoing challenge, we can use the Social Constructivist Digital Literacy (SCDL) framework. This model draws on a social constructivist theory developed from Vygotsky's and Bruner's work from the 1970s. It is beyond the scope of this book to present an in-depth analysis of constructivist or social constructivist learning theories. Therefore, a brief overview follows and, should you wish to delve deeper, you will find suggested readings on this topic listed at the end of this chapter.

SOCIAL CONSTRUCTIVISM

This theory of learning positions the individual as having interactions with the world around them and then using these interactions to make meaning and learn new knowledge. It 'emphasises the importance of culture and context in understanding what occurs in society and constructs knowledge based on this understanding' (Kim et al., 2012).

A social constructivist perspective sees learning as a social action, enacted between individuals, within their context. An individual develops a personal meaning from their interactions with others, but knowledge is initially developed between humans and their environments.

An example of social constructivism in the online world is the use of blogging in classrooms. As you write a blog post, you are presenting your understanding of a topic or concept. As your peers respond to your post, they may agree, critique or present other examples. From this new information, the group must together make sense of what this means as a whole. The next time you post to the blog, the responders may be different, bringing different perspectives and understandings. Your understanding of the concept may further change as you interact and socially construct new knowledge with this new team.

Social constructivists see knowledge as a human product that is influenced and changed by the people and environment around them. Learning is active, co-created and does not exist until humans work together to create it.

AN OVERVIEW OF SOCIAL CONSTRUCTIVIST DIGITAL LITERACY FRAMEWORK

Reynolds' (2016) framework builds on Reynolds and Caperton's (2009) work that highlights digital literacy skills that students were demonstrating in schools. Reynolds' 2016 study sought to compare students' use of technology at home and in school. In better understanding the skills students demonstrated when using technology, Reynolds hoped to have a clearer sense of their digital literacy abilities. To achieve this Reynolds developed six 'practice domains'. These domains frame the learning practices that students demonstrated, and offered a perspective of learning that takes into account the way that students are using technology to learn outside of the classroom.

This framework is developed from a single research project that is relatively new (Reynolds, 2016). It, therefore, offers suggested avenues for future research, rather than definitive answers. However, the framework in itself is useful for teachers in the classroom. The framework reinforces the socially constructed nature of student learning through digital technologies. Indeed, Reynolds claims her study 'posits that learners build knowledge socially through dialogue and interaction' (Reynolds, 2016, p. 741). Reynolds also claims this framework is more useful than previous ways of measuring or categorising digital literacies, as it does not list specific tools, websites or skills. It is therefore presented as less quickly outdated (Reynolds, 2016, p. 757). To understand this claim, we need to explore the framework itself.

THE SOCIAL CONSTRUCTIVIST DIGITAL LITERACY FRAMEWORK

Six practice domains explain different student actions with digital technologies. It is important to note that the domains are not considered to be hierarchical. Each area is seen to offer specific learning opportunities and a strong learning experience for students would draw on all six domains as appropriate to the learning outcomes. The structure of the framework does, however, propose that the domains of Socialise, Research, Surf/Play are skills that students need in order to demonstrate their abilities in the domains of Create, Manage, Publish, and so there is an interdependency implied within the framework that we need to consider.

HOW MIGHT WE USE THIS FRAMEWORK?

Having explored the SCDL framework (Reynolds, 2016), we need to consider how we might use these concepts as tools for teaching and learning. While Reynolds did not specify that the framework was useful for classroom teaching, there are some ways that the concepts have framed learning experiences for students in schools so far.

We might begin by using the SCDL framework to audit the learning experiences we offer our students. If you pulled out your lesson and unit planners for the last term or semester and categorised how you made use of technology, this could offer an insight into your technology use and preferences. Research is emerging that suggests that teachers bring their knowledge of technology from their personal use into the classroom (Blannin, 2017). This suggests that your personal preferences when using technology impact your teaching choices. We know that effective teachers use pedagogical strategies that meet their student learning needs (Zierer and Hattie, 2017), not the teacher's. Undertaking an audit of your practice against the SCDL framework could highlight areas for further development, and of course areas you are demonstrating expertise.

In a similar vein, the SCDL framework can help us explore other options for learning experiences. Consider the lesson planning, topics, content or activities that you are seeking to implement. Use the framework to evaluate your choices for student learning. Is your planning only focused on searching for information? Perhaps your planning asks students to publish their work online without a focus on the pre-skills of surf/play, research and/or socialise. The SCDL framework can offer a lens to inform our planning across our teaching and encourages reflection on the pedagogical choices we are making.

The SCDL framework can also provide us with a way to connect our teaching with the ways that students already use technology. That is not to say that we should only use technology in the ways represented by the framework. Our students use technology in ways that suit them and their out-of-school learning. As teaching professionals, we have pedagogical knowledge that our students likely lack. We must bring our pedagogical skills to the classroom and make informed decisions about technology use. The SCDL framework does, however, offer us an insight into the skills many of our students may have.

The SCDL framework (Reynolds, 2016) is relatively new. We need to see more empirical data before we can firmly say that students should develop these skills in school. For now, it offers us another frame to consider technology use in our classrooms.

The following short snapshots offer insight into how two teachers have used the SCDL framework for teaching and learning.

IN THE PRIMARY CLASSROOM

MK is teaching a group of Year 5 students about our solar system and planets. Having watched a short video about Mars, 10-year-old Seb asks a question about gravity on the planet Mars. MK is not sure of the answer and so asks Seb to research the answer on the classroom computer and then share with the class. Seb opens a browser and enters the search term 'Mars floating away'. As the other students begin a different task, MK moves to work with Seb. MK realises that the search term that Seb has used is returning results that are not answering his question. Instead of finding information about gravitational forces on Mars, Seb is reading about rotational planes of planets and their orbiting paths.

1. *Which domain* from the SCDL framework do you think Seb is finding challenging at this point?
2. How might MK use the *domain of 'socialise' in the online space* to help Seb find the answer he is seeking?
3. How might MK have *better scaffolded Seb's online research* before he began searching on the computer?

IN THE SECONDARY CLASSROOM

Riku is in Year 9 and is 14 years old. Riku's teacher is Miray, a graduate teacher with one year of classroom teaching experience. In today's Economics and Business class, Miray has planned for the class to research how a product on eBay (www.ebay.com.au) arrives at their school. She is seeking to address the critical curriculum question: 'How do participants in the global economy interact?'

Miray's students have begun by choosing an item to research on eBay and have formed into groups to complete their project. Riku's group have chosen a digital camera and have begun their research by seeking out the seller of the camera online.

Miray approaches Riku's group and begins to take notes based on the Economics and Business curriculum outcomes and the SCDL framework.

1. *Choose two of the SCDL framework domains* and explain how this activity addresses them.
2. *What question would you ask Riku's group* to understand better their ability to 'manage' their technology use and data?

BACK TO THE CLASSROOM

Our teacher has returned to teach her Year 8 students. She has provided access to three different websites and now asks the learners to model several fractions with the blocks, as they did last lesson. She knows it is important to 'tune them in' to their prior learning, as during this lesson she hopes to build on those experiences.

After modelling several fractions and decimals with the blocks, she directs the students to open their laptops and go to a fraction website. This is the same site their classmates were using last lesson. She explains that their work with the blocks has prepared them to be successful at this online task and shows them how to drag the on-screen blocks together to represent the fraction shown.

As they begin working, she notes that three of the four students are using the physical blocks to support their online work. They build the fraction with blocks, then build the same fraction on the screen. The fourth student appears to no longer need the physical blocks at all and moves straight into the online representations of fractions. This is a great outcome for both the students and the teacher. By manipulating the blocks in the classroom and then connecting this modelling of fractions to the online examples, she hopes to have provided a bridge between the concrete world and the abstract concepts of fractions and decimals.

The teacher will continue to monitor the group over the next few weeks as they focus on fractions and decimals. She also reminds herself that she may also need to return to physically modelling the concepts before moving to the abstract, online space as the concepts become increasingly challenging.

CONCLUSION

Using these frameworks can offer a language and examples of how technology can be used in the classroom. When we engage with TPCK (Mishra and Koehler, 2006), Bloom's Revised Digital Taxonomy (Churches, 2008) or the Social Constructivist Digital Literacy framework (Reynolds, 2016) we are choosing to be critical consumers of educational technology. We seek to make choices about how, when and why we are using technology for learning based on credible frameworks and empirical evidence.

Later in this book, we will explore more ways to investigate, make choices and implement technology that meets our students' learning needs. The next chapter, however, presents strategies for critiquing the safe and appropriate use of technology with children and young adults. Being safe and ethical, and modelling appropriate behaviour, is as essential in the online world as it is in the physical classroom, and the following chapter presents questions, strategies and resources for your professional, educational use of technology.

FURTHER READING

Read this paper for further examples of how Bloom's Revised Digital Taxonomy has been used in classrooms:

Krouska, A., Troussas, C. & Virvou, M. (2018). Computerized adaptive assessment using accumulative learning activities based on revised Bloom's taxonomy. In M. Virvou, F. Kumeno & K. Oikonomou (eds), *Knowledge-Based Software Engineering: 2018*. JCK-BSE, August. *Smart Innovation, Systems and Technologies*, vol. 108 (pp. 252–258). Cham: Springer doi:10.1007/978-3-319-97679-2

This paper goes deeper into the background of TPCK and its roots in Shulman's PCK:

Phillips, M. & Harris, J. (2018). PCK and TPCK/TPACK: More than etiology. In E. Langran & J. Borup (eds), *SITE 2018: 29th International Conference – Society for Information Technology and Teacher Education* (pp. 2109–2116). Waynesville, NC: Association for the Advancement of Computing in Education (AACE). Retrieved from www.learntechlib.org/noaccess/182817/ (accessed 30 June 2021).

In this paper, Reynolds discusses the use of a constructivist approach to digital literacy:

Reynolds, R. B. (2019). Game design in media literacy education. *The International Encyclopedia of Media Literacy*, 1–9.

REFERENCES

Allen, M. (2009). Tim O'Reilly and Web 2.0: The economics of memetic liberty and control. *Communication, Politics & Culture, 42*, 6–23.

Ang, K. H. & Wang, Q. (2006). *A Case Study of Engaging Primary School Students in Learning Science by using Active Worlds.* In R. Philip, A. Voerman & J. Dalziel (eds), *Proceedings of the First International LAMS Conference 2006: Designing the Future of Learning* (pp. 5–14). Sydney: The LAMS Foundation.

Australian Bureau of Statistics (2011). *Household Use of Information Technology.* Canberra: Australian Bureau of Statistics.

Australian Bureau of Statistics (2016). *Household Use of Information Technology.* Canberra: Australian Bureau of Statistics.

Australian Curriculum, Assessment and Reporting Authority (2015). *Australian Curriculum: Digital Technologies.* Retrieved from www.australiancurriculum.edu.autechnologiesdigital-technolo giesrationale (accessed 30 June 2021).

Australian National Audit Office (2011). *Building the Education Revolution Guidelines.* Retrieved from www.anao.gov.au/work/performance-audit/building-education-revolution-primary-schools-21st-century (accessed 30 June 2021).

Basulto, D. (2012). Why Ray Kurzweil's predictions are right 86% of the time. *Big Think,* 13 December. Retrieved from https://bigthink.com/endless-innovation/why-ray-kurzweils-predic tions-are-right-86-of-the-time (accessed 30 June 2021).

Beeson, M. W., Journell, W. & Ayers, C. A. (2014). When using technology isn't enough: A comparison of high school civics teachers' TPCK in one-to-one laptop environments. *Journal of Social Studies Research, 38*(3), 117–128.

Blannin, J., (2017). Accounting for teachers' choices to use, or not to use, Web 2.0 technologies in upper primary school classrooms (PhD dissertation, University of Melbourne). Retrieved from https://minerva-access.unimelb.edu.au/handle/11343/208015 (accessed 5 July 2021).

Bloom, B.S. (1956). *Taxonomy of Educational Objectives. Vol. I: Cognitive Domain.* New York: McKay.

Churches, A. (2008). *Bloom's Digital Taxonomy.* Retrieved from www.academia.edu/30868755/ Andrew_Churches_Blooms_Digital_Taxonomy_pdf (accessed 30 June 2021).

Crook, S., Sharma, M., Wilson, R. & Muller, D. (2013). Seeing eye-to-eye on ICT: Science student and teacher perceptions of laptop use across 14 Australian schools. *Australasian Journal of Education Technology, 29,* 82–95.

Desjardins, J. (2018). What happens in an Internet minute in 2018. *Visual Capitalist,* 14 May. Retrieved from www.visualcapitalist.com/internet-minute-2018 (accessed 30 June 2021).

Digital Education Advisory Group (2013). *Beyond the Classroom: A New Digital Education for Young Australians in the 21st Century.* Retrieved from https://wlps.wa.edu.au/wp-content/ uploads/2015/10/deag_final_report-2.pdf (accessed 30 June 2021).

Doherty, I. (2011). Evaluating the impact of educational technology professional development upon adoption of Web 2.0 tools in teaching. *Australasian Journal of Educational Technology, 27,* 381–396.

Education Services Australia (2016). *Unpacking the Curriculum.* Retrieved from www.digitaltech nologieshub.edu.au/teachers/australian-curriculum/unpacking-the-curriculum (accessed 30 November 2018).

Gregory, S. & Lloyd, I. (2010). *Accepting choices: To ICT or not to ICT: Engagement!* In D. Gronn & G. Romeo (eds), *ACEC2010: Digital Diversity. Conference Proceedings of the Australian Computers in Education Conference 2010,* Melbourne, 6–9 April. Carlton, Victoria: Australian Council for Computers in Education (ACEC).

Gudmundsdottir, S. & Shulman, L. (1987). Pedagogical content knowledge in social studies. *Scandinavian Journal of Educational Research, 31*, 59.

Hattie, J. (2009). *Visible Learning: A Synthesis of Over 800 Meta-analyses Relating to Achievement.* Abingdon: Routledge.

Jenkinson, J. (2009). Measuring the effectiveness of educational technology. *Electronic Journal of E-Learning, 7*(3), 273–280.

Kamel Boulos, M. N. & Wheeler, S. (2007). The emerging Web 2.0 social software: An enabling suite of sociable technologies in health and health care education. *Health Information & Libraries Journal, 24*, 2–23.

Kim, H., Choi, H., Han, J. & So, H.J. (2012). Enhancing teachers' ICT capacity for the 21st century learning environment: Three cases of teacher education in Korea. *Australasian Journal of Educational Technology, 28*, 965–982.

Krathwohl, D. R., Anderson, L. W. & Bloom, B. S. (2001). *A Taxonomy for Learning, Teaching, and Assessing : A Revision of Bloom's Taxonomy of Educational Objectives.* New York : Longman.

Lee, S. J., Srinivasan, S., Trail, T., Lewis, D. & Lopez, S. (2011). Examining the relationship among student perception of support, course satisfaction, and learning outcomes in online learning. *The Internet and Higher Education, 14*(3), 158–163.

Livingstone, S., & Helsper, E. (2007). Gradations in digital inclusions: Children, young people and the digital divide. *New Media & Society, 9*(4), 671–696. Retrieved from https://doi.org/10.1177/1461444 807080335

Martin, A., & Grudziecki, J. (2006). DigEuLit: Concepts and tools for digital literacy development. *Innovation in Teaching and Learning in Information and Computer Sciences, 5*(4), 249–267. https://doi.org/10.11120/ital.2006.05040249

Mishra, P. & Koehler, M. J. (2006). Technological pedagogical content knowledge: A framework for teacher knowledge. *Teachers College Record, 108*, 1017.

Murugesan, S. (2007). Understanding Web 2.0. *IT Professional, 9*, 34–41.

Passey, D., Rogers, C., Machell, J. & McHugh, G. (2004). *The Motivational Effect of ICT on Pupils.* Research Report 523, Department of Educational Research, Lancaster University.

Reynolds, R. (2016). Defining, designing for, and measuring 'social constructivist digital literacy' development in learners: A proposed framework. *Educational Technology Research and Development, 735.* doi:10.1007/s11423-015-9423-4

Reynolds, R. & Harel Caperton, I. (2009). *The Emergence of 6 Contemporary Learning Abilities in High School Students as they Develop and Design Interactive Games and Project-based Social Media in Globaloria.* Annual Convention of the American Education Research Association (AERA) Conference Paper, 12–17 April, San Diego, CA.

Selwyn, N. & OECD (2010). Web 2.0 and the school of the future, today. In *Inspired by Technology, Driven by Pedagogy* (pp. 23–43). OECD Publishing. doi:10.1787/9789264094437-4-en

Shulman, L. S. (1981). Disciplines of inquiry in education: An overview. *Educational Researcher, 10*(6), 5–23.

Shulman, L. (1987). Knowledge and teaching: Foundations of the new reform. *Harvard Educational Review, 57*(1), 1–23.

Regional Australia Institute (2016). *The Future of Work: Setting Kids Up for Success.* Retrieved from www.regionalaustralia.org.au/home/wp-content/uploads/2016/11/The-Future-of-Work_ report.pdf (accessed 30 June 2021).

Zierer, K. & Hattie, J. (2017). *10 Mindframes for Visible Learning: Teaching for Success.* Abingdon: Routledge.

Zylka, J., Christoph, G., Kroehne, U., Hartig, J. & Goldhammer, F. (2015). Moving beyond cognitive elements of ICT literacy: First evidence on the structure of ICT engagement. *Computers in Human Behavior, 53*, 149–160. doi:10.1016/j.chb.2015.07.008

3

CYBER-SAFETY AND ONLINE LEARNING

IN THIS CHAPTER YOU WILL LEARN:

- What we mean by cyber-safety and digital citizenship in education
- The significance of a digital compass to your teaching and learning
- How online and offline worlds are connected for today's students
- How to maintain students' privacy in online learning
- Strategies for managing inappropriate online behaviour.

INTRODUCTION

Today's media seem intent on presenting the negative side of technology use in schools. From cyber-bullying to the latest hacking scandal, we read, hear and see examples of inappropriate technology use every day. These are, of course, serious issues that need to be addressed quickly and effectively. Bullying of any kind is unacceptable and using technology to harass, intimidate or share upsetting content should be of concern to us as teachers.

This chapter explores what we mean by inappropriate technology use and provides strategies and practical ideas for maintaining a safe and welcome learning environment for today's students.

To begin, you will read a case study of one classroom. Jaylin is 12, and his online work has become the subject of comedy and mean comments amongst his classmates. Following this case study, we will explore how Jaylin's teacher might respond to this behaviour in the classroom.

IN THE CLASSROOM TODAY

In a Year 7 classroom, 12-year-old Jaylin is in English class. His teacher Jan has asked everyone to upload their completed essay to the class shared online space, called Google Classroom. Each student has uploaded their essay about the environmental impact of their transportation to school. They researched and explored how different modes of transportation impact on the air, water and soil quality at their school. Jaylin uploaded his essay last night. He was rather pleased with his final essay and is keen to share it with his classmates.

The next day, the teacher asks the students to go into the Google Classroom space and chose the work of two of their peers. Next, they need to add comments that identify the positives of the work and two areas for improvement. The class has worked on how to provide useful feedback for the last week, and Jan wants to see how they apply that learning to this feedback activity.

Jaylin eagerly opens the online space and adds some thoughtful comments to two of his classmates' work. He is polite and respectful and offers ideas that could improve the essay. Next, Jaylin opens his essay to read the feedback he has received. Sadly, the classmates who have provided feedback have not been as polite as Jaylin. One comment, written online for all to see, says, 'OMG, this is a ridiculous title!'. Another has added, 'Yeah, he can't even spell easy words. Soooo stupid!'. Another writes, 'Wow, I can't believe he chose such a boring topic to write about. Loser.'

As Jay scrolls through the feedback, he becomes increasingly upset, particularly when he notices that several of the mean comments are from students he considered friends. He gets up and leaves the room in a hurry. Jan sees him leave and goes to Jaylin's computer to investigate. Jan is very upset with the comments online and is frustrated that his hard work to teach proper online behaviour has been ignored.

Jan knows he needs to address this behaviour. But where to start?

ONLINE REALITIES

How would you advise Jan to address this problem? Would you delete the online space? Perhaps you would call in the school leader and let them assign appropriate consequences.

Behavioural challenges such as these are often seen in classrooms. It is essential to identify that this type of behaviour, as unpleasant as it is, had existed long before computers were used in schools. Thirty years ago, these same disagreeable comments would likely have been shared in different ways. Children might have drawn a mean picture or passed a note around the classroom. Of course, these days technology makes it much easier to both act inappropriately and to maintain some anonymity at the same time. We are not, in this chapter, negating any profound and deeply hurtful bullying behaviour that is repeated, targeted and often involves social exclusion. That bullying remains a terrible part of some students' lives should be a major concern. Schools and educational settings need to consider how to best address these challenges through specific policies, practices and social skills training for students and teachers.

Later in this chapter, a section called 'Managing challenging behaviours online: Digital dramas' provides insight and strategies into dealing with behaviours that either are, or are close to being, identified as online bullying.

For now, we explore the types of challenges identified in the opening vignette. How would you advise Jan to proceed?

ONLINE VERSUS OFFLINE BEHAVIOURS

Online behaviour is, naturally, often a reflection of offline behaviours. This may be true for the majority of your students. However, we need to remember that some people do seem to maintain a somewhat more aggressive online persona than their offline personality would lead us to believe. Your face-to-face knowledge of that child may not reflect the ways they engage online.

Part of the challenge of online behaviour is the rapid change in how humans, and young adults, in particular, interact and engage in social networks. In only the past five years, the computer world has changed, and much of that change can be attributed to a single computer device: the iPad. The tablet computer, and the smartphone before it, have led to a shift in the ways that social relationships can be initiated, negotiated and maintained. Through tablet computing and the Internet, today we can find a group with the same hobby as us, the same favourite book, favourite player and even a new life partner. Twenty years ago, the majority of these interactions took place offline, often with a local community.

Today, we have access to a range of online activities. These include massive multi-player online games, collaborative computer coding, video-making sharing, podcasting and live-streaming video. Each of these digital activities can also include social interactions. Whether you and your friend are live-streaming at your local football game from two different perspectives, fighting zombies in a virtual reality as part of a team or co-developing an app to solve an identified problem, social interactions are very much a part of the online world. This leads, inevitably, to behaviours that are considered difficult, challenging or even abusive. The social nature of humans appears in the online space as much as it does in the offline world.

The primary difference with today's communications tools for us teachers and our students is anonymity. These days, students as young as 10 can mask their computer's identifiers and essentially become invisible. Using virtual private networks (VPNs), fake user and dummy email accounts, students can make themselves almost entirely undetectable as the source of any content.

As an example of what we mean here, consider this: without any prior experience, you could set up a VPN in about 10 minutes. This means that instead of your computer's Internet connection coming directly from your local Wi-Fi to your computer, your connection is re-routed through a virtual network in another city, state or country. Once re-routed the connection is re-accessed through your local Wi-Fi. This redirection means that when you click submit on that content, your computer's identifier (called an 'IP address') appears to the receiver as from your VPN's city, state or country. So, you might sit in Melbourne, Australia and post that review or comment; the receiver, however, sees your location as Madrid, Spain or whichever place you have chosen.

As you hopefully now understand, VPNs provide a further level of anonymity that can create significant challenges in schools, and also increasingly in the broader workforce. The hacking scandals we hear about in the media often identify that a server, somewhere, was breached and users' personal information was stolen. From here, forensic computer scientists have to trace the source back through many VPNs, firewalls, fake user accounts and so on.

As such, there is an increasing demand for forensic skills in computer science. These skilled individuals spend hours, days and months to solve online crimes and prevent future repeats of the same issues. In our schools, we are unlikely to have access to this level of sophisticated support. We do, however, have existing skills we can draw on that focus less on the technological trail and more on the behaviours of our students.

WHAT DOES THIS MEAN FOR US AS EDUCATORS?

For many years, research has often identified that 'schools have a fundamental role in ensuring their students' safety' (Wishart, 2004, p. 193). This means that we, as educators, have a direct responsibility to ensure that students are safe whether in our classroom, science room, playground or online. We have an ethical obligation to engage with online learning, for the opportunities that technologies offer our students but also to ensure that they develop appropriate online behaviours and strategies.

WHAT DO WE MEAN BY 'ETHICS' IN AN ONLINE SPACE?

As a teacher, the development of students' digital skills should be designed not only to complete a task but also to develop their confidence in working, learning and playing online. The rapid rate at which technology is evolving means we cannot aim to teach students how to function appropriately in every technology tool or platform. Instead, we need an ethical approach that sees us engage in activities and discussions that raise questions and concerns about how social interactions online might work.

As teachers, we have a level of responsibility accorded to us by the students, their parents, our school leaders and perhaps the government. Within Australian schools, teachers are held to a level of responsibility known as 'Duty of Care'. This term is connected to the legal field of negligence and positions teachers as holding responsibility for the educational, social, physical and emotional well-being of students in their care. This 'duty' is 'commonly described as the care that would be taken by a reasonable parent' (Sleigh, 2011, p. 16).

As human beings, teachers bring their morals and ethics into the classroom. Indeed several Australian states have gone further and developed an ethical code of conduct for teachers. These codes of conduct present expectations for how teachers engage in, and perceive, their role as a teacher. Beyond a simple job description to transfer our knowledge to students, we are charged with developing citizens who can contribute positively to society.

Around the world, the positioning of teachers as ethical practitioners continues to grow. Seeking to become an educator is now often expressed as a vocational quality or a calling. From this perspective, 'a purposeful teacher is always an ethical teacher with moral purposes' (Tirri, 2018, p. 2). When we have a definite purpose as a teacher, we naturally bring morality and ethics into achieving that purpose.

Further, a moral teacher is 'first and foremost an ethical person, someone in whom such central moral virtues as fairness, respect, trustworthiness, honesty, and kindness, have become settled dispositions which reveal themselves in the teacher's every interaction with students and constitute the very manner in which he or she teaches' (Campbell, 2003, p. 104).

This moral and ethical approach to education has become increasingly significant as expensive technology creates more of a divide in our community, homes and schools. Some students do not have technology resources at home or family members with skills to help them learn. Other students may have a mother who is a computer scientist and is surrounded by a wide range of technology resources. How we as teachers plan, implement and review our teaching practice with technologies should consider this inequity as a part of our ethical responsibility. As teachers, we often see and engage with inequity in our classrooms. The next step is to consider these challenges when we engage with technology for learning or teaching.

As we engage in online spaces with students, we bring our own ethical and moral practices that are informed by our 'duty of care'. When using technology, this might include developing our skills and experiences in the online space so that we can develop those skills in our students. Ethics for us might mean ensuring equity in access to resources independent of a student's socio-economic background (Mascheroni et al., 2016) or engaging in gender-neutral strategies for activities that might address the imbalance of females in STEM subjects (Gutiérrez et al., 2019).

PRIVACY AND INTELLECTUAL PROPERTY IN THE ONLINE SPACE

In our classrooms, teachers often work in several spaces. These might include the classroom, an innovative open-plan learning space, outdoors in a playground, the library, the science classroom. These spaces each have unspoken rules that dictate the way we act. For example, a student playing football in the playground is likely more socially acceptable than kicking a ball and running back and forth in the library.

A philosopher called Shotter (2012) discusses how we use spaces and how humans develop clear, yet invisible rules for moving through and interacting with those spaces. Focused on physical spaces, Shotter says, 'when someone acts, their activity cannot be accounted as wholly their own—for a person's acts are inevitably "shaped" in part by the acts of the others around them, and also in part by their reactions to their overall surroundings (both social and physical)' (Shotter, 2013, p. 142).

Shotter is explaining that, in a social space, we are influenced by those around us. Learning in online spaces is relatively new, particularly for schools. This is of interest to us as we engage with online learning spaces and resources. The behaviours in the online space may reflect the behaviours of others, or perhaps even the lack of positive behaviour models.

While we do not yet have a full understanding of how learning occurs in the online world, we do have significant research that informs the way we learn offline. We can draw on research from experts such as Shotter and Campbell to make informed choices about how, when and why we engage with digital technologies in the classroom.

UNDERSTANDING ONLINE SPACES

Shotter's notion of different types of spaces having different types of permitted social actions is one that Professor Stephen Heppell has developed (2016). Professor Heppell is a pioneer in educational technologies and often engages with cutting edge digital pedagogies. Through his international work he has identified three types of online spaces. These three categories are useful for teachers from both a pedagogical perspective (how does this help my students learn?) and an ethical perspective (is this online activity equitable, safe and focused on student learning?).

The spaces are labelled 'Me', 'We' and 'See'. These terms are purposefully simplistic so that language does not hinder a student's understanding of their technology use. Whatever digital technology you use, your students will engage in one of these three types of spaces.

Considering this simple framework during your planning can help maintain safe, equitable and ethical practices in your classroom.

ME SPACES

A Me Space is any digital technology that is private. Examples include a file on a private computer, a private online account or a private cloud storage system. A private 'me' space enables students to reflect, record their thoughts, take responsible risks and try new things. A student's work in a Me Space may later be moved to another space, depending on the outcomes that the teacher is seeking to address. For example, a student writes a blog post in a word processor, then receives feedback from the teacher only. Next, the blog post is uploaded to the classroom blog; this is set up as a We Space.

WE SPACES

In a We Space, students are engaged with other people that they know. They might share the online space with their classmates or teammates or with another school. The difference from a fully open platform is that the members of the shared space are selected and invited based on a shared goal, interest or perspective. This collaborative 'We' space provides a place to share student work with a known group of peers or colleagues. Engaging students in peer to peer feedback is often a focused goal for using a We Space.

SEE SPACES

If your pedagogical goals include engaging with the general public or an unknown group of people, then you will likely set up a See Space. This is a public space where the whole world can 'See' the students work and potentially engage with them. An example of this is a Wikipedia page. You can view a page on Wikipedia, and you can provide some general comments, or report errors. You are not, however, the creator of the original content. Of course, if you were a Wikipedia editor, then you would be using Wikipedia as a We Space for editing and moving into a See Space for viewing.

Me, We and See. Three easy to remember terms that provide a useful definition for teachers and students to reflect on the purpose of their online work. Do you need to post your feedback to a student in a See Space? For what purpose? Could you use a We Space instead?

In making informed decisions about how your students will share, create or interact online, you will, hopefully, limit their challenging behaviours. However, we know that we have to teach appropriate skills, knowledge and strategies. We cannot expect our students to understand the social expectations of digital technologies. As Shotter has explained, behaviours are developed socially within a space. As teachers, we need to ensure that positive behaviours are established and moderated for our students.

Next, we explore the concept of becoming a Digital Citizen and how a teacher can impact on a student's values and ethics when they work online.

BECOMING A DIGITAL CITIZEN

For many years, educators have used the term 'cyber-safety' to define the strategies that teachers and students need to practise when maintaining safety on the Internet. The term 'cyber-safety' has undergone several changes, and most recently the replacement term 'digital citizenship' has emerged. Citizenship reflects the shift in focus away from safety in specific digital technologies to a broader approach of generalised behaviour.

An example of a cyber-safety practice is when a teacher asks students to log in to a website but to use a nickname. A digital citizenship approach to logging in to the same site would see teachers asking students what they think they should use as a username and to discuss why that is appropriate. There may appear to be little difference in these two examples. However, the former shows the teacher ensuring her students are safe and telling them what to do. The latter case engages students in making decisions about their behaviours and justifying their choices.

Underlying the term digital citizenship is an acknowledgement that we, as teachers, cannot supervise every online interaction a child has.

A DIGITAL COMPASS

From a broader concept of being a good citizen when using digital technologies, the idea of a digital compass has become more widely used. This term references a physical compass, traditionally used by navigators and explorers to make decisions about where to go next and which path to take.

Similarly, the concept of developing a digital compass seeks to provide students with the necessary skills, understanding and knowledge to make informed choices about their actions. Where should they go? What path is the best and safest to get there?

A digital compass brings together ethical decisions, specific skills and positive behaviours. As a group, this compass can direct students to appropriate behaviours when engaging in the online world.

Avoiding or dealing with cyber-bullying, of course, continues to be a significant challenge for today's teachers. A digital citizenship approach to online safety does not limit how we respond to the inappropriate behaviour that is bullying. As we will explore in the next section, your offline practices will support you in managing the challenges of cyber-bullying.

Outside of the repetitive nastiness of bullying, however, are a large number of lesser but still significant challenges that teachers face when engaging with digital technologies in their classrooms. These challenges might include managing personal information online or dealing with everyday behaviours such as grumpy students, online arguments or appropriate social media use.

Research, however, continues to find that lessons on specific cyber-safety skills have a limited impact on online behaviours (Luke et al., 2017). As technology becomes more pervasive and online resources include more interactive features, a more holistic, ethically based approach to appropriate online behaviour is needed. As educators, we need to focus on developing a positive 'digital compass' in all our students. We can start by focusing on the language of ethics and choices, and less on the terms 'cyber-safety' and 'cyber-bullying'.

There are four main areas that teachers should address with students to begin developing a positive and effective, digital compass. These four areas are each explored in the next section:

- Managing challenging behaviour online: Digital dramas
- Personal identity in the online space
- A digital tattoo
- Social media and teaching.

MANAGING CHALLENGING BEHAVIOURS ONLINE: DIGITAL DRAMAS

Working with children and young adults, you have likely already experienced the role that teachers play in the social and emotional development of their students. From early childhood to high school, students increasingly face 'digital dramas' that occur both during and outside of school hours. We need to work to develop a transparent approach for our students to these disagreements, misunderstandings or inappropriate behaviours. In this way, we are seeking to frame our students' responses as their responsibility both online and offline.

There are several key strategies for addressing online, challenging behaviours. As the teacher, it is, of course, best to engage with the students involved in a face-to-face meeting. As students grow older, they might decide to manage an online problem themselves; however, we should model that when you disagree with someone online, an offline discussion should take place. Taking an argument or unpleasant interaction offline can diffuse some of the drama and, in many cases, draw students together to make sense of what was said online. Often these negative, online behaviours can be traced to a misunderstanding or misinterpretation. If a conversation is challenging, moving to a private, offline space, where others are not observing the interaction, can be a first step to mending relationships and moving forwards.

Six main concepts should underpin your work with students dealing with challenging online behaviours:

1. The first key message is that digital dramas can happen to anyone. Misunderstandings can occur unintentionally, and we can hurt others' feelings without realising it. Without the benefit of body language and tone we are not always able to make sense of online comments. We need to ensure students gain an understanding that language can be misinterpreted, and that online communication requires a clear and careful approach to language and conversation.

2. Teachers can support their students by offering examples of how to manage difficult situations before they happen. This pre-emptive approach derives from the idea that a digital compass relies on regularly calibrating our online interactions to the audience and ensuring we are clearly understood. Case studies, role plays and writing tasks are all useful to help our students develop clear communication skills.

3. As we have discussed, students should be supported to talk face to face when faced with a digital drama. Working through issues offline is, of course, a skill in itself and we need to provide opportunities for students to rehearse and explore these skills. Some teachers engage students in an 'online' chat in the real world, before moving to the online space. For example, the students write phrases on large paper to show to a partner. When they hold up a statement on a given topic, for example 'the spelling in this paper is terrible', their partner then draws an emoji in response. How is this feedback, without body language or facial expressions, received? The teacher then leads a discussion about the anticipated message and the received message. Once students can express their meaning clearly, they can move to interacting in the online space.

4. There is sometimes a perception that younger children are not able to interact online. Children as young as 3 years old can understand cause and effect and can usually make some inference about the feelings of others. This means we can begin working with children from a young age, in particular to understand that other people behind the screen have emotions just as they do. Students need to learn that while you might not see

a person's face, a real human is behind the screen. From this understanding we build towards a deeper understanding of shared ownership and shared creatorship in the online space, sometimes a challenge for young children.

5. Bystanders to digital dramas have an important role in guiding others to take their dramas offline. As with other forms of bullying, challenging behaviours online can often involve students who do not contribute directly but, by their presence, tacitly support the negative behaviour. When unpacking a problem that has emerged online, it is often useful to include students who saw or experienced the interactions. Helping the bystanders understand their role in the situation can help rebuild friendships.

6. Finally, a student's digital compass can help them make informed and appropriate decisions. Hopefully these skills include avoidance of online arguments, bullying or the purposeful isolation of others in online spaces. The skills our students need to develop mirror the offline behaviours we hope to see. The more we can help students to make a connection between their online and offline behaviours, the easier it will be for the student to make careful, and informed, choices.

REMOVING TECHNOLOGY ACCESS?

In the offline, physical world, students are sometimes exposed to unpleasant comments. As teachers we need to model how to be safe and provide opportunities in moderated spaces for students to practise these skills. When challenging behaviours occur, one approach some school leaders take is to remove the technology entirely.

However, for everyday challenges, we should consider the implications of simply disconnecting the child. Often, if we permanently remove technology from our students this does not stop their online interactions. It will, however, push them to hide their online lives from us.

According to the Australian Bureau of Statistics, at around the age of 10 children begin to develop social lives online (Australian Bureau of Statistics, 2011). Were we to remove the technology entirely, we also remove their social connections. A further challenge of removing technology devices is that we are not preparing students to be proactive online users. As adults, our students will have to engage with technology and, if we ban the use of technology when they are younger, they will have had no experiences or models of best practice.

It is important to note that we are discussing the removal of technology for an ongoing, or substantial time. As with other behaviours there will likely be consequences and the removal of access to devices as consequences for poor behaviour choices. We should consider the challenges that restricting our students to only an offline world can create. They may miss out on learning experiences, friendships and social activities of their peers.

In some instances, online behaviour is outside the normal coping strategies of a teacher or a school. In this case, it is important to remember that the laws of the land can provide support. To understand the legal boundaries and supports available to you in your state, you should approach the local police station. You can ask for advice on dealing with bullying, inappropriate media sharing, underage access to certain online resources and any other concerns you have. There are an increasing number of laws being enacted around the world. These, hopefully, will help the police and victims to end inappropriate behaviour online more quickly and with less paperwork.

PERSONAL IDENTITY IN THE ONLINE SPACE

Your personal identity is private and valuable. In the online world, we often see students sharing too much information and giving away all that makes them identifiable in the eyes of the law. For example, signing up to a new website service can be fun. However, what details is the website owner collecting? Do they really need to know your birthdate? What about your ethnic background or marital status? As adults we take responsibility for our personal information; as teachers we need to go further and model for our students how to protect ourselves online.

THE RULE OF THREE

When it comes to personal information, such as a name, address, birth date or car registration number, we should remember a mnemonic device called 'The Rule of Three'.

To steal an identity, do damage to a reputation, to hack an online account, or do other inappropriate things to a computer or an online account, Internet hackers generally only need three pieces of information. It might be a first name, a last name, an address, a school name, football team, street name or a car registration number. When you are registering with a new website, take note of the details that you are being asked to provide. Note, in particular, the use of asterixes *. These generally signal that the information is compulsory. If there is no asterix next to a text box, feel free to leave it empty. Never provide more personal information than is necessary.

Reflecting carefully on what information you are sharing is particularly important when taking or using photographs or videos in your teaching.

A photo of a student playing in their football team with their team name on the jersey is one piece of identifiable information. If the football shirt has the player's name on the back and the name of his homeroom teacher on his backpack, you have provided three pieces of personal information. Consider cropping or removing the photograph.

As a teacher, what else do you share online on behalf of your students? It may be that you are sharing images within a secure school-provided platform. However, there are still potential issues. You might share a photo to a class page, where parents can see the students holding up their beautiful artwork. However, what other details are you sharing here? In Australia, many students wear uniforms with their school name on them. Perhaps the photo shows the location of the photo (in the playground, or the art room). The timestamp on the photo could now tell an unsavoury viewer when a particular student at that school will likely be in the art room or playground each week.

Remember that all digitised images can be copied and saved, either by right-clicking and saving or by using a screen capture tool. This means that any online personal information in a photo is potentially able to be distributed. A photo of your school swimming team with the team captain holding up the cup is an awesome achievement. You need to ask, however, is every parent happy with this photo being posted online? Hopefully the school has sought permission from parents to use photos of the students within the school. If the swim team photo is posted in the school newsletter you will need separate, specific permission from each family to share the image.

While these potential challenges can seem impossible, we should remember that avoiding technology use altogether is not a realistic option for us or our students. Today's learners will enter a workforce that capitalises on technology. We need to teach students from a young age about personal safety and sharing in the online environment. In doing so, we are preparing them to be confident digital citizens who can manage their online profile with care and consideration.

A DIGITAL TATTOO

Perhaps you have heard the term 'digital footprint'. A popular phrase in the past 15 years, a digital footprint denoted the concept that no matter what you visited online, whatever you created, wrote, downloaded or viewed, a record of your visit would be created.

Today, we need to reconsider this concept. A footprint is no longer a sufficiently compelling metaphor (Han et al., 2018). A footprint can be retrodden, hidden in the sand, re-routed, perhaps erased – unlike today's Internet-enabled world where everything online is held on ubiquitous cloud servers.

Instead, we need to help our students to understand that their digital actions are creating a permanent, unerasable record of their lives. To some this may not be a worrisome thought; for most of us, however, we understand that children and young adulthood are places in which we need to make mistakes. We need to be able to fail, pick ourselves up and move on.

Increasingly, though, our students are becoming tarnished by their online lives before they even join the workforce. An inappropriate photograph taken at a party at age 17 can be found by a future employer five years later and potentially cost them a job.

For around 100 Australian dollars, employers can pay investigators to research a possible employee. This relatively small amount of money will usually provide access to the person's social media accounts, even when security protections are in place. From here the investigator can often find out your friends, their friends and so on.

A tattoo is a commitment into the future, it is a permanent record. Removing a tattoo is possible, but painful, long-winded and involves other people to be successful. This is the way we need to explain the permanence of content on the Internet to our students. Their contributions online are not ephemeral footprints, but can become bold markers in their lives, either positive or negative.

We have to be comfortable that everything we post online should be appropriate for our parents, grandparents and employers to read or view.

SUPPORT STRATEGIES: AN EXAMPLE

What if your student has already encountered this problem? Perhaps they shared a photograph of a classmate without permission. The student who posted the photograph did not mean for their peer to be ridiculed to this extent. But what can be done?

First of all, ask the student to remove the original image from whichever platform/s it was posted on. Next, ask all students who have the image on their device to delete it. Not all students will delete it; however, this is their opportunity to do the right thing. Next, ask your school technician to locate any copies of the photograph file on the school server. This should eliminate a majority of the copies.

From here, we need to focus on behaviours. Students who shared the image are brought together and asked to explain how their actions may have made their classmate feel.

Working through the perspectives and feelings of all parties involved is a restorative approach to challenging behaviour that has been shown to have a positive impact on the relationships of those involved (Gregory et al., 2016). The approach is designed 'to strengthen social connection and responsibility for one another by increasing opportunities for affective communication' (Gregory et al., 2016, p. 4).

As a teacher, you can also work with the student's parents. They can sometimes approach the owners of the platform or website on which the photograph appeared and ask for it to be removed, particularly if the student is underage. Become familiar with the reporting buttons that are available on all social media platforms. These buttons should be used as necessary to ensure the safety and privacy of our students.

If the issue is not resolved at this stage, other experts may be invited to support the student group. This might be a counsellor or social worker within the school or a specialist from the school authority. You should also remember that the police are available for support, should you wish to take the issue further.

SOCIAL MEDIA AND TEACHING

Social media can be a useful tool for teaching and learning. You can create group activities, co-develop online research pages and communicate with parents. Social media offers a relatively easy-to-use approach to interactive collaborative learning.

However, you do need to be aware of potential challenges. Social media has a dominant and growing presence in the world. In some cases, social networking platforms are overtaking email in use in education.

In a survey conducted at one large primary school in Australia, 68 per cent of students (aged 5 to 12) were members of at least one social network. A large number of the remaining

32 per cent had seen a social network and interacted with others online in some other way (Blannin, 2017).

On some social media websites, a child can become 'friends' with any other player. Rather than banning social media tools, or removing their devices to keep them safe, we need to ensure that our students have appropriate boundaries in place.

These might include:

- Only become friends online with people you know offline.
- Be sure you know who you are talking to.
- Plan for students to meet their friends online at a specific time, and set a time limit.

As teachers, we likely have social media profiles that we use in our private lives. Modelling best practice to our students is key to engaging them in safe practices. Do you know everyone in your 'friends' list?

BACK TO THE CLASSROOM

Jan is reviewing the comments that the students have posted on Jaylin's essay. Jan notes that the essay is very well written and meets all the criteria. The comments were very unhelpful and have upset Jaylin greatly. Jan decides he needs to meet with the group of students who posted the comments on Jaylin's work.

Jan makes a meeting for the next break time. Using the analytics in the online shared space, Jan can see that five students have 'viewed' Jaylin's work, although only three have made comments. Jan decides to include the bystanders in the discussion so that they can all have input into the discussion and outcomes. Jaylin is also, reluctantly, present.

Jan begins by explaining the situation and that he is very disappointed in this behaviour online. Sam, who viewed Jaylin's work, comments that he 'didn't do anything'. Jan explains that Sam is there precisely because he didn't do anything. He could have helped Jaylin in the online space.

As the conversation progresses, it emerges that Rylie, who wrote the first comment, did not realise that everyone, including Jaylin, would view his words. He thought they were his private notes. Realising his mistake, however, he chose to not delete his comments. Instead, he goaded the other students into making more comments. Jan leads them through a discussion of how Jaylin may have felt, how Sam, Rylie and the others feel, and what might need to happen next. This has now become an issue about behavioural choices and not about technology.

Rylie and Jaylin agree that the comments were mean and unnecessary. Jaylin feels humiliated in front of his other classmates, who have all seen the mean comments on his work. Seeking to rebuild his friendship with Jaylin, Rylie offers to explain to the class that he made a mistake and is sorry he upset Jaylin.

Jaylin agrees to this next step.

To conclude, Jan reviews the three types of spaces that we work in: Me, We and See. The students come up with a definition for their shared online space. It is a 'We' space. The students agree to keep private work to themselves and to be more careful when working in the shared space. Jan makes a time to meet with them in a week to check in on how things are going.

CONCLUSION

This chapter has explored how technology can present us with challenging behaviours and inappropriate uses. While these issues are of course confronting, we have explored how ethics, digital citizenship and appropriate behaviour management strategies should be used. Focusing on the behaviour first, and the technology second, is shown to provide authentic contexts for students to learn how to act online. We have seen that it is important to clearly delineate between Me, We and See spaces so that students make informed choices about their online interactions. As teachers, we have a role in providing our students with a safe and supportive space to learn online, one that provides opportunities to take risks and practise appropriate online behaviours.

FURTHER READING

This website provides a range of resources for teachers seeking to learn more about online behaviours and cyber-safety. This regularly updated website offers podcasts, vodcasts and texts focused on all aspects of safety, including 'e-safety'. The website is also popular with parents of school-aged children as it offers advice, strategies and information on emerging technology and its applications at home.

www.lifeeducation.org.au/teachers/resources

Digital citizenship is the focus of this not-for-profit organisation's website. Based in the USA but with applicable resources for teachers around the world, CommonSense offer lesson plans and teaching resources for students aged 5 to 18.

www.commonsense.org/education/digital-citizenship

This paper discusses a 2016 Canadian survey of teachers. Their findings indicate that digital citizenship, while seen as necessary, has yet to be fully integrated into classrooms. Teachers instead maintain their focus on teaching technical aspects of digital literacy. This paper is a useful exploration of the difference and overlap between cyber-safety, digital literacy and digital citizenship.

Steeves, V. & Regan, P. M. (2018). Teaching Digital Citizenship in the Networked Classroom. *International Journal of Public Administration in the Digital Age (IJPADA),* *5*(4), 33-49. doi:10.4018/IJPADA.2018100103

REFERENCES

Australian Bureau of Statistics (2011). *Household Use of Information Technology.* Canberra: Australian Bureau of Statistics.

Blannin, J., (2017). Accounting for teachers' choices to use, or not to use, Web 2.0 technologies in upper primary school classrooms (PhD dissertation, University of Melbourne). Retrieved from https://minerva-access.unimelb.edu.au/handle/11343/208015 (accessed 5 July 2021).

Campbell, E. (2003). *The Ethical Teacher.* Maidenhead: McGraw-Hill Education (UK).

Gregory, A., Clawson, K., Davis, A. & Gerewitz, J. (2016). The promise of restorative practices to transform teacher–student relationships and achieve equity in school discipline. *Journal of Educational and Psychological Consultation, 26*(4), 325–353.

Gutiérrez, J., Barth-Cohen, L., Francom, R., Greenberg, K., MacArthur, K. & Dobie, T. (2019). *An Emerging Methodology for the Study of Preservice Teachers' Learning about Equity in STEM Education.* Presented at the Proceedings of the 41st annual meeting of the North-American Chapter of the International Group for the Psychology of Mathematics Education.

Han, R., Blackburn, J., Hosseinmardi, H., Lv, Q., Huang, B. & Mishra, S. (2018, April). *International Workshop on Cybersafety: Chairs' welcome & organization.* In *Companion Proceedings of the Web Conference 2018* (pp. 981–982). International World Wide Web Conferences Steering Committee.

Heppell, S. (2016). *Me, We, See.* Retrieved from https://fuse.education.vic.gov.au/Resource/LandingPage?ObjectId=a3d94eb9-446b-4404-919e-4b09515f0df2&SearchScope=EarlyChildhood (accessed 27 July 2019).

Luke, A., Sefton-Green, J., Graham, P., Kellner, D. & Ladwig, J. (2017). Digital ethics, political economy and the curriculum: This changes everything. In K. A. Mills, A. Smith, J. Z. Pandya & A. Stornaiuolo (eds), *Handbook of Writing, Literacies and Education in Digital Culture* (pp. 251–262). New York: Routledge.

Mascheroni, G., Livingstone, S., Dreier, M. & Chaudron, S. (2016). Learning versus play or learning through play? How parents' imaginaries, discourses and practices around ICTs shape children's (digital) literacy practices. *Media Education, 7*(2), 261–280.

Shotter, J. (2012). Agentive spaces, the 'background', and other not well articulated influences in shaping our lives. *Journal for the Theory of Social Behaviour*, *43*(2), 133–154.

Sleigh, D. (2011). A teacher's duty of care. *Education Today*, 9, 16–17.

Tirri, K. (2018). *The Purposeful Teacher*. Retrieved from www.intechopen.com/books/teacher-education-in-the-21st-century/the-purposeful-teacher (accessed 2 July 2021).

Wishart, J. (2004). Internet safety in emerging educational contexts. *Computers & Education*, *43*(1–2), 193–204.

EVALUATING TECHNOLOGY PRACTICES

4

IN THIS CHAPTER YOU WILL LEARN:

- Ways to evaluate if technology is supporting learning
- Ideas for choosing technologies to meet learning needs
- Digital literacy and evaluating what our students are learning.

INTRODUCTION

When we choose to use technology in the classroom, we accept that there is a risk that our lesson may not go as planned. The same can be said, on a smaller scale, perhaps, of any lesson we teach. Your lesson plans will be successful depending on many factors, including:

- The depth of your planning
- The students
- The time of day or day of the week
- The previous or following lessons on their timetables
- Their life outside school including sports, drama, music and other clubs
- Their family, friends and relationships.

With this number of factors potentially impacting on your lesson, we need to be sure we evaluate technology resources before we use them, and hopefully avoid any challenges where we can. There are two ways to think about the evaluation of technology:

1. The content and its reliability
2. The use of technology and any challenges.

In this chapter we will explore what this looks like in the classroom and present ideas for countering potential issues.

IN THE CLASSROOM TODAY

Anh is 17 years old and is in Year 11. Yoshi, Anh's teacher, is planning a lesson for a Science class tomorrow. Yoshi knows that there are some great simulations online to explore cell division and does a quick Google search to find one that looks useful and closes the laptop.

Next morning, as Anh's class enter the room, Yoshi explains, 'Today we are going to take the laptops and use an online simulation'. The students are excited and rush to get a laptop from the trolley at the front of the room. As Anh and her group open the computer and get online, the problems start.

One group calls out to Yoshi, 'My computer says it needs some software to run the website?', and another says, 'Why won't it open in my browser?'. Finally, Anh says, 'It's working on our laptop, but the pictures don't look the same as the video you sent us?'. Yoshi is feeling flustered and heads over to Anh's group. One look confirms that the simulation is indeed inaccurate, and it is still not working for the other groups. Yoshi mutters under her breath and tells the students to close their laptops and pull out their textbooks.

Yoshi realises that she needs to rethink her use of technology for the next lesson. She has read that simulations can support student understanding, but how can she avoid the same problems?

What does Yoshi need to do before introducing a new technology or digital resource into the classroom?

CONTENT AND RELIABILITY

Is what you are reading reliable? Does it make sense based on what you knew already or what others have claimed?

These are the key questions to ask about any resource you find online. There are, of course, some websites that can be seen as more reliable than others. Webster's dictionary, for example, has a long history of trustworthiness and reliability. When we consult the dictionary, we rarely need to double-check a definition or synonym. The organisation behind that definition is trusted. Therefore, we believe the content.

This is not always the case, however. Take, for example, definitions of terms provided on the websites of political parties. A cleverly crafted definition of an important term can bring more voters to a cause or move them away from the party altogether. In 2019, both the Conservative and Liberal-National parties in Australia spoke at length about the impact of drought on rural citizens and the need to stimulate economic growth in these often remote areas. They drew on similar studies and sometimes the same experts. However, their political statements always reinforced their world view. Compare the following two quotes:

> The National party has been working very hard on a policy as a group, and our policy involves working with the community at a local level, furnishing them with a substantial amount of money per shire and letting the community make decisions at a local level about what the best use of it is. (Martin, 2019)

> Labor's agriculture spokesman Joel Fitzgibbon also said there was 'no case for stealing money away from infrastructure projects'. (Sullivan, 2019)

If our students came across these quotes, would they know which was the most accurate way of interpreting this debate? Should money be taken from agriculture and given to farmers, or should the government build infrastructure and develop drought solutions at a federal level?

Answering these questions, and knowing to ask them in the first place, is how we help students become critical of the reliability of what they read, view and watch online.

Assessing the reliability of information requires three primary skills:

1. Understanding who created the information and what their biases or beliefs are
2. Developing skills to trace claims back to their roots and make their own decisions
3. Reading widely and comparing information from different sources to find a convincing final argument.

Once we have moved through the above three stages, we need to decide whether the information is reliable or not. An informed citizen should be able to summarise the various arguments and facts and be able to express an opinion that is based on evidence.

In today's world of fake news, when truth is often clouded, ignored or denied, we need to build our students' abilities in seeking out the truth. Indeed, lies spread faster than the truth, according to an extensive study of more than three million Twitter users. Vosoughi et al. (2018) intentionally spread a serious of inaccurate rumours on Twitter and found that false news reached, on average, up to 100,000 people. In contrast, the truth 'rarely diffused to more than 1000 people' (Vosoughi et al., 2018, p. 1146). The authors put this extreme imbalance down to the fact that false news is more emotionally stimulating and novel than the truth. Humans seek amusement and entertainment despite apparent fallacies. What does this mean for our students? It means we need to expose false news and become detectives of the truth!

The concept of truth is challenging as people will always hold different opinions, based on their beliefs, ideas and world views. However, we need today's students to be able to mine through the data and make an informed judgment. That judgment might even be that we don't know the answer yet.

USING TECHNOLOGY FOR LEARNING AND POTENTIAL CHALLENGES

The last time you were using a computer device, what went well and what went wrong?

Technology is becoming increasingly reliable. Gone are the days of entire networks disappearing or software crashing without backups. The stability and accessibility of hardware and software for schools have increased dramatically in recent years, helped, in part, by changes in hardware and software. Simplicity is a crucial component of design for many hardware and software designers. Simplified designs should lead to less potential challenges. Less potential problems, in turn, should lead to more reliable technology. This suggests we can use hardware and software in our classrooms with less and less concern about how technology will function (or if it will function at all).

As we read in the vignette for this chapter, Yoshi was keen to use technology. She had learned that 'good' teachers use simulations in science class and, being a 'good' teacher, she was eager to try it out. Trialling new strategies for teaching and learning is to be commended. In this case, however, Yoshi may have jumped in too soon.

Yoshi looked for one key aspect of the software, the representation of cell division, and then took it into the classroom. To avoid making Yoshi's mistake, here are eight questions to ask before using technology in the classroom:

1. Will this work on any device and operating system? If not, how will I ensure everyone can access it?
2. What devices do we have in my classroom (or have access to)? Will these work for this tool?
3. What are the things my students need to know before they use this tool? How will I introduce the technology to them?
4. Does this tool demonstrate the key learning concepts I am targeting this lesson? If not, is it appropriate?
5. Can I try this with a small group before the whole class uses it? Or should we all learn together?
6. What are the potential technical challenges I might face in using this digital tool? (Access to specific software, device user permissions, cyber-safety concerns, battery life of devices, shared or independent work around a device.)
7. What are the potential challenges around the content?

   - Is the information accurate, up-to-date, and does it offer sufficient detail?
   - What doesn't the tool show or represent or explore?
   - How will I plan my teaching to fill these gaps?

8. Finally, consider the potential benefits of this tool:

- Does it offer collaborative learning opportunities?
- Peer feedback?
- Repetition activities to strengthen concept knowledge?
- Individual knowledge testing?
- Differentiated learning?
- Self-correction opportunities?
- Teacher guidance at specific points?

These are just a few of the questions you need to consider when choosing technology for your classroom. This may seem like a long list. However, the final, eighth point seeks to help you evaluate whether your work to set up this tool is justified in the potential learning benefit to your students. The more you work with technology for learning and teaching, the easier it becomes to evaluate a new tool, resource or device. Your experiences will inform your future technology use and help you be a critical consumer of technology alongside your students.

Be sure to balance your effort in learning new technology skills with the potential for positive student outcomes.

BEYOND DIGITAL LITERACY

Digital literacy is a term that has been used for more than 20 years in education (Becker et al., 2017). This term is often used when we begin talking about technology in education. Sometimes governments and international organisations also use this term and throw down the challenge that we, as teachers, must ensure that students are 'digitally literate'. Often, however, what this term means for students and their teachers is not clear. In this section, we explore the term digital literacy and consider how this term influences what we do, or do not do, in our classrooms.

WHAT DOES LITERACY MEAN?

To begin, we need to explore briefly what we mean by digital literacy. There are many definitions and discussions about the meaning of this term and these debates continue to evolve.

For this chapter, we will draw on a wide-ranging study conducted in 2009 by Sefton-Green et al. This team reviewed the terminology and implementation of digital literacies programmes. They discovered several ways to understand and define the term. These include:

- Empowering learners to develop specific skills with technology
- Developing a sense of 'being technologically literate' with all technologies

- An aspiration of government bodies to develop their country's overall skills and potential for economic and social development. They term this the 'civic aspirations' of a nation.

Empowering learners through the development of digital literacy skills, appears to include engaging with new and emerging technologies. These experiences may serve students well into their adult lives. Students are empowered by developing skills and knowledge about how to use technologies. This might include how to create a slideshow presentation, how to film and edit a video, or how artificial reality can be a useful learning tool. Empowerment, with regards to digital literacy, is at some levels about equity; ensuring that all students have equitable opportunities to engage with technologies and to develop specific, core skills.

A further level of digital literacy, as discovered by Sefton-Green et al. (2009), is to focus on the literacy component of the phrase. This requires us to consider what we mean by literacy. Traditionally, literacy has been used as a synonym for reading, writing, speaking and listening. Developing these core communications skills has long been considered a human right (Law et al., 2018). Ensuring that children have opportunities to develop literacy skills has been part of the goals for many countries for more than 200 years. Of course, other literacies are part of a person's daily life. If you were from an Indigenous background, for example, you might consider yourself 'literate' if you demonstrated knowledge of medicine, animal tracking, oral history memorisation, and so on. Literacy, as we know it in the Western world, is by no means the only type of literacy that has proven necessary, useful or sought after for our ancestors around the world.

WHAT DO THESE DEFINITIONS OF LITERACY MEAN FOR US?

Being literate has become to represent an ability to engage fully in society, to communicate effectively and to create, develop or respond to the literacy practices of others. In the classroom, this means we approach technology use as a requirement. Our students have the right to these experiences and engagements with technology so that they can be literate users. This goes beyond how to use technology and instead engages students in:

- Decision-making processes (What tool would suit this task? What might technology offer to solve this problem?)
- Trial and error (That didn't work, what can I try next?)
- Structured play (I wonder what is possible with this technology resource?)

Developing literate students requires more than teaching a list of specific skills. Literate students, according to this definition, are fluent in technology. They understand the nuances and potential of digital resources and make informed decisions.

Finally, some definitions of digital literacy refer to more substantial scale changes and programs of policies within governments. These might be national or international governments who have identified a need for increased technology literacy in their populace. This might include a desire to improve their economies or to ensure the ongoing health and safety of citizens.

An interesting example of this definition of digital literacy can be seen in Israel. A small country facing challenges of war, international trade and economic dependence, Israel's political leaders have increasingly moved its citizens towards technological expertise in recent years. Policies, beginning in the 1960s, promoted the development of technology resources to support agricultural research and development (Israeli Ministry of Science and Technology, 2013). Driven by a desire to make their unforgiving desert landscape more conducive to farming and agriculture, funding for research into science and technology was made available.

Today, Israel is committed to developing an innovations industry, with the government claiming they now count the most scientists and technicians for any country in the world per capita (Israeli Ministry of Foreign Affairs, n.d.). Indeed, 'Israel is one of eight countries in the world that have the technological ability to build and launch their satellites' (Israeli Ministry of Foreign Affairs, n.d., p. 2).

In its education system, Israel has developed specific curriculum programmes to meet this national focus on innovation and technologies. From the age of five, students learn the building blocks of computer coding. As they grow, students learn more complex skills which offer them opportunities to participate in cyber-security or software development industries as adults. The former prime minister of Israel has put the country's goal of leading innovation and technologies research squarely on the shoulders of today's students. Becoming digitally literate is now almost a nationalistic duty for these young adults. As Benjamin Netanyahu has said:

> You students need to strengthen us with your curiosity. Your years in the security services will be golden years for the security of the nation. (Quoted in Estrin, 2017)

Developing the digital literacy of Israeli citizens has been integral to the success of Israel's focus on innovation and technology. Israel continues to identify as the world's 'Cyber Nation' (Israeli Ministry of Economy and Industry, 2014). As such, digital literacy, including the use, development and design of technology, is positioned as important as reading, writing and mathematics for today's learners.

This third definition of digital literacy, focused on nation-building, positions all members of society as needing to develop digital literacy skills so that they can contribute to their own and their country's development.

In exploring three ways to define digital literacy, we come to understand that the term is complex, changing and based on the context of the person or persons using the term. The following examples summarise the way that digital literacy can be seen in the classroom:

- You might teach digital literacy skills in the classroom by ensuring students can type a letter, turn on a computer or complete other essential skills – Empowering learners to develop specific skills with technology
- You might engage students in using 3D printing to develop an ability you see as necessary for their future workplaces – Developing a sense of 'being technologically literate' with all technologies
- You might, however, believe that teaching students how to code computers, build digital devices or innovate solutions to complex problems is your duty as a member of society who needs those particular skills – The 'civic aspirations' of a nation.

WHY DOES DIGITAL LITERACY MATTER TO US?

Understanding what is meant by digital literacy is increasingly vital for us as teachers. We are tasked with developing a country's youngest citizens and ensuring they are capable of engaging with social, economic and industrial changes in the world. This has led schools to engage more with digital literacy alongside traditional reading and writing literacies. Different terminology has also emerged in an attempt to delineate between the various definitions and better understand the role of education in digital literacy. One example of this is the term 'digital competence'. Digital competence is a broader and more general term for literate practices with technology. Beyond teaching how to use technology, digital competence has been defined as:

> Digital competence is defined as consisting of (1) technical competence, (2) the ability to use digital technologies in a meaningful way for working, studying and in everyday life, (3) the ability to evaluate digital technologies critically, and (4) motivation to participate and commit in the digital culture. (Ilomäki et al., 2016)

As Ilomäki et al. demonstrate, there is a need in education for many different types of digital literacy and digital competences. In addition, the Organisation for Economic Co-operation and Development (OECD) suggests that governments should ensure that teachers learn to identify and conceptualise the required set of digital skills and competences for their education system, and then incorporate them into the educational standards (OECD, 2019). The OECD also promote developing students' digital literacies (and competencies) as a strategy to reduce the socio-economic divide in use and access to technologies in many countries around the world.

> People, education and learning lie at the heart of these issues [of bridging the digital divide] and their solutions. The machines and sophisticated ICT equipment are useless without the competence to exploit them. Nurturing this competence is in part the job of schools and colleges, where the foundations of lifelong learning and 'technological

literacy' are laid. In part, it is dependent on the learning that takes place throughout life in homes, communities, and workplaces. Education and learning are now the lifeblood of our 21st-century knowledge societies, and ICT has become integral to them. (Organisation for Economic Co-operation and Development, 2019)

Having read this section, it is hoped you now see digital literacy as more complicated than only teaching how to use technology. Indeed, the OECD has charged the education profession with maintaining the 'lifeblood' of today's societies. Ensuring that today's students have access to technology is essential. Perhaps even more important, however, is that students are provided opportunities for learning and experiencing the potential impact of technology on a global scale.

The next section of this chapter further explores how teachers who use technology effectively make decisions about technology in their classrooms.

USING TPCK

We have learned from recent research (Blannin, 2015) that several factors inform how teachers use digital technologies in their classrooms. It seems that, most often, teachers begin to think about technology for learning by connecting with their ideas about pedagogy. By pedagogy, we are referring to the strategies that we use for teaching and learning. Teachers use many different pedagogies in one day. From lecturing and group work to tests, presentations and making posters, pedagogical choices represent how students learn and make connections to what they already know.

Having explored the Technological, Pedagogical and Content Knowledge Model (TPCK) (Mishra and Koehler, 2006) in Chapter 2, we learned that TPCK is a useful model of teacher knowledge that represents the various cognitive domains that an effective teacher uses for learning. TPCK, however, does not provide us with a framework for our teaching. Indeed, it was not intended for that purpose.

In recent research, it has been discovered that teachers bring together their knowledge of learning needs and pedagogical skills to explore the affordances of the technology. To make sense of these choices, a redesigned TPCK Model (Mishra and Koehler, 2006) is proposed here. It is seen to represent more clearly how teachers choose to use technology in their classrooms.

In some research literature, the TPCK model has been seen as contentious and is suggested to be both highly significant for teacher technology use and, more recently, as incomplete (Angeli et al., 2014; Kramarski and Michalsky, 2014). The revised model (Blannin, 2017) that follows offers adaptations and refinements to the original TPCK model and presents a new theory of what teachers need to know to use technology effectively.

Significant to this newly revised model is Graham's (2011, p. 8) statement that the visual simplicity of the TPCK model, 'hides a deep underlying level of complexity, in part because all of the constructs being integrated are broad and ill-defined'. Graham (2011) therefore challenges researchers to continue to develop and work with the TPCK model and to move beyond a focus on technological knowledge (TK), as he suggests so far has been the case in teacher education and professional learning:

> it is clear that in order for the model to be viable long term, it must lead researchers and practitioners to understand the technology, pedagogy, content knowledge constructs in more depth without becoming so complicated that it is inaccessible to all but a few elite researchers. (Graham, 2011, p. 9)

To this end, the refined TPCK model (Blannin, 2017) seeks to graphically represent the ways the constructs of technology, pedagogy and content knowledge have been drawn upon by teachers who use technology effectively in the classroom. We know that teachers' pedagogical content knowledge has an impact on student outcomes, both positively and negatively (Dinham, 2016). Dinham (2016) states that teachers are seen to connect with either pedagogy or content when using technology. This research (Blannin, 2017) indicates, however, that teachers who make choices to use Web 2.0 positioned themselves as pedagogues first and content experts second. This means that teaching is about pedagogy for these primary school teachers; their job is first informed by how students learn and then by what students learn.

RE-THINKING THE TPCK MODEL

In the TPACK model, the original authors presented an equal overlap in their visual representation of content, pedagogy and technology knowledge (Mishra and Koehler, 2006). In this research (Blannin, 2017), however, data analysis has suggested that teachers in phase one did not articulate that the three areas of technology, pedagogy and content held equal weight in their decision-making.

The research uncovered a pattern of engagement with technologies that differed from the TPCK model. This provides us with a strategy for thinking about how and when we can use technology for learning. The number and type of teacher interactions suggested that teachers were motivated and driven, initially, by the pedagogical needs of their students.

They first asked, how will the students learn? Next, they engaged with the technological skills that the pedagogy may require and asked, what can technology use offer students' learning if anything? Finally, teachers considered the specific learning content for individual students: what does each student need to know at the end of this learning experience? These teachers demonstrated a transparent pedagogical approach to learning. Their context might influence this. These teachers worked in primary schools and were 'generalist' teachers who taught a range of subjects. They focused on how students would learn best and did not engage with the specific content outcomes until later, although they had a concept of what they were teaching.

A teacher's thought process in this study is summarised in the following example:

My class will be looking at light and sound in Science next week. When we did Science last term, they reflected well on their work, but they didn't really understand what peer feedback meant. I know that feedback is important to their learning, so I'll need to make sure that we work on their peer feedback skills. So maybe I could use an online form to get them to give each other feedback. Then we could look at the remarks together. I think that we could also use a shared online folder. Then they can all access and practise giving feedback on a sample piece of work. Ok, I know that Jake's small group will need a bit more support with this, so I think I'll manage their online folder so that it takes some pressure off. I want Jake and his group to focus on the feedback examples, and I'll provide them with a few videos of good feedback in their shared folder. I'll also need to teach some of the students how to use the online shared folder. I'll do that first and make it an open session so any student can attend. Sammy's group could likely work on some more complex problem-solving work with light and sound concepts. I think that a WebQuest online will meet their needs. I'll find one that is appropriate for them. At the end of this unit of work, all the students should be able to identify the properties of light and sound and should be able to give useful feedback to each other. I'll be able to evaluate their learning using our feedback rubric.

The following sections walk you through the modified TPACK model.

PEDAGOGICAL KNOWLEDGE

Teachers have consistently highlighted the impact of their pedagogical knowledge on their use of technology. In fact, in this study, their pedagogical knowledge had more impact on their technology use than their content knowledge. Teachers discussed their strategies for teaching more than the content of their teaching.

Classroom observations showed that teacher-to-teacher discussions were focused around the pedagogical choices that teachers were making, rather than the content of the learning experience. Teachers' thinking about technology is perhaps not as balanced as is represented or understood in the original TPACK model (Mishra and Koehler, 2006).

INCREASED TEACHER FOCUS ON HOW TO TEACH

In this research (Blannin, 2017), teachers demonstrated a clear focus on the purpose of teaching: learning specific educational content. While noting that content knowledge was a continuing focus, these teachers, however, instead began their planning by drawing on their pedagogical knowledge to inform both lesson planning and professional development.

Content knowledge does not appear to have had a significant impact on teachers' choices to use or not to use, technology for learning. David's comment below shows an example of the language participants used to talk about their teaching. They were focused on their pedagogical choices, rather than the content they were teaching:

> Because I know if I was to stand at the front and lecture and basically teach the same thing, some students already know it, some students have a pretty good idea of it, some students have no idea what I'm talking about. So just being able to cater for pretty much everyone [with technology] along the way. (David, Royal Park Primary School, Interview 2)

OVERLAPPING CONCEPTS OF TECHNOLOGICAL AND PEDAGOGICAL KNOWLEDGE

The research (Blannin, 2017) pointed to a relationship and a strong connection between pedagogical and technological knowledge. As Rachel notes below, her use of technology was strategically connected to her pedagogical choices:

> I feel like I can do a lot more with IT. I can teach my lessons in a lot more ways using IT, whereas if I didn't have it ... so I can use websites, I can use videos, I can use blogs, I can use ... whereas if I think about if I didn't have that, my creativity would be limited. (Rachel at a Primary School in Victoria, Australia)

Rachel says, 'I can teach my lessons in a lot more ways using IT', highlighting her use of technology as a pedagogy, or way of teaching.

TECHNOLOGICAL KNOWLEDGE AND CONTENT KNOWLEDGE

Finally, technology was positioned as a pedagogical tool, rather than a separate aspect of the practice of teaching. Teachers developed specific learning strategies to learn new skills, both technological and pedagogical. Teachers did, however, learn technological skills in different ways, in different spaces, and separately to pedagogical skills. Teachers' technological knowledge was mediated by their pedagogical knowledge and, as such, indirectly connected to teachers' content knowledge.

This redesigned TPACK model proposes that there may be a false assumption at play within the design of the original TPACK model (Mishra & Koehler, 2006); teachers do not appear to access content, pedagogical and technological knowledge with an equal focus.

Using this redesigned model, we can explore how we use the types of knowledge represented in the TPACK model (Mishra and Koehler, 2006). When choosing to use, or not to use, technology in the classroom, try engaging with pedagogical strategies first, then consider how to make sense of the content through that pedagogy. Finally, decide what technological knowledge might be needed.

MAKING INFORMED DECISIONS

The previous section explored the higher-level decision-making practices of some school-teachers. To ensure that these practices are useful, we next focus on three key stages for using technology: (1) Reflect (on the tools available, your context, the students' learning needs); (2) Review (what is possible, and what technology resources are available to you); (3) Reconsider (what traditional ways of learning might be replaced with technology-enabled learning).

What do we need to do? To address digital literacy development in the classroom, we must answer two questions:

First, we must consider what students need to know across the curriculum.

- What aspect of the curriculum are we seeking to explore? How is the learning connected to the twenty-first-century world in which we live?

Of course, there are skills and knowledge that remain constant despite technological innovations. It is essential to consider, however, that new skills and expertise are now necessary for a successful life. An example of this is in mathematics. Thirty years ago, students needed to learn how to solve division problems by hand, creating long algorithms on paper and working through multiple steps to get to an answer. Today, we have computers and calculators. A quick visit to a website such as Wolfram Alpha (www.wolframalpha.com/) will provide a quick answer. What we need to teach in today's maths lesson has changed. Our students need to understand how to phrase a mathematical question. The questions can now be more complex and multi-layered, enabling students to explore mathematical problem-solving more deeply and more efficiently. As any mathematicians will tell you, asking the right question is the key to becoming a capable mathematician (Di Teodoro et al., 2011: Terrell, 2003). Today's schools can provide these experiences to their students, and potentially develop mathematics skills that are well beyond what was possible for previous generations.

Having considered the learning outcomes or focus, we must next consider how technology can help students learn about both the technology and the content.

- What technology will help students learn this skill or knowledge?

There are many ways to use technology in your teaching. Consider these verbs: integrate, substitute, replace, research, create, develop and design. What role might technology take in your lessons? Will you integrate technology so that students use it as they need to? Or will students use technology to design and create expressions of their new knowledge and understanding?

With an understanding of the knowledge and skills we seek to teach, and the technology or technologies that might help, we next follow three steps: Reflect, Review and Reconsider. To connect these stages, we are using a scenario. Five students in a Year 5 classroom need more support with understanding how to create sentences using appropriate punctuation.

As the teacher, you are keen to use technology to provide these students with effective learning experiences. To begin, we will reflect on what tools are already available to you.

REFLECT

This first stage asks you to pragmatically list the tools available to you and your students in your specific context. You will likely only need to create or update this list a few times a year, depending on how your educational setting updates or changes the technology resources. Each time you consider using new technology, either hardware or software, in your classroom, you should refer to and update the list as needed.

REVIEW

The reviewing stage is straightforward. Consider the list you created in the reflection stage and highlight resources that might be useful for supporting students.

In this example, we may have identified some hardware, software and a person who can help us support our five students. From here we need also to consider what we don't yet have access to in the school. This might be other websites, ideas or learning strategies. To explore, we need to consider what we 'don't know yet'. This might mean we talk with other educators, either in person or online. We might search online for keywords and strategies for teaching, 'punctuation + learning + primary school'. This might lead us to add new resources to our reflection table.

RECONSIDER

With a shortlist of resources, we now need to reconsider our plans. We initially had outlined the ways that technology might help our students learn new skills. Remember the verbs you highlighted above?

- Integrate
- Substitute
- Replace
- Research
- Create
- Develop
- Design

Add to these verbs to reflect the opportunities that your shortlisted resources provide. For example, using a website that asks students to Find Errors or Create Examples could be added to your list. Now we create a final plan for teaching and learning.

This approach to planning for technology use has been introduced in several hundred classrooms. Feedback has told us that the process can feel cumbersome at first and that it takes some time to create these detailed plans.

However, the process is designed to draw on research that identifies pedagogical connections to technology should inform how technology is used. This understanding leads to new ways of teaching and learning, and in time will become a more embedded approach to using technology. Experience teaches us that you will not need to create detailed planners forever!

In some schools, classroom teachers create these planners in teams, following Reflect, Review and Reconsider. Their work can be shared with other colleagues to use. This is one way of developing a bank of useful planning documents within a school.

As teachers, we know that we often have to modify plans to meet the unique needs of our students; however, if we share our projects, ideas, discoveries and areas of learning, we can hope to receive similar support in return.

BACK IN THE CLASSROOM

After the school day has finished, Anh sits at her classroom desk to review her day and plan for tomorrow's teaching. What had gone so wrong in the lesson? The simulation looked fine last night. Anh decides to ask some questions about the online simulation and try to understand what went wrong. Anh completes a quick review of the lesson, using the questions we outlined in the 'Using technology for learning and potential challenges' section of this chapter.

1. Will this work on any device and operating system? If not, how will I ensure everyone can access it?
    *   On closer look, the website works best on only one web browser – and it is not the one that the school uses. It should work in a different browser though. But next time, Anh will ask the school technicians to install the new browser. It looks like other simulation websites use the same browser.

2. What devices do we have in my classroom (or have access to)? Will these work for this tool?
    *   The classroom laptops were ready to use, and there were no significant issues with the laptops themselves.

3. What are the things my students need to know before they use this tool? How will I introduce the technology to them?
    *   The students had explored the basic concept of cell division in the previous week. It is clear though the class needed a refresher before jumping into the simulations.

4. Does this tool demonstrate the key learning concepts I am targeting this lesson? If not, is it appropriate?

- It does seem appropriate, but it seems to use slightly different language than Anh. This isn't a problem, but Anh needs to explain that there are few ways to explain the concepts in the lesson.

5. Can I try this with a small group before the whole class uses it? Or should we all learn together?

- Anh thinks that if she had spent a few minutes at the beginning of the lesson reviewing the main concepts, the students could all have worked on the simulations more effectively.

6. What are the potential technical challenges I might face in using this digital tool?

- There are no specific technical challenges Anh can identify beyond using the correct browser for the simulation. However, she realises she needed to ensure that the students remained on track and were not searching the Internet for irrelevant, or inappropriate, content. Anh will make time to check on this during the next lesson.

7. What are the potential challenges around the content?

- Upon closer inspection, it is clear that the content in the simulation is accurate, despite Anh's initial thoughts that the material was wrong. Anh realises that the students needed to be led into using the simulation by reminding them of their prior learning. In this way, they could have made sense of the different terms and images.

8. Finally, consider the potential benefits of this tool:

- Anh is still keen to use the simulations in the next class. She realises that the simulations offer collaborative learning opportunities for the students. Anh can see that asking students to work together was a good idea. This gave them a chance to problem-solve together. In the next lesson, she will try using the simulations again. She wishes she had answered these questions before today's lesson – never mind, she can try again next week.

CONCLUSION

In this chapter, we have explored several ways of making decisions about how, when and why we might use technology in the classroom. With so much technology now available to teachers, we discussed the need to demonstrate careful and considerate use of digital resources.

To begin this chapter, we explored what it means to be a critical consumer of technology in today's world. This led us to consider what we mean by digital literacy. We noted that while the term is used widely in the media, as teachers, we need to consider what we mean by literacy in this context carefully. Developing a clear understanding of why we are using technology for learning will help us make informed choices.

A theoretical section in this chapter next explored the TPACK model, developed by Mishra and Koehler in 2006. This model provides an understanding of the types of knowledge we draw on when we effectively engage with technologies for learning. We then unpacked the TPACK model and considered emerging research which reimagines the model to represent the thinking processes of teachers who use technology in their classrooms.

We ended the chapter with a practical strategy for choosing which technologies to use, or not to use, in our classrooms: Review, Reflect and Reconsider. This strategy drew on the reimagined TPACK model and offered examples of how to plan for effective technology use. Finally, we reviewed the initial vignette and used some of the strategies we learned in this chapter to help our hypothetical teacher reconsider her teaching.

From here, we can apply what we have learned in this chapter to our own, unique, educational settings. This might mean you review and reflect on the technology you have previously used or plan to use in your classroom. How might this chapter inform your next steps? What might you need to explore, consider or learn to meet the challenges of using new technologies in your classroom?

FURTHER READING

Explore how the media and today's society are increasingly intertwined and dependent on each other:

Croteau, D. & Hoynes, W. (2018). *Media/Society: Technology, Industries, Content, and Users.* **London: Sage Publications.**

Learn how the idea of 'truth' is linked to changes in how society understands the world around us:

Corner, J. (2017). *Fake News, Post-Truth and Media–Political Change.* **London: Sage Publications.**

Investigate how the way in which we use technology influences what and how our students learn in the classroom:

Beeson, M. W., Journell, W. & Ayers, C. A. (2014). When using technology isn't enough: A comparison of high school civics teachers' TPCK in one-to-one laptop environments. *Journal of Social Studies Research,* **38(3), 117–128.**

REFERENCES

Angeli, C. & Valanides, N. (2009). Epistemological and methodological issues for the conceptualization, development, and assessment of ICT–TPCK: Advances in technological pedagogical content knowledge (TPCK). *Computers & Education, 52*(1), 154–168. https://doi.org/10.1016/j.compedu.2008.07.006

Becker, S. A., Cummins, M., Davis, A., Freeman, A., Hall, C. G. & Ananthanarayanan, V. (2017). *NMC Horizon Report: 2017 Higher Education Edition.* Austin, TX: The New Media Consortium.

Blannin, J. (2015). The role of the teacher in primary school Web 2.0 use. *Contemporary Educational Technology.* http://cedtech.net/articles/63/632.pdf

Blannin, J., (2017). Accounting for teachers' choices to use, or not to use, Web 2.0 technologies in upper primary school classrooms (PhD dissertation, University of Melbourne). Retrieved from https://minerva-access.unimelb.edu.au/handle/11343/208015 (accessed 5 July 2021).

Dinham, S. (2016). Leading learning and teaching. *ACER Press.* https://ezp.lib.unimelb.edu.au/login?url=https://search.ebscohost.com/login.aspx?direct=true&db=nlebk&AN=1438265&site=eds-live&scope=site

Di Teodoro, S., Donders, S., Kemp-Davidson, J., Robertson, P. & Schuyler, L. (2011). Asking good questions: Promoting greater understanding of mathematics through purposeful teacher and student questioning. *Canadian Journal of Action Research, 12*(2), 18–29.

Estrin, D. (2017). In Israel, teaching kids cyber skills is a national mission. *Times of Israel,* 4 February. Retrieved from www.timesofisrael.com/in-israel-teaching-kids-cyber-skills-is-a-national-mission/ (accessed 2 July 2021).

Graham, C. R. (2011). Theoretical considerations for understanding technological pedagogical content knowledge (TPACK). *Computers & Education, 57*(3). doi:10.1016/j.compedu.2011.04.010

Ilomäki, L., Paavola, S., Lakkala, M. & Kantosalo, A. (2016). Digital competence: An emergent boundary concept for policy and educational research. *Education and Information Technologies, 21*(3), 655–679.

Israeli Ministry of Economy and Industry (2014). *From Startup Nation to Cyber-Nation.* Retrieved from https://itrade.gov.il/romania/?p=709 (accessed 20 November 2019).

Israeli Ministry of Foreign Affairs (n.d.). *Commitment to Innovations.* Retrieved from https://mfa.gov.il/MFA_Graphics/MFA%20Gallery/Documents/Innovations2010-En.pdf (accessed 20 November 2019).

Israeli Ministry of Science and Technology (2013). *Science and Technology.* Retrieved from https://mfa.gov.il/mfa/aboutisrael/science/pages/science and technology.aspx (accessed 20 November 2019).

Kramarski, B. & Michalsky, T. (2014). Effect of a TPCK-SRL model on teachers' pedagogical beliefs, self-efficacy, and technology-based lesson design. In *Technological Pedagogical Content Knowledge* (Vol. 1 – Chapter 5, pp. 89–112). Springer US. https://doi.org/10.1007/978-1-4899-8080-9_5

Law, N., Pelgrum, W., & Plomp, T. (2008). *Pedagogy and ICT Use in Schools around the World: Findings from the IEA SITES 2006 Study* (Vol. 23). Springer. http://books.google.com.au/books?hl=en&lr=&id=urCHH10HK_0C&oi=fnd&pg=PR13&ots=m8LBMI7Gpo&sig=XgGNvcWjSNHAXcfrdgxvnDi5npA&redir_esc=y#v=onepage&q&f=false (accessed 21 July 2021).

Martin, S. (2019). Nationals push for $1.3bn in drought relief to help party keep seats in next election. *Guardian,* 23 October. Retrieved from www.theguardian.com/australia-news/2019/oct/24/nationals-push-for-12bn-in-drought-relief-to-help-party-keep-seats-in-next-election (accessed 2 July 2021).

Mishra, P. & Koehler, M. J. (2006). Technological pedagogical content knowledge: A framework for teacher knowledge. *Teachers College Record, 108*(6), 1017.

Organisation for Economic Co-operation and Development (OECD) (2019). *Bridging the Digital Divide*. Retrieved from Schooling for Tomorrow: Knowledge Bank website: www.oecd.org/site/schoolingfortomorrowknowledgebase/themes/ict/bridgingthedigitaldivide.htm (accessed 24 December 2019).

Sefton-Green, J., Nixon, H. & Erstad, O. (2009). Reviewing approaches and perspectives on digital literacy. *Pedagogies: An International Journal, 4*(2), 107–125.

Sullivan, K. (2019). Labor refuses to back PM's Future Drought Fund. *ABC News*, 13 February. Retrieved from www.abc.net.au/news/2019-02-13/labor-ditches-drought-fund/10806472.

Terrell, M. (2003). Asking good questions in the mathematics classroom. *Mathematicians and Education Reform Forum Newsletter, 15*, 3–5.

Vosoughi, S., Roy, D. & Aral, S. (2018). The spread of true and false news online. *Science, 359*(6380), 1146. doi:10.1126/science.aap9559

5

USING THEORY TO INFORM OUR PRACTICE

IN THIS CHAPTER YOU WILL LEARN:

- How technology helps learners think
- Theories of learning and how they translate to the classroom
- Why theory is important to technology use in our classrooms.

INTRODUCTION

In this chapter, we explore some theoretical frameworks that can help us when we use digital technologies. These theories can shape our own and our students' learning. We position these theories as types of pedagogical theory that are similar to more general pedagogical practices. In particular, we will explore the theories of Constructionism and Connectivism as these theories offer deep insights into the use of technologies for learning.

IN THE CLASSROOM TODAY

Rami is reviewing his teaching from last week. He introduced his 8-year-old learners to a history activity that asked the learners to create a timeline on a large piece of paper. It did not go as planned. After a frustrating lesson, Rami is left with several diagrams of the historic event that do not seem to have any sequence or relevance to a timeline. What is going on here? Rami asks. The students understand the historic event but have not been able to create a timeline. Surely that is straightforward enough? He will need to review his thinking before the next lesson.

CONSTRUCTIONISM

Constructionism is a theory of learning developed by Seymour Papert that purports to engage learners in cognitive development through computers. Papert's seminal book *Mindstorms* (Papert, 1980) presented a detailed argument for the use of technology and computers in school education. He identified ways in which computers can aid the development of student thinking and offer new, different ways of learning that can be very useful in schools. Indeed he claims, from his vantage point of the 1980s, that computers can and should change the way we think. He proposed that the emergence of commercial computing and the move towards personal computers would, 'in more essential, conceptual ways, influencing how people think even when they are far removed from physical contact with a computer' (Papert, 1980, p. 4).

Today, we are faced with a range of technologies at home, at work and in the classroom. Wearable technology such as smartwatches, minicomputers/mobile devices and artificial intelligence software are part of everyday life. How then have Papert's predictions and claims of technology's potential been realised? And do they have relevance in today's schools?

Papert's work drew heavily on the work of Piaget (1964), whose constructivist theory identified that children create (or build) understanding through direct experiences. This book does not claim to dive deeply into Piaget's theories as it is believed these are covered in many, if not most, educational texts. However, it is essential to understand where Papert took up Piaget's ideas and where they connect.

Importantly, Piaget saw the child as the instrument of learning. A child develops knowledge and understanding by building on previous experiences, and these experiences impacted how the learning was understood. Piaget saw childhood development as progressing through four distinct phases, and his theory suggests that every child will move through the four phases, but each child will do so at their own pace (Piaget, 1964). These four stages, summarised from Piaget's writings (1964), are:

- Sensory-motor, pre-verbal stage
  - Up to around 18 months of age, children are developing an understanding that objects exist outside their physical location: a sense of object permanency.
- Pre-operational representation
  - Up to around 7 years, children are starting to develop concepts of language and symbols: a sense that their own perspectives define the world.
- Concrete operational stage
  - Up to around 11 years, children can think about things logically if they have access to physical objects or materials: a sense that they can work things out in their head.
- Formal operational stage
  - From 12 years, children develop their abilities to think logically when they don't have physical objects in front of them: a sense of being able to follow hypothetical or abstract arguments in their heads.

From these four pillars of development, Papert extrapolated that making and engaging with concrete materials is a significant part of learning and that learning and practice should occur together. Papert presents computers as a way of ensuring learning 'construct[s] a meaningful product' (Papert, 1986, p. 20). Papert saw computing as a resource to move learners from concrete to formal learning. Referring to the above summary of Piaget's four stages, Papert sees the computer as a bridge for students to move between stages three and four and perhaps accelerate a child's development in the process.

As a part of this focus on moving between concrete and formal cognition, Papert advocates for learning, that is 'more active and self-directed' (Papert, 1986, p. 21). He presented the idea that computing and computers can help students to develop new abstract thinking skills and formal cognitive processes without first having to have fully developed concrete thinking. In his words, 'Knowledge that was accessible only through formal processes can now be approached concretely' (Papert, 1986, p. 21).

If we accept that computers can indeed offer these types of learning, we need to understand better how these thinking processes occur. In turn, this knowledge can help us understand what technologies might offer students in our classrooms and how learners might be best supported to engage with computers and technologies. We will explore Constructionism through four main ideas, or pillars, that Papert identified as crucial to Constructionism. The following are summaries of central themes that have emerged from reading a range of papers that explore Constructionism. As Bers et al. (2001) have noted, these are the four common-alities that emerge when we read about Constructionism.

LEARNING MUST BE ACTIVE

This first tenet of Constructionism identifies that some object or artefact should be at the outcome of the learning. As Papert identifies, a computer or virtual environment should be 'where learners can become the active, constructing architects of their own learning' (Papert, 1986, p. 122). With these active learning experiences, we refer to the child actively making sense as they engage in some activity, not necessarily with a real-world physical object. Programming a computer or creating something virtually are good examples of this.

Consider using an iPad to read an ebook compared to creating an ebook. These two differ-ent tasks may not seem to have much difference in the classroom. At the end of each, students will presumably have engaged with some new content. With a focus on Constructionism, we might see that active learning with and through computers can better support children's cog-nitive development. When they create their own ebook, children are 'learning by doing' (Bers et al., 2001, p. 4).

OBJECTS SUPPORT US TO UNDERSTAND ABSTRACT IDEAS

Computers support learning by providing ways to create objects that represent our mental models. A mental model is an image or conceptual understanding we hold about some concept. When we use computers to understand abstract ideas, we provide a way to experience abstract concepts that would not be possible without computers. As Fischer and Ostwald comment, 'Experiential artefacts allow us to interact with the world. They provide information that enables us to interpret a situation through our perceptions' (Fischer and Ostwald, 2005, p. 19).

TECHNOLOGY OFFERS NEW WAYS OF THINKING

Using technology, we learn to interact with devices in specific ways such as buttons, touch screens, a mouse or a stylus. In thinking through technology, we can learn to think differently, too. Papert saw this new type of thinking as particularly important for future generations, who, presumably, will have access to increasingly sophisticated and accessible technologies. Papert phrased it this way: 'Coding enables children to think in systematic and sequential ways while encountering powerful ideas from computer science and other domains of knowledge' (Bers, 2017, p. 2)

SELF-REFLECTION IS IMPORTANT

Drawing again on Piaget's learning theory of how learning occurs, Papert identifies that we need to scaffold learners to build knowledge and mental models. Self-reflection, then, is designed to enable students to engage with what they knew before and what they know now. In so doing, they can build knowledge that connects to their prior learning and understanding of the world. In the classroom, this means we should be asking learners to present their ideas as they develop and support them to make connections between what they knew before and what they know now.

To conclude this section on Constructionism, it seems fitting to hear from Papert (1986) himself. As you read the following quote, take a moment to reflect on what you knew about learning before reading this section and how Piaget and Papert might influence how you think about teaching and learning.

> Constructionism – the N-word as opposed to the V-word – shares constructivism's con-notation of learning as 'building knowledge structures' irrespective of the circum-stances of the learning. It then adds the idea that this happens especially felicitously in a context where the learner is consciously engaged in constructing a public entity, whether it's a sandcastle on the beach or a theory of the universe. (Papert, 1986, p. 11)

CONNECTIVISM

Following the previous section in which we explored Papert's theory of Constructionism, we next explore the ideas of Connectivism. This section is drawn from research conducted in several Australian primary schools (Blannin, 2017). The study sought to understand better why some teachers used technology more effectively and efficiently than others.

In some schools, one person was seen as the 'tech teacher'. Whether they had a formal leadership role or not, this was the person to whom other teachers would go for quick fixes and new ideas for teaching.

Why was it then that in other schools, there was not only one person designated as having high-level technical skills, but rather an entire team of teachers or the entire school?

The research discussed here suggested that there seemed to be a shared responsibility for learning and teaching, and the teachers functioned in a highly connected and reliant way. While the actual teaching was sometimes carried out together, there was something else at play beyond the careful hiring practices of the school leaders. One outcome of the research was that another theory, called 'Connectivism', was seen as being enacted. This connected approach to learning and teaching appeared to be a critical factor in ensuring that teachers could learn, enact and reflect on their teaching to the ultimate benefit of their students.

Connectivism, as defined by Siemens in 2004, offers a way to understand how learning occurs in today's technologically enabled world. The fundamental principle of this theory is that 'Learning is a process that occurs within nebulous environments of shifting core elements – not entirely under the control of the individual' (Siemens, 2004, p 89).

Siemens was interested in new ways of understanding learning, moved beyond traditional learning ideas, and considered the many changes to information and communications technologies. Siemens (2004) proposed that these changes impacted on how we learn in the twenty-first century. In 2004, Siemens first suggested looking beyond ourselves, as individuals, to understand learning:

> Over the last twenty years, technology has reorganised how we live, how we communicate, and how we learn. Learning needs and theories that describe learning principles and processes should reflect underlying social environments. (Siemens, 2004, p. 1)

In this research study, we found that teachers used many different ways to learn, often including teachers and students learning from each other. This interactive learning approach demonstrated that they were learning through connections with others, as Siemens' (2004) hypothesised. Siemens (2008) said we need to change how we learn:

> The growing prominence of networked technologies for formal and informal learning suggests substantial pressures for education institutions to adapt their models to suit better the interests and digital literacy skills of a growing percentage of the learner population. (Siemens, 2008, p. 7)

CONNECTIVISM IN THE CLASSROOM

Siemens' (2008) reflection that educational institutions need to change their teaching approaches to 'better suit the interests and digital literacy skills' of learners (Siemens, 2008, p. 7) was clear in my research, as teachers talked about how they learn new skills through others. They said, on numerous occasions, that they wanted to learn new pedagogical and technological skills so that they could meet the changing needs of their students. This was a driver for change and was strongly connected to a sense of connection to other teachers within and beyond their school.

Siemens (2008) further explains this approach of Connectivism, saying:

> When knowledge is seen as existing in networks and learning as forming and navigating these networks, many existing aspects of academia are subject to change. (Siemens, 2008, p. 19)

Siemens' (2014) later work presented a case for changing the future of learning across society. Not only in schools but also workplaces and homes, he sees learning as:

> a continual process, lasting for a lifetime. Learning and work-related activities are no longer separate. In many situations, they are the same. (Siemens, 2014, p. 1)

The concept that learning is ongoing and 'lasting for a lifetime' (Siemens, 2014, p. 1) was also shown in the study (Blannin, 2017) where one teacher in a primary school said:

> Even if you are working on your own, we still, you know, all work in the back office so that we can be like – look, I'm really stuck, I don't know how to do the maths lesson for the younger or, the lower group, does anyone have an idea? So, it's like really yeah collaborative in terms of that. (Sarah, Interview 2, Gregstone Primary School)

CONNECTIVISM AND COLLABORATION

The teachers in Sarah's school are a learning resource for each other. Siemens' (2014, p. 4) Connectivism concept helps us make sense of Sarah's theories about how learning occurs. His statement that learning is no longer a personal act that occurs within an individual shows us how to make sense of ongoing, multi-strategy learning. In this research, the learning strategies used by teachers indicated that learning was not seen *only* as an internal event but rather an external and dynamic activity that occurred in the space between individuals. As Siemens states:

> We can no longer personally experience and acquire learning that we need to act. We derive our competence from forming connections. (Siemens, 2014, p. 4).

Sarah again offers an example of this networked learning space, which was also expressed and validated by all nine participants in this study.

The connections that Sarah's team made between themselves were both personal and professional. There was a sense of personal connection in her willingness to express her lack of knowledge when she says, 'Look, I'm really stuck'. In expressing her lack of knowledge, she appeared to be seeking connections on a personal level. She positioned herself as someone who needed and willingly accepted help from her colleagues.

Hannah also highlighted this mixture of personal and professional connectedness within the teaching teams at each school:

> when we plan, whether it's individually or with a partner or a team you constantly sort of trying to think about, well, how can we enhance this ... (Hannah, Interview 1, Gregstone Primary School)

Hannah provides a sense of collaborative learning and Connectivism in this statement. Her use of the term 'we' suggests a shared approach to problem-solving and shared learning at her school. Even when planning alone for an upcoming lesson, Hannah sees the team as a shared resource or 'hive mind' that can, together, solve problems. Siemens (2014) connects Hannah's understanding of shared knowledge shift to the fast-paced growth in technology and global changes:

> In today's environment, action is often needed without personal learning – that is, we need to act by drawing information from outside of our direct knowledge. The ability to synthesise and recognise connections and patterns is a valuable skill. (Siemens, 2014, p. 3)

The concept of knowledge being 'outside of our primary knowledge' was also relevant to this study (Siemens, 2014, p. 3) and showed that Connectivism could be a valuable way to think about learning in our schools. Teachers in the study appeared to access new knowledge and skills through connections within and beyond the school. They demonstrated an ability to synthesise new information from various sources, including social media, teachers at other schools, online videos, blogs and other online resources.

Sally, from MacArthur Primary School, commented on the need to validate other teacher's contributions so that they create and maintain supportive teams of learning partners in a networked learning environment:

> Like these people are doing amazing ... yeah. I think people need to be validated. So, I think they need to know that what they're doing is good and it's good enough, like they're not missing a step, that they are doing quite well, but they also need to know that next step of being better, and it's not that you need to get better, it's just that you can get better. (Sally, MacArthur Primary School, Interview 1)

In contrast to Sally's comments, Matt, from Homedale Primary School, discussed a perceived lack of technical support from other teachers at his school. He had, instead, made connections beyond the school, with colleagues whom he believed had more experience than him:

> Some of my friends are more advanced, they're actually technical sort of coordinators in schools, like ... implementing the use of technology ... and so he was a really good resource to use in the classroom. (Matt, Homedale Primary School)

Matt appeared to have actively sought connections with other teachers and brought them into the classroom as a strategy for learning. The colleague to whom he refers above was never physically in his classroom or school, as he lived a long distance away. Matt, however, speaks of his external colleague as a 'really good resource ... *in the classroom*' (emphasis added). Matt, in conversation, suggested that he felt connected to his external colleague and suggested that he felt connected despite not being physically connected.

Matt could be said to be 'deriv[ing] our competence from forming connections' (Siemens, 2004, p. 4). Matt's learning strategies, which were as varied as other participants, had led him to build connections with other people beyond his school. For Matt, knowledge existed both inside and beyond his school and was accessed based on the teacher's learning needs.

There is much ongoing debate about why it can be difficult for teachers to engage effectively with technologies in the classroom. O'Connor et al. (2004) and Office of the Auditor General Western Australia (2016) suggested a lack of support, research or practical technology models in schools. This deficit, they argued, had limited the effective use of technology in classrooms. Suppose we consider the impact and implications of Connectivism. In that case, however, it may provide us with a new way of thinking about learning and teaching: a group of connected and networked teachers who learn and teach together.

CONNECTIVISM FOR YOUR CLASSROOM

As we reflect on the ideas of Constructionism and Connectivism, it can be helpful to consider how you learn as an adult and how this might be reflected in your teaching. Your strategies for learning may not suit the students in your classroom, and so it can be helpful to consider different types of learning.

Drawing on the same research project as previously, Table 5.1 provides an overview of the types of learning that teaches engaged in to improve their digital literacy and technology skills.

There are collaborative and individual learning strategies that proved helpful and ensured that teachers could learn in many 'modes' of learning. Multi-modal learning, as this can be called, is a helpful framework for considering your teaching approach. These complex and varied strategies seem to have provided support in learning both technology skills and new pedagogy. Just because we teach does not mean that students learn, and as teachers, it is our responsibility to ensure that both happen in our classrooms.

Table 5.1 Teaching and learning strategies that may support connectivism in learning

Individual learning strategies	Collaborative learning strategies
Personal exploration online	Team teaching with new technologies
'Playing online'	Learning together in same physical space
Seeking assistance from their own children	Modelling skills to their peers (practising)
Observing students in the classroom	Seeking online support from others (Skype, email, Facebook)
Collecting ideas into a resource folder 'for later'	Chatting with peers in informal spaces (staff room, hallways, before/after meetings)
Observing their peers learning and teaching	Making appointments with technical support staff
Searching 'how-to' online	Asking questions on online forums, blogs and social media spaces
Trialling new pedagogical and technological skills – as a team and individually	

Each of the teachers in this research spoke about their a personalised 'toolkit' of learning strategies. They shared that they wanted to develop a range of ways to learn new skills so that they could meet the diverse needs of their students. The term 'toolkit' is used to express the purposeful way teachers appeared to draw on different 'tools' or learning strategies to meet different needs. Each tool (or strategy) was chosen for a specific purpose that met a specific need, just as a handyperson would choose the right tool for the task at hand. These teachers often spoke of using several strategies to meet their own learning needs, drawing on different approaches as they were helpful to them.

David provided an example from Royal Park Primary School during an interview. He commented that he had watched a teacher use a technological resource and made his own notes on how it worked. David then went away and explored the tool in his own time, on his computer at home. Finally, David searched online for specific answers to his questions, asking 'how to make something happen in the classroom'.

David's varied learning strategies suggest to us that learning new skills included 'multiple opportunities to learn new information and understand its implications for practice' (Timperley et al., 2007, p. xxxvii).

Having 'multiple opportunities' (Timperley et al., 2007, p. 15) to learn a new skill seemed important for teachers to develop new skills, mentor their colleagues and share their knowledge and skills.

For your learning as a teacher, these findings suggest that you need to make space to engage in a few different types of learning: collaborative and individual, formal and informal.

CONNECTING STUDENT LEARNING TO TEACHER LEARNING

Teachers in this research (Blannin, 2017) made connections between how they learnt and how they wished their students could learn. There was no distinct line between how a teacher learned a new skill or technology resource and how a student learned similar concepts.

Victoria shared this view when she reflected on how her students learned new skills:

> the other thing we find a lot of the time is that the students are often sort of more expert in ICT than we are you know and have better ideas, or will come in and say, oh, I've got this app, and I think this would be really good, and you know they're spending time discovering apps at home. (Victoria, Royal Park Primary School, Interview 1)

As teachers, we need to be open to learning from others, including from our students, to lift the load of constant new technologies appearing in our classrooms.

Connectivism (Siemens, 2014) may support us to make sense of new pedagogies and technologies.

BACK TO THE CLASSROOM

Rami has been reviewing learning from his university classes. He has reminded himself of Constructivism and Connectivism. These two ways of theorising learning has led Rami to rethink his teaching. In the next lesson, he will provide concrete resources to create a timeline. He has created a physical, paper timeline along the length of the classroom wall and then created a series of small picture frames. Each frame contains an explanation of an event but is missing a date. In small groups, the learners will be asked to investigate each event and uncover the missing date (or date range). Having done this, the learners will then come together as a class and explain where their event should be positioned on the timeline. Rami has reframed his lesson as a space where the learners are moving from abstract (dates) to concrete (the timeline) and back to abstract (the dates in relation to others). He has provided several ways to present the learning and to engage with the concepts and ideas. Rami is particularly proud that he has provided a space for self-reflection when the groups present to the class. He is excited to teach this lesson and can't wait to see how it will be received by his students.

CONCLUSION

This chapter has seen us explore two major theoretical concepts that can help us make informed decisions when using technology in our classrooms: Constructionism and Connectivism.

Through Constructionism (Papert, 1986), learning is framed as external-to-internal knowledge-building that occurs through:

- Active learning
- Giving abstract concepts a concrete expression
- Considering technology as providing new ways of thinking and developing knowledge
- Ensuring that we build new mental models through self-reflection.

Siemens' (2014) Connectivism is, in many ways, a complementary approach to Papert's Constructionism, in that it gives us a way to think about where the knowledge we are seeking to understand can be found. In reflecting on the ideas of a connected network of learners, in which everyone holds some part of the information, we can understand that the external models of Constructionism that we construct for our learners are framed within a networked understanding of knowledge itself.

FURTHER READING

Learn more about Connectivism in our twenty-first-century classrooms.

Kivunja, C. (2014). Do you want your students to be job-ready with 21st century skills? Change pedagogies: A pedagogical paradigm shift from Vygotskyian social constructivism to critical thinking, problem solving and Siemens' digital connectivism. *International Journal of Higher Education*, 3(3), 81–91.

Explore how Constructionism might look in a literacy classroom:

Moon, A. L., Francom, G. M. & Wold, C. M. (2021). Learning from versus learning with technology: Supporting constructionist reading comprehension learning with iPad applications. *TechTrends*, 65(1), 79–89.

Reflect on how Constructionism relates to other theories you may have explored:

Laurillard, D. (2020). The significance of Constructionism as a distinctive pedagogy. Constructionism 2020. Constructionism Conference. Available at: www.construction ismconf.org/keynotes-and-panels/.

REFERENCES

Bers, M. U. (2017). The Seymour test: Powerful ideas in early childhood education. *International Journal of Child–Computer Interaction, 14*, 10–14. doi:10.1016/j.ijcci.2017.06.004

Bers, M. U. (2018). Coding as a playground: Programming and computational thinking in the early childhood classroom. *Information Technology in Childhood Education*. New York and London: Taylor & Francis.

Blannin, J., (2017). Accounting for teachers' choices to use, or not to use, Web 2.0 technologies in upper primary school classrooms (PhD dissertation, University of Melbourne). Retrieved from https://minerva-access.unimelb.edu.au/handle/11343/208015 (accessed 5 July 2021).

Fischer, G. & Ostwald, J. (2005). Knowledge communication in design communities. In R. Bromme, F. W. Hesse & H. Spada (eds), *Barriers and Biases in Computer-Mediated Knowledge Communication* (pp. 213–242). New York: Springer. doi:10.1007/0-387-24319-4_10

O'Connor, K., Goldberg, A., Russell, M., Bebell, D. & O'Dwyer, L. (2004). *USE IT Report Three: Teacher's Beliefs about Access, Use, Support and Obstacles in Using Instructional Technology*. Boston College, Technology and Assessment Study Collaborative.

Office of the Auditor General Western Australia (ed.), *Information and Communication Technology (ICT) in Education*. Retrieved from: https://audit.wa.gov.au/reports-and-publications/reports/information-and-communication-technology-ict-in-education/ (accessed 11 June 2017).

Papert, S. (1980). *Mindstorms: Children, Computers, and Powerful Ideas*. New York: Basic Books.

Papert, S. (1986). *Constructionism: A New Opportunity for Elementary Science Education*. Massachusetts Institute of Technology, Media Laboratory, Epistemology and Learning Group.

Piaget, J. (1964). Cognitive development in children: Piaget. *Journal of Research in Science Teaching, 2*(3), 176–186.

Siemens, G. (2004). Connectivism. *International Journal of Instructional Technology and Distance Learning, 2*(1), 2–10.

Siemens, G. (2008). *Learning and Knowing in Networks: Changing Roles for Educators and Designers*. IT FORUM for Discussion.

Timperley, H., Wilson, A., Barrar, H. & Fung, I. (2007). *Teacher Professional Learning and Development Best Evidence Synthesis*. Auckland: Iterative Best Evidence Synthesis Program.

TECHNOLOGY USE FOR LITERACY LEARNING

6

IN THIS CHAPTER YOU WILL LEARN:

- How technology has changed what we mean by Language Arts and Literacy
- How to engage with multi-modal literacies in your teaching
- Ideas for teaching with technology in your literacy or English Language Arts classroom.

INTRODUCTION

Teaching literacy has long been the basis of education. From the days of the 3Rs of reading, writing and arithmetic, schools have understood that engaged and successful citizens are those with the ability to read, write and learn. With the increased use of technology in the classroom, today's students have new ways of developing, using and exploring literacies.

In Chapter 4, we explored what digital literacies might mean for our students and how we might address these needs. In contrast, this chapter will focus on how technology can support the development of traditional literacies such as reading, interpreting and creating texts. Of course, the meaning of the term 'text' has changed since the original definition of 'printed words on paper'. This chapter will address the text types our students engage with and therefore how they need to use the literacy skills of reading and writing in new ways.

Flanagan and Shoffner (2013) identify a clear connection between technology and literacy learning, and claim that technology integration still has a way to go to be effective in teaching English Language Arts (that is, teaching English to English-speaking students). While there are many different opportunities to engage with literacy through technology, this has yet to be the case in many classrooms:

> Technology plays an integral role in the English Language Arts (ELA) classroom today, yet teachers and teacher educators continue to develop understandings of how technology influences pedagogy. (2013, p. 242)

Since the initial use of technologies such as cassette tapes and videos in the classroom in 1970s, we now have the chance to bring much more authentic texts into the classroom. These might include live feed videos of political speeches, up-to-the-minute news reports or short-films by citizen-makers. Each of these examples offers insights into texts and the evolution of this text.

For example, a news report may be updated as facts emerge or fallacies are put to rest. In exploring the evolution of a text, technology provides opportunities for our students to develop critical thinking skills that inform their judgments. They might ask: 'If this fact has been shown to be false so quickly, how might I check that this new piece of information is valid?'.

Engaging with authentic materials means that we, as teachers, become curators of content. We can no longer rely on a textbook to provide every text example that students need to explore. Indeed, we need to develop our own skills as critical thinkers to develop sets of texts, data or online resources that provide focused learning experiences. As we begin this chapter, it is important to note that teachers are not being asked to create every digital text themselves; there is an ever-growing repository of potential learning resources on the Internet. Our role is to bring a pedagogical lens to each resource we find online and to understand its potential benefit to our students' learning. Using existing digital resources has been promoted as a tool for teaching literacy for over a decade, and continues to be a great way to access authentic learning experiences (Dudeney & Hockly, 2007).

In this chapter, we will explore the possibilities for using technology for teaching literacy skills such as reading and writing. We will provide examples of what 'good practice' looks like in the classroom and also discuss some potential challenges that you might face.

A short vignette follows this section and provides some practical context for the rest of the chapter. As you read, be sure to refer back to this classroom scenario so that you consider the theoretical ideas within a practical context.

IN THE CLASSROOM TODAY

In Miray's English class today, her Year 9 students are developing their skills in critical analysis. In yesterday's class Miray asks each student to review the transcript of a recent political speech made in Parliament. The speech focused on the inequity of access to health care for Australians living in rural and remote areas and demanded action from the prime minister. Riku is a student in Miray's class. She has not read a political speech before and she has noticed that it reads more like an argument than speeches she has heard before. There are lots of short sentences, people's names used, and some words she doesn't understand.

Miray explains today's task: each small group of the students will look at one of five online newspaper articles about the speech. Once they have read the article, they need to go back to the original transcript of the speech and ask themselves, has the journalist provided a fair account of the speech?

To help the students develop an answer to this question, Miray has provided access to the online newspapers and asks them to read the article in full, look at the images used and the headline of the article.

As Riku and her group begin reading the newspaper article online, Riku notices that the page says 'updated three hours ago'. This means it might have changed. Calling Miray over, Riku explains that they can't complete the task, as the article could already be out of date. Miray is pleased that the group noticed this and begins to explain that newspapers are constantly updating their work. 'But how do we know what is true then?', asks Riku. Miray thinks carefully. This is an important teaching moment, but how to explain to these 15-year-olds that 'truth' is a tricky concept in the online space?

Deciding she needs more time to reflect, Miray asks Riku's group to continue the activity and use the current version of the article. After class, Miray is concerned that she hasn't met her students' needs today. How might technology help her explore this important concept?

TECHNOLOGY IN LITERACY LEARNING

The rapid pace of change in technology has also impacted on both what we mean by literacy texts and what we mean by language. In this section, we explore these changes and what they mean to you as technology-enabled literacy teachers.

WHAT DO WE MEAN BY A TEXT?

A major challenge for literacy and English teaching in recent years has been the shift in what we can now consider as a 'text'. Traditionally, a text was a book or other document, on paper, printed or handwritten. Today, of course, we have access to so many types of texts (State Government of Victoria, Australia, 2019). Table 6.1 shows some of the types of texts that are available to us in our technology-enabled literacy or English classroom.

Table 6.1 Different types of texts

• Online games	• Blogs
• Infographics	• Wikis (co-created, editable websites)
• Online quizzes	• Digital posters
• Newspapers	• Digital artwork
• Web pages/websites	• Slideshows
• Podcasts	• Interactive stories
• Social networks	• Digital magazines
• Email	• Online advertising

The list in Table 6.1 is not exhaustive and can never be, as new ways of presenting and engaging with texts continue to emerge. The list does provide some ways to think about what types of text we are exposing our students to in our classrooms. Indeed, some data suggests that people spend up to 463 minutes a day engaged with media (Watson, 2020). Some of this time may be spent with traditional texts but most appears to be digital in nature. Consider that in 2009, statistical analysis suggested that an average person read 100,000 words a day, with only 9 per cent of that word count being read in a printed form (Nusca, 2009). More than 10 years later, it is safe to say that digital texts have increased in quantity exponentially.

The fast growth and increasing diversity of digital texts means we need to reflect on how we are preparing students to be literate in today's society. As we discussed in Chapter 4 digital literacy is a unique and at times contentious term. Digital texts, however, are less challenged and increasingly accepted as necessary foci for the literacy and English classroom. Having explored what we mean by the term 'text', we next discuss the idea of multi-modal or multi-media resources for learning.

MULTI-MODAL LITERACIES

First, let us clarify the difference between multi-modal learning and multi-media resources. Lauer (2009) provides a useful definition. Multi-modal learning is concerned with the ways in which learners engage with content, essentially asking, 'What is the mode of content delivery, written, spoken or drawn?'. Multi-media, on the other hand, is concerned with the tools used to create the content.

Let's review an example. In the classroom, a student can engage with a video that explains a new concept such as how to use a semi-colon. The video itself is a multi-media resource. As the student watches the video she engages with different modes of expression such as imagery and spoken words. In this way, a single multi-media resource can engage students in a number of modes of literacy learning.

Over the past decade, an imperative to ensure students are exposed to a range of multi-modal literacies has gained prominence in literacy research (Sewell and Denton, 2011). There are several reasons for this that may resonate with you in your classroom, including the reality that texts are no longer static pieces of information:

> Multimodal literacy recognizes that for many children, knowledge construction has shifted away from the static, printed text to dynamic texts supported by sounds and pictures. Furthermore, knowledge construction is much more social and, hence, bound upon situational contexts. (Sewell and Denton, 2011, p. 39)

How might these multi-media resources influence your teaching? The use of technology in the literacy or English classroom gives us a range of strategies that we will explore further later in this chapter. Technology itself does not offer pedagogical resources. It is, as we have noted in previous chapters, you as the teacher who takes an online resource and creates from it a pedagogically relevant tool for learning. This means that the teacher needs to engage with online resources, including those from the list above, to ensure that you maintain a current understanding of what texts, multi-media and multi-modal learning are available to you.

Consider the idea of multi-literacies in the online space. This might mean teaching a new concept using a video, an infographic and a printed text. Students need to be able to navigate between different types of texts and modes of learning. This idea of bringing multi-media resources together within a single learning experience is not new. Researchers have been promoting a multi-modal approach for a number of years:

> Rather than focusing solely on the single literacy of print, English teachers navigate multiple literacies (or multiliteracies) in the classroom, working across print, visual, and media literacies. (Flanagan and Shoffner, 2013, p. 243)

It is within this idea of multiple literacies that technology emerges as a supportive resource for the classroom. Today's teachers cannot create every resource from scratch, nor do they have time to personalise everything they create for each student in the classroom.

Technology, then, provides access to a range of modes of learning and an almost infinite library of multi-media. From YouTube and online newspapers to interactive ebooks and educational podcasts, technology is the link between the changing demands of literacy and English teaching and actual learning experiences in the classroom.

PASSIVE AND ACTIVE LEARNERS

Another issue to consider when bringing technology into the classroom is exactly how the learning will take place. Flanagan and Shoffler (2013) usefully ask us to consider whether we are engaging in high- or low-tech learning. A teacher's perspective on what learning is impacts on this and we should seek to consider what literacy learning means to you.

Does literacy learning mean reading books? Writing essays? Responding to comprehension questions? Perhaps watching a video or using images is your idea of a strong literacy lesson?

While technology can undoubtedly enhance learning in these ways, each of these previous examples are rather passive activities. We can consider how technology is used in our literacy or English classrooms by equating high-tech learning to active learning, wherein students create, share and comment on a range of digital texts. Low-tech learning, then, is more likely to be passive and require students to view, read, watch or listen instead of making or doing.

Consider how student learning might be made more active. What are students doing during the learning? Viewing, reading and writing can all be made more active with the introduction of technology. For example, in watching a video, students could use a back-channel app to discuss what they see as they see it. A video about the extinction of bees can therefore become a discussion of students' understanding and perceptions of the importance of bee colonies. The conversation can be in real time while the video is playing. What might this activity offer in terms of student understanding and engagement? Perhaps it produces more focused student questions or relevant discussions, or perhaps this is one way to ensure that students are actively 'at-work' while a video plays.

This is only one example of how technology can be an active learning experience for your students. You should also consider students as content creators, rather than only being consumers. In this way, students will have a clear purpose to view, watch, explore and engage with examples of texts. Then, they use their learning to create their own content. Imagine asking students to listen to a podcast about species extinctions. Following this more passive activity, students are guided to create their own response podcasts that will be shared with the entire school community. Technology, in this case, is providing a real-world connection to learning and an audience to provide feedback and advice on their learning.

CRITICAL LITERACIES

With the ever-increasing growth of online, digital content, it has become increasingly important to ensure that our students are able to discern bias and influence within the texts they explore. This might mean understanding a news website's political leanings or the way that landscapes are painted by First Nations people compared to colonisers. Each of us brings our own political beliefs into the classroom. Our teacher identity is influenced by our beliefs about how we should live and engage with the world around us. Often these beliefs are developed from childhood and can be deeply held. In our classrooms, we should consider how we have positioned discussions and what alternative beliefs and political backgrounds our students may hold. As Shor and Freire (1987, p.46) reflect:

This is a great discovery, education is politics! When a teacher discovers that he or she is a politician, too, the teacher has to ask, What kind of politics am I doing in the classroom? That is, in favor of whom am I being a teacher?

We raise this issue of politics and teacher beliefs here because of the changed nature of texts and literacy learning. As students explore digital texts, and create their own, they need to become aware of the nature of what is 'true' and what is not. While some may argue that reality is a fixed concept that everyone experiences in the same way, it is hard to substantiate this case when we engage with digital texts.

Students who leave formal education without an understanding of bias and the ability to critique texts are at a disadvantage. Instead, we need to ensure students are prepared for their future, whether this means further, tertiary study or entering the workforce. In particular, the ability to find references that reliably support their arguments and references that contradict their opinions is a necessary literacy skill for life in the twenty-first century (Julia and Isrokatun, 2019).

In many countries, teachers have been teaching critical thinking for decades, and this present discussion does not seek to minimise the work they have been doing. Instead, teachers are now challenged to consider the broad range of texts with which students will engage and seek to understand how bias is represented in these new, digital and growing modes of information.

Technology access in our literacy and English classrooms means that we can more easily bring opposing views into our classrooms. We can ask students to read an online newspaper article and compare it to a political cartoon on the same topic. Our students can compare a blog post written by a citizen-journalist to a video news reel from an established news organisation. They can play an online game to explore the characterisation of players and compare their observations to Wikipedia articles about the cultural groups represented. Teachers, of course, are at the heart of this type of learning. Active, engaged and critical learning experiences, that make the most of digital texts are framed by teachers who understand the importance of these learning activities. By ensuring that we as teachers are skilled in finding, comparing, creating and critiquing digital texts, we become an informed guide for students in our classrooms. Indeed, 'it can be said that the process of technology integration needs to be carried out consciously and in a planned way in order to make significant contributions to the use of technology, which is an essential task for teachers' (Gunuç and Babacan, 2018, p. 355).

To conclude this section, we pose several statements for your consideration and reflection:

1. The content that students learn is as important as the types of digital texts they use.
2. Active and passive learning approaches can both offer explorations of a range of texts, however, if students learn only to passively consume digital texts, they miss the opportunity to become more engaged as active content-creators.
3. Student creation of digital texts provides a way to engage an authentic audience and discussion in classroom learning activities.

Having reflected on your opinions around the above statements, we will next consider some potential barriers that have been known to impact on the use of technology in the classroom.

By exploring some of the possible constraints and controversies that surround digital technologies' use in literacy and English teaching, we hope you will be able to plan and counteract their impact on your teaching more readily.

CHALLENGES AND CONTROVERSIES IN TECHNOLOGY-ENABLED LITERACY LEARNING

Moving to the use of digital technology in the literacy or English classroom presents some unique challenges that may not have existed 10 years ago. In the following sections, we consider what you will need to know as successful teachers of twenty-first-century literacies.

PRIVACY

One area that challenges every teacher who uses technology in the literacy classroom is maintaining the privacy of ourselves and our students. As we use websites and resources we find online, we also need to consider what information we are giving away. In Chapter 3 we explored how we might support students to make informed and ethical choices. Privacy is another aspect of literacy learning through technology that we need to remember.

In brief, privacy means our personal details and any information that might identify us. It is important for our students to understand that they have a right to privacy and a right to refuse to give away their personal details.

Using creative technologies such as blogs means that we need to ensure we have permission for students to log in to the site and that students understand how to be positive digital citizens.

In addition to personal privacy, we also need to consider the concept of copyright. While copyright laws differ in every country it is fairly standard practice for individuals to be able to create and share their ideas and creative output online with some sense that their ownership remains with them. Creative Commons website offers ways to provide free and easy copyright agreements to anything you create online. If your students create a digital slideshow about a topic, they can use Creative Commons licences to declare who owns the slideshow and how others might be able to use it. You can choose to apply a number of different licences to your work from open licences that enable others to take your work, modify it however they like and present the final result as their own, to more strict licences that constrain use of the content to a certain website and with specific rules around attribution. You can search for Creative Commons online to learn more.

The ideas of copyright and privacy are significant areas for learning in the literacy classroom as students explore online resources, access the work of others and make choices about their own texts. For example, in exploring how emotive language is used in the classroom students can find many articles online. Before sharing them with the class we need to support them to understand if we have permission to use this text outside of its original website. In this way we ask students to respect the authorship rights of others and develop a sense of how they might share their literacy learning online in a safe and private way.

PRIORITIES (SPELLING, HANDWRITING, GRAMMAR?)

When technology began to become a major part of society and schooling around 20 years ago, there were many concerns raised over the impact of technology use on the development of traditional skills such as spelling, handwriting and grammar. According to those concerned, we were at risk of raising a generation of learners who couldn't communicate effectively in writing. A number of those concerns remain, and journalists appear to frequently decry the lack of spelling and handwriting skills in today's students. In 2019, the *Washington Post* newspaper ran an article that asked, 'Does it matter that my son can't spell?' (Denn, 2019). As a parent of a primary school child, the author describes her frustration with the amount of spelling errors that her child makes. Language experts, however, join with technology gurus to see a different side to the story. While technology does remove children's autonomy in spelling it may enhance their ability to recognise misspelled words. Spell-checking software has been available for a number of decades and continues to improve. Beyond the built-in spelling and grammar checkers in our word-processing software, there are many software packages focused only on improving the readability and conformity of your writing. These tools provide a back-up for those who prefer to write and then edit later. Some research has also highlighted that technology can support students with specific learning needs to develop and rehearse spelling and grammar skills (Benmarrakchi et al., 2017; Green, 2017).

Handwriting, grammar and spelling have traditionally been perceived as taught in the primary years of schooling, with expectations that by secondary school students have a strong grasp of written communication conventions. In today's world, where learners read more, write more and express themselves in numerous ways, we need to ask whether a focus on traditional communication forms is enough. This means that our students need to be able to communicate in many more ways than only through reading and writing. With increasingly busy classrooms and curricula, it is hard to advocate for increasing a teacher's workload. Perhaps it is now time to consider handwriting, spelling and grammar as co-curricular foci. In positioning these literacy skills alongside other learning outcomes, we can provide an authentic context for learners to improve.

The introduction of tablet computing and touch-screen computers will undoubtedly impact on how students develop spelling, grammar and handwriting skills. The ability to write, annotate and draw on a digital screen enables learners to:

1. Practise their handwriting
2. Erase and retry without the mess of erasers
3. Use writing recognition software to turn their handwriting into text.

Of course, just because touch screens enable this learning doesn't mean that students will learn these skills with teachers. It is us as experts in pedagogy who ensure that learning occurs for every student.

As technology continues to mutate and develop, it may not be long before all computing is voice-driven. What will that mean for handwriting and spelling lessons? We will have to wait and see.

DIGITAL WRITING AND CHANGING RULES OF EXPRESSION

Spelling, grammar and handwriting are not the only learning areas that have been impacted by the introduction of technology into the literacy classroom. Indeed, as we ask students to engage with and create multi-media and multi-modal texts we are challenged to reflect on the new rules of digital communications. As an example, consider the prevalence of acronyms and language used in SMS texting. Most, if not all, of us would be familiar with many of these:

- LOL – laughing out loud
- BTW – by the way
- TYVM – thank you very much
- IDK – I don't know

Language teachers have long known the power of social media and texting to engage their learners (Shi et al., 2017). Instead of writing a conversation in a second (or third) language, creating a text conversation provides an authentic context, a space to explore less formal language and possibly to discuss more topics of interest to the learner.

Should literacy and English teachers be teaching social media language? There are a number of researchers who believe these new acronyms and terms should be part of a school education. It is believed that young adults form and develop their sense of identity by using social media language and grammar (Tagg, 2016). The use of punctuation, emojis and abbreviations ('wot' instead of 'what') have been seen as a unique way of expressing oneself to the message receiver. If this is the case, it might be necessary for literacy and English teachers to dive into social media principles in their teaching.

In Tagg's (2016) research, for example, the student conversations she analysed demonstrated spelling and grammar that went against conventions. However, these were not simple errors but rather standardised misspellings that were repeated several times. There appeared to be an unwritten rulebook for communication that was followed, almost as rigidly as the spelling and grammar rules in a traditional written piece. In one example, all members of a conversation used the spelling 'wot' instead of 'what'. Similarly, the word 'ya' was consistently used in place of 'you'. These might be considered time savers as each example creates less letters to type; however, with the sophistication of today's predicative text applications it may also be a conscious choice to use these non-conventional spellings.

New terminology, phrasing and acronyms can raise concerns for teachers who are uncomfortable with changes to what is seen as the 'correct' way of communicating. There is a sense of loss of the traditional rules to which we have adhered for a long time. Language, however, cares not for our feelings! It is a living thing that evolves with each generation (Hamoodat et al., 2020). It may, therefore, be time to accept that new ways of expression are not only valid communication devices, but that familiarity with them is a necessary learning focus in our classrooms (Bischoff & Palea, 2019).

KEY CONCEPTS FOR TECHNOLOGY IN LITERACY LEARNING

In this section we explore two concepts that can frame technology integration in literacy learning. There are numerous ways to integrate technology, and as new software and hardware emerge we will likely continue to learn and adapt our teaching to meet the needs of our students. As virtual reality, machine learning and voice-controlled devices become more accessible in the classroom, new pedagogical approaches will be needed. The concepts chosen for discussion here have a strong evidence-based background developed over at least a decade. They provide an entry point into technology integration for literacy learning and offer some ideas for reflecting on your pedagogical practices.

DIGITAL STORYTELLING

Storytelling has been a part of the human experience for as long as we have records. In Australia, our First Nations people have used stories for many millennia. Yarning, as storytelling is called, provides a way to share and pass on important information about culture, history and survival and is even an emerging research methodology in its own right (Geia et al., 2013). Storytelling as it developed in Europe has similar roots. Aesop's fables and Hans Christian Andersen's stories and fables sought to codify behaviour practices and make sense of the world around them.

Technology offers a way to extend this tradition with new media and modal presentations. Digital storytelling, then, is framing an idea or concept with technological enhancements. As Figg et al. (2010) remind us, 'developing 21st-century skills is a function of individuals expressing their [student's] own voice using written and oral language, as well as many other electronic formats and media'.

In the classroom, digital storytelling can be either factual or fiction. Your students might create a video that presents a report on some topic. This would involve collaborating with other students, writing a script, designing the storyboard for the video, recording and editing the video. The numerous steps in this kind of project means it is often advisable to group students together to share the workload.

There is a misconception that digital storytelling refers only to video. This is not accurate as digital storytelling can also mean:

- Using animation software
- Creating a stop-motion video
- Creating a photo-based slideshow
- Designing and building 3D worlds (such as in Minecraft).

There is also some research that digital storytelling can improve our students' writing and presentation abilities (Figg et al., 2010). This exciting outcome appears to be connected to the authentic audience with which digital storytelling engages. In a traditional story-writing activity, a student's work might be read aloud to their class or submitted to the teacher; beyond this there is no further audience and, potentially, no further motivation to review and refine their work (Kreamer and Heny, 2019). Digital storytelling, then, not only enables students to present their ideas in new and innovative ways, but also provides accessible creations that can be shared online in many different ways.

Digital storytelling builds on humans' desire to share experiences and learn from those around them. The addition of digital technologies to this age-old tradition opens up possibilities of text types, collaborative creation and sharing that were previously impossible in the classroom.

WIKIS/CO-CREATION

In classrooms today students can access all types of information online. Some of this is formal, and some is informal. As we have discussed, the language used in each type of environment can change and social standards can emerge in each platform. What happens when students write and create together? In a wiki space students can co-create and, importantly, co-edit their texts.

Wikipedia is probably the most famous type of wiki, and one that you have no doubt consulted. You are likely aware that Wikipedia is a platform full of user-generated content. By editing content on a Wikipedia page, your explanations, opinions and claims are readily critiqued by other experts in the field. The more content you add or edit that is endorsed by others, the higher your status as a Wikipedia editor grows. In this way, facts can be updated much more quickly than a traditional encyclopedia, and verified by an international community of experts. Co-creation and collaborative writing are increasingly skills demanded by industry. Indeed, a large-scale survey of industry leaders identified that collaborative abilities are the second most demanded skills:

> Communication and collaboration tools will evolve, and Australian workers will need to be skilled in new media literacies, for example communication through social media. (Australian Industry and Skills Committee, 2020)

Skills in collaborative creation and communications can be developed within a wiki space. This might be a private wiki, managed by your school or a private software company, or it could mean engaging with the world's largest wiki, Wikipedia.

In Wikipedia, your students are able to create, challenge and question the work of experts and provide evidence for alternative views on any subject. One recent study asked students to do exactly this and found some tangible positive outcomes for learners (Vetter et al., 2019). These included the development of critical thinking, source evaluation and peer-review skills.

In the classroom, you might begin with a class exploration of a Wikipedia entry, relevant to a topic of study. From here, students can be asked to explore the article's reference list and contributors. In exploring who the creators of this content are, we are asking students to make informed judgments about whose opinions are presented or prioritised, leading to critical questioning and evaluation activities.

In a similar way, creating their own wiki pages or articles can provide an authentic audience and real-time critique for their work. Students will need to develop communications skills and collaborative strategies to successfully co-create a wiki page. For example, with 10-year-old students, a class wiki page might be developed that explains how to play an online game. As each student adds their contributions, they may also suggest edits to the work of others. How they offer these edits, negotiate changes and develop a final agreed-upon version of the text will provide teachable moments and developing strategies for effective communications. Wikis created by students also provide a sense of authorship and ownership over the text. This might improve student engagement in developing literacy skills.

Wiki as an Internet tool are generally considered to be part of the Web 2.0 development beginning in the early to mid-2000s. Not soon after, in 2009, research began to demonstrate the impact of wikis as an educational tool. Dymoke and Hughes (2009) used a wiki with their pre-service teaching students to share their personal poetry writing over the course of a year. The outcomes were encouraging. At the beginning, the students often demonstrated reluctance and hesitation about sharing their poetry publicly in the wiki; at the end of the year the same students demonstrated increased confidence in their own writing abilities and in their ability to provide insightful feedback to their peers. Other findings indicated that some students took more risks with their writing and were more willing to trial new poetry genres. Although this book is not focused on tertiary students, there are lessons to be learned from this and similar studies. Students can be supported to share, co-create and peer review their literacy practices, and can enjoy positive behavioural outcomes such as increased confidence and willingness to try and fail at new approaches. Surely these are important behaviours for literate learners in the twenty-first century.

EXAMPLES OF PRACTICE

In this section we present some examples of technology in the literacy classrooms. In these examples we suggest teaching strategies that rely on technology and ideas that use technology to enhance what may already be happening in classrooms.

Each example identifies a specific context for the learning activity. Whether these activities and pedagogical choices would be appropriate for your educational context is for you to decide. We advise you to reflect carefully on your context, your students' learning needs and the prior learning assumed in these examples.

LITERACY AND TECHNOLOGY IN THE EARLY CHILDHOOD SETTING

In MK's classroom today, the students are developing their skills with letter recognition. As an early childhood educator, MK understands that her learners need to explore the concept of shapes as letters in a number of ways so that they develop cross-contextual skills. To provide these experiences, MK has set up four learning stations around the room. Each learner will engage with all four activities, but MK is keen to understand how each activity appeals to and supports their learning.

At the first activity, five children are gathered around the sand box. They have a set of laminated cards and are tracing letters into the sand with their fingers. One child makes a common mistake but another child quickly wipes the sand clean and says, 'That's wrong!'. Tears ensue as the child who made the error (drawing b instead of d) complains that he wasn't finished yet and now he has to start again. MK intervenes to restate the behaviour expectations – no touching other people's letters – and moves on.

Two other groups are working with large pieces of paper and thick crayons to support their fine-motor skills. Each of these groups has a slightly different task. One must cover the page in the designated letter, in this case the letter 'p', the other must attempt to draw the same letter on lines across a page. These tasks seem to be progressing well so MK moves to the final group.

Here, the children are using the iPads and a letter-tracing app. On the screen a letter from a pre-defined set appears. MK has chosen long-stem and short-stem letters to integrate this activity with the others. As the letter appears, the iPad reads the letter, and provides three examples of words which begin with that letter. 'P, P is for Pot, Puppy and Paper', says the iPad. Next the children are guided to trace the letter p on the screen. As they succeed in tracing the letter, the tracing lines slowly become increasingly transparent until the children are writing the letter p unaided.

As she reflects on the learning that took place during this lesson, MK is interested to note that as the children rotated through the tasks they did appear to improve their letter recognition and writing skills. The physical task in the sand box seemed to provide a way to play while writing. The paper drawing groups had varied success in writing on lines but were developing consistency in their letter writing. As children engaged with the iPad task, they did seem to remain engaged longer as the challenge level increased as their abilities improved. MK can see that the iPads offered a way to provide personal support to the learner that is hard to offer consistently in the busy classroom. MK also understands, however, that young children need to explore ideas and concepts in the physical world. There is a place for technology in her early childhood teaching practice, alongside more traditional activities.

LITERACY AND TECHNOLOGY IN THE PRIMARY SCHOOL SETTING

Rami, in his Year 2 classroom, is excited for today's literacy activity. His teacher David has told him that there will be drawing and recording on the iPads. David brings the class back to attention and explains today's activity. Using a book they read together in shared reading time yesterday, they will be adding their own ideas and drawings to each page. Using a digital storytelling app on the iPads, the students will work in groups of three to create their own version of the book.

Before they begin David leads a brief recap of the book. Who were the characters? What happened and in what order? The students help David create a short timeline on the interactive whiteboard.

As they move into groups, Rami begins a discussion with the group about the main character, who was lost in a forest and needed to escape to be home in time for dinner. 'What if she could fly?' he asks. The group consider the idea. 'Wouldn't that make the book really short though?' asks a teammate. The discussion that ensues leads the group to begin creating an outline of the book in the app. They draw the basic outline of the forest and the main character and decide that flying is not a good idea, but maybe roller skates could work. The group continues to develop their version of their story, with the main character now navigating the hills and valleys of the forest on wheels. By the end of the lesson, they have re-read the original book three more times, incorporated and then removed a number of ideas that were eventually set aside and created a final version of the book.

After the lesson, David has some time to explore the students' work. As a teacher, David knew this was a comprehension activity that aimed to demonstrate some strategies for understanding texts. By drawing the key actions in the texts and modifying characters and events, students had been led to engage with the text more deeply. Tomorrow he will make this learning clear to his class and ask them to reflect on their understanding of the story after today's activity.

What did the app activity add? Could this task have been completed offline, using paper and pencils? Perhaps, admits David, but what paper could not offer was the ability to re-think and re-do ideas as they emerged. Each time an idea was rejected, students could erase and begin again with a clean page. They could also re-order their ideas to better reflect their original story. Finally, the app enabled each child to have equal input into the group creation. As they worked in the shared space on their own iPads, they were developing collaboration and communication skills. In challenging the ideas of their peers and accepting edits and changes to their own work, they are beginning to understand writing and reading as collaborative practices. Understanding that they can learn from each other is a critical skill that David will continue to explore in his teaching. In this example, the app and iPads provided a useful, easy-to-use and accessible space to do this.

LITERACY AND TECHNOLOGY IN THE SECONDARY SCHOOL SETTING

Jan is preparing an English lesson for her Year 8 class. The focus of this unit of work, over four weeks, is developing critical literacy skills. Jan has noticed that the majority of her students appear to accept everything they read online as true, and often read only the first item that appears in their Internet search. In previous lessons, she has provided texts to the students that present opposing ideas about current events. Topics have included climate change, political elections and sporting victories. Her students, however, seemed to have already formed opinions on these topics prior to her lessons and so asking them to critique their established opinions has proven challenging. They are not easy to sway in their ideas! This has made highlighting critical thinking skills more difficult.

To move their thinking forwards, Jan has developed a lesson that engages students in a debate they may not yet have encountered – the right to vote for under-18s. This will draw on their recent debates around politics and elections but ask students to broaden their perspectives.

As class begins the next day, Jan asks the class to raise their hands if they have ever voted for anything. About half the students raise their hands and share their experiences: voting on a holiday destination with their families, choosing a captain of their sports team, deciding where fundraising funds should be sent. From here Jan asks who gets to vote in our federal elections? Most students agree that those who are over 18 have the right to vote in elections.

Jan now asks students to consider what that actually means and invites students to spend 10 minutes exploring the federal government website to find out. With a definition created by the class, Jan now challenges the students by asking, why can't you vote? You just found that you could read and make sense of the rules about voting, but why is 18 the age for voting?

The following activity, Jan hopes, will support the students to engage more deeply with online resources and begin developing critical literacy skills. Jan explains that search engines work by prioritising articles that are linked to other trustworthy articles. This means that the first page of a search result shows you the most popular, most linked webpages – not necessarily the most accurate. If we want to find out why voting is restricted to those over 18, we might need to look at more than the most linked websites – these are likely the most popular websites, because most people accept that 18 is the best voting age, and the federal government webpage is a highly referenced (linked to) and trusted website. What if we challenge the assumption that 18 is the best age to begin voting?

In groups of two, Jan asks students to find articles that support under-18 voting. They are to add articles they find to a shared digital space she has created. As articles begin to appear, Jan takes notes. At least half the articles are from individuals (bloggers, activists and solo journalists). Most of the articles argue that the voting age should be 16. All the articles appear on the second page of a search when she checks online – this is encouraging.

After the lesson Jan reflects on the activity. There is still much learning to draw out of the activity, including how we choose and prioritise sources and authors and how we validate claims made online. The purpose of the lesson, however, appears to have been achieved. The list of 32 articles in the shared online space all provide arguments for lowering the voting age.

The discussion at the end of the lesson was also interesting. Students had begun to develop their own opinions and make claims backed up by their reading. Excitingly, their classmates had also begun to challenge them with counter-claims and their own ideas. Critical thinking practices were beginning to emerge. Engaging with real-world data and providing ways for students to generate opinions based on their findings has been invaluable, and was only made possible by access to the vast range of digital texts available online.

BACK TO THE CLASSROOM

Miray is back in her classroom with her Year 9 students. Many groups continue to work on their task: comparing the political speech to the newspaper article that reports on it. However, several other groups have raised concerns that their article isn't 'true' or doesn't really represent what was said in the speech. One group has even decided that the journalist who wrote their article must have been at a different speech.

Miray, however, has a plan. She has decided that students could learn about critical analysis of online content by creating and evaluating their own articles.

Using the classroom blogs that are already established, Miray brings up a post she wrote last night. As the class read through it together, there are mumbles and groans. Not everyone agrees with Miray's article about the political speech. Using Miray's post to begin the discussion, the students identify that there are three main interpretations of the political speech within the class:

1. One group believed that the politician was uninformed and did not make a good case for improving health care access in rural and remote areas.
2. A second group felt the politician was well informed but his speech was mis-understood by the journalists.
3. Finally, other students felt that the journalists had purposefully changed the meaning of the politician's words to better suit their own opinions.

Miray asks the students: Which group is correct and why are there so many different versions of the speech in the newspaper? To bring the ideas of 'truth', critical analysis and opinions together, Miray asks students to write a blog post as if they were journalists. Which version of the speech will they present? What biases or personal opinions can they read in their classmates' posts?

In the next lesson, Miray will ask the groups to comment on the posts and offer a critique that identifies any bias or different interpretations.

CONCLUSION

In this chapter we have explored how technology can impact on the literacy and English Language Arts classrooms.

We began by understanding and describing what we mean by technology in the literacy classroom and identified a number of ways that the notion of a 'text' has changed in our everyday lives. While literacy and English teachers have always taught critical skills, today's ever-increasing range of texts, authors and media has heightened the demand for our students to become critical users of online content. We explored the role of our students in literacy learning as both active and passive content consumers and suggested that a balance of consuming and creating might best provide experiences in critical thinking.

We engaged with several challenges that have impacted on technology-enabled literacy learning, including concerns about privacy and copyright when we use and create texts online. We also discussed how priorities in literacy can be seen to be changing, from a focus on handwriting, grammar and spelling to a rise in authorship and text creation. This discussion will likely continue, but perhaps the rise of tablet computing, increasingly accurate digital stylus and the use of text-enhancing software may mitigate these concerns in the longer term.

A final challenge discussed was the changing nature of language and the informal but often consistent language of social media and other online spaces. We understood acronyms, abbreviations and changed spelling to be a part of identity formation for today's youth and discussed that this language is widely used and perhaps requires some space in literacy curricula. As more and more employers use social media to hire staff, and use social media platforms for intra-office communications, the formal language of today's résumés and workplaces may become less prevalent. The rise of emojis as devices of digital communication was briefly presented. This emergent communication tool will undoubtedly prompt more research and interrogation in the coming decades as we perhaps move full circle towards the hieroglyphic communications of ancient times.

As we moved from discussing challenges to the possibilities offered by technologies, we investigated several teaching strategies with technology for use in your classroom. These strategies were underpinned by longer-term research outcomes and offered a starting point for your planning. Digital storytelling was proposed as an evolution of human's natural design to tell and pass on stories. The technology in this strategy provides a collaborative platform that can engage an authentic audience, beyond the classroom, in authentic student-created texts. The use of wikis further provided collaborative, co-creation opportunities for learners that positioned each student as a co-author, encouraging peer review, acceptance of feedback and critical reflection.

We concluded this chapter with three practical examples of how a technology-enabled literacy classroom might look. We shared lessons, taken from practice, for early childhood, primary and secondary classrooms. Each example offered insight into the teachers' thinking, their planning and implementation behind the use of technology. As you reflect on the use of technology for teaching you are welcome to trial any of the ideas you have connected with in this chapter.

As teachers, we are all literacy leaders, either by receiving specific titles such as English Teacher or Literacy Coordinator, or through our teaching and communication of ideas.

No matter, your role as a teacher, modelling strong, relevant and informed literacy practices are part of what makes you a great teacher. You will likely need to keep learning and
developing your skills throughout your career, just as your students will.

FURTHER READING

Technology-enabled literacy learning is a growing and fast-changing field. The following
readings offer an extended evidence base for your teaching and may provide you with further
motivation and ideas for your classroom practice:

Aobaid, A. (2020). Smart multimedia learning of ICT: Role and impact on language
learners' writing fluency – YouTube online English learning resources as an example.
Smart Learning Environments, *7*(1), 1–30.

Chen, Y., Zhou, D., Wang, Y. & Yu, J. (2017). Application of augmented reality for early
childhood English teaching. In *2017 International Symposium on Educational Technology* (pp. 111–115). doi:10.1109/ISET.2017.34

Ding, L. (2018). Exploration of key technologies in a personalized English learning system. *International Journal of Emerging Technologies in Learning (iJET)*, *13*(07), 85–96.

Guan, N., Song, J. & Li, D. (2018). On the advantages of computer multimedia-aided
English teaching. *Procedia Computer Science*, *131*, 727–732.

Wulandari, M. & Pasaribu, T. A. (2020). *Technology for English Language Learning*.
Yogyakarta: Sanata Dharma University Press.

REFERENCES

Australian Industry and Skills Committee (2020, 19 February). *Collaboration Skills*. Retrieved from
https://nationalindustryinsights.aisc.net.au/national/collaboration-skills (accessed 5 July 2021).
Benmarrakchi, F. E., El Kafi, J. & Elhore, A. (2017). Communication technology for users with specific learning disabilities. *Procedia Computer Science, 110*, 258–265.
Bischoff, A. V. & Palea, A. (2019). A communicational analysis of the evolution of symbolic language case study: Emojis. *Professional Communication and Translation Studies, 12*, 59–71.
Denn, R. (2019). In the era of spellcheck and auto-correct, does it matter that my son can't spell?
Washington Post, 4 February. Retrieved from www.washingtonpost.com/lifestyle/2019/01/29/
era-spellcheck-autocorrect-does-it-matter-that-my-son-cant-spell/ (accessed 5 July 2021).

Dudeney, G. & Hockly, N. (2007). *How to Teach English with Technology*. Harlow: Pearson Longman.

Dymoke, S. & Hughes, J. (2009). Using a poetry wiki: How can the medium support pre-service teachers of English in their professional learning about writing poetry and teaching poetry writing in a digital age? *English Teaching: Practice and Critique, 8*(3), 91–106.

Figg, C., McCartney, R. & Gonsoulin, W. (2010). Impacting academic achievement with student learners teaching digital storytelling to others: The ATTTCSE digital video project. *Contemporary Issues in Technology and Teacher Education, 10*(1), 38–79.

Flanagan, S. & Shoffner, M. (2013). Teaching with (out) technology: Secondary English teachers and classroom technology use. *Contemporary Issues in Technology and Teacher Education, 13*(3), 242–261.

Geia, L. K., Hayes, B., & Usher, K. (2013). Yarning/Aboriginal storytelling: Towards an understanding of an Indigenous perspective and its implications for research practice. *Contemporary Nurse, 46*(1), 13–17.

Green, S. (2017). A critical reflection on how information communication technology can facilitate high quality teaching and learning for dyslexic children and their spelling. *The STeP Journal (Student Teacher Perspectives), 4*(4), 61–69.

Gunuç, S. & Babacan, N. (2018). *Technology Integration in English Language Teaching and Learning*, (Vol. 1). Vernon Press.

Hamoodat, H., Aswad, F., Ribeiro, E. & Menezes, R. (2020). A longitudinal analysis of vocabulary changes in social media. In H. Barbosa, J. Gomez-Gardenes, B. Gonçalves, G. Mangioni, R. Menezes & M. Oliveira (eds), *Complex Networks XI*. Springer Proceedings in Complexity. Cham, Switzerland: Springer. doi:10.1007/978-3-030-40943-2_18

Julia, J. & Isrokatun, I. (2019). Technology literacy and student practice: Lecturing critical evaluation skills. *International Journal of Learning, Teaching and Educational Research, 18*(9), Article 9. www.ijlter.org/index.php/ijlter/article/view/1621 (accessed 5 July 2021).

Kreamer, H. M. & Heny, N. (2019). The power of authenticity: Empowering student writers through meaningful, real world writing experiences. *Virginia English Journal, 69*(1), 36–47.

Lauer, C. (2009). Contending with terms: 'Multimodal' and 'multimedia' in the academic and public spheres. *Computers and Composition, 26*(4), 225–239.

Nusca, A. (2009). Americans consume 100,000 words of information each day, study says. *ZDNet*, 9 December. Retrieved from www.zdnet.com/article/americans-consume-100000-words-of-information-each-day-study-says/ (accessed 5 July 2021).

Sewell, W. C. & Denton, S. (2011). Multimodal literacies in the secondary English classroom. *English Journal, 100*(5), 61–65.

Shi, Z., Luo, G. & He, L. (2017). Mobile-assisted language learning using WeChat instant messaging. *International Journal of Emerging Technologies in Learning (IJET), 12*(02), 16–26.

Shor, I. & Freire, P. (1987). *A Pedagogy for Liberation: Dialogues on Transforming Education*. Westport, CT: Greenwood Publishing Group.

State Government of Victoria, Australia (2019). *Creating Multimodal Texts*. Retrieved from www.education.vic.gov.au:443/school/teachers/teachingresources/discipline/english/literacy/multimodal/Pages/createmultimodal.aspx (accessed 5 July 2021).

Tagg, C. (2016). Heteroglossia in text-messaging: Performing identity and negotiating relationships in a digital space. *Journal of Sociolinguistics, 20*(1), 59–85.

Vetter, M. A., McDowell, Z. J. & Stewart, M. (2019). From opportunities to outcomes: The Wikipedia-based writing assignment. *Computers and Composition, 52*, 53–64. doi:10.1016/j.compcom.2019.01.008

Watson, A. (2020). *Topic: Media Use: Statistics & Facts*. Statista. www.statista.com/topics/1536/media use/ (accessed 21 July 2021).

TECHNOLOGY
FOR MATHEMATICS

7

IN THIS CHAPTER YOU WILL LEARN:

- How to use technology to enhance student mathematical learning
- Why you should consider technology as a key tool when teaching mathematics
- What technology in mathematics can look like in a range of contexts.

INTRODUCTION

Mathematics teachers have long used technology to enhance their students' learning and their teaching practices. Calculators, overhead projectors and traditional technologies like slide rulers are now seen as a normal part of the maths classroom. Today, we generally understand technology to mean 'digital' technology, and that's what we will be exploring in this chapter. Beyond calculators, we will explore how technology can fundamentally change the learning experience in the classroom. Where students have traditionally learned mathematical concepts through repetition and rote learning, abstract formulas and pages of calculations, technology offers real-world contexts, auto-corrected repetition practice and problem-solving activities.

Technology can also offer speed of access to millions of examples and resources and even experts around the world. There are a few ways that we can think of mathematics learning, but most often there is a distinction made between mathematics and numeracy. Understanding the difference is essential for us as we explore how technology can be used in our classrooms. To simplify, mathematics is the processes and tools for understanding how numbers work in the world. Numeracy is the application of this learning in our lives (Li et al., 2014). To be fully numerate, we need to have skills in both areas. This means that even if we are not mathematics teachers, we are still teachers of numeracy. Indeed, national curriculum documents such as the Australian Curriculum now recognise that numeracy and literacy teaching is the responsibility of all teachers, regardless of whether they teach science or sports.

Early digital technology use saw a sweeping array of apps, software programs and websites that enabled students to practise the skills that they had been taught in traditional classrooms.

As an 8-year-old, perhaps you used a computer to play something like a leapfrog game on a website. To practise your multiplication tables, you would have to find a number pattern (3, 6, 9, 12 …) hidden amongst several lilypads on the screen. Correct identification of the next number in the pattern meant that your 'frog' would happily croak and jump to the lilypad. A false move and your frog ended up in the water. The frog became progressively wetter, and you become progressively frustrated. After a while, you perfect the counting pattern, and the frog reaches the far shore safe and sound. What have you learned? Perhaps that frogs (strangely) don't enjoy the water. Perhaps that number patterns have to be memorised. Have you learned ways to explore patterns? Have you examined why number patterns are useful or helpful? Probably not.

This is not to say, of course, that some memorisation isn't necessary for mathematics learning. There remains a place for rote learning in today's classrooms. The challenge, though, is whether rote learning in itself is enough for today's learner.

Hopefully, the frog example above makes you reflect on how and why technology is being used in this way. Are there other possibilities for the digital resources you have? Should technology be relegated to practising of skills after the teacher has provided direct instruction? Is there another way that technology might instead teach new skills, explore ways to use technology and ensure our students are both mathematically literate and numerate?

In this chapter, we will explore what technology has to offer all teachers, in our role as teachers of numeracy.

IN THE CLASSROOM TODAY

In today's maths class for some Year 3 students, the 8-year-olds are working on their understanding of place value in our number system. They are rolling dice and using blocks to model the number they've made. Unfortunately for one student, the building stage of the activity is proving challenging. He keeps losing track of his number.

The teacher heads over to help the group and asks them to build the number 768 using the blocks. Cameron's group, however, seems to have made the number 786. The teacher begins explaining why this is wrong and how the place value determines the value assigned to an individual digit. However, Cameron's group just become more confused. They've got a pile of hundreds, a pile of tens and a pile of ones, and it looks right to them! The teacher rings the bell and calls the class to an end for the day.

In maths class, the following morning, Cameron's group tries again with the same result, more confusion and the misrepresentation of the number using the blocks. The teacher wonders how to help. She knows that technology can help with the representation of mathematical ideas and considers how she might use technology to support the students. She doesn't only want them to practise the skills; she wants them to learn and develop a deeper understanding of the concept of place value.

After school that day, Cameron's teacher sits down to consider where to begin with these students. She has found several activities online that support children to understand the place value system, but she's looking for more than simple repetition. In looking at the resources in front of her, she asks, which would best meet the needs of this group of students?

TECHNOLOGY IN MATHS TEACHING

In 1980, Seymour Papert published his book *Mindstorms*. As we explored in Chapter 5, Papert was concerned with how we make knowledge through technology. Beyond rote and drill, and repetition, he argued for a Constructionist approach to learning that created a space for learning that was active and creative.

Keeping in mind this theory that technology can provide more than merely a rehearsal space for offline learning, we can frame technology use in the maths classroom in three ways:

1. Technology as a replacement for teachers
2. Technology as a teacher's aide in today's classroom
3. Technology as a problem-solving space.

As Hoyles and Lagrange (2010, p. 138) explain:

> If we consider mathematics to be a fixed body of knowledge to be learned, then the role of technology in this process would be primarily that of an efficiency tool, i.e. helping the learner to do the mathematics more efficiently. However, if we consider the technological tools as providing access to new understandings of relations, processes and purposes, then the role of technology relates to a conceptual construction kit.

TECHNOLOGY AS A REPLACEMENT FOR TEACHERS

Technology is often used to replace teachers in the classroom by providing direct instruction to students through online games, videos or presentations. As an international focus on providing a personalised education increases, teachers are asked to create personalised learning programs for every child in their classroom (Ogden and Pierce, 2019). Although research tells us this is the desirable way for all students to learn effectively (Walkington and Hayata, 2017), it, of course, can be challenging to implement in a classroom.

How does one teacher create, implement, monitor and refine a mathematics learning plan for 25 or 30 students? It is here that technology often arises as a support mechanism. As teachers identify the learning needs of the students, websites, software and technology resources become increasingly relied upon to provide initial learning experiences in maths concepts. While this can be an excellent approach, the teacher, who, of course, knows their students best, has little control over how information and concepts are presented through these resources. As students progress through online resources, how do teachers or how should teachers make sense of what students are learning and understanding and what need to know next?

It's important to remember that nothing in the realm of technology is either inherently positive or negative when it comes to mathematics learning. The number of resources that one can now find online means that we have a role as a curator in today's classrooms. We cannot be expected to build from scratch a learning resource for every single student, every single week, across the school year. So technology does have a place in the teaching of today's students.

Technology as a replacement for teachers is not necessarily effective unless we as teachers make the pedagogically informed decisions for the students' use of the technology. Indeed, it's not yet viable that any piece of software or technology hardware can fully replace the teacher in the classroom! Despite the advances of artificial intelligence and machine learning, we still rely on our knowledge as teachers of our students to make informed decisions. It's important to understand that technology cannot replace the teacher. We are trained to understand the pedagogical and curriculum demands of today's classrooms. So while the task a child undertakes online or inside a piece of software might seem to be replacing a face-to-face conversation or learning experience with a teacher, it is the teacher as a curator that is the key to success here.

For example, should a student be identified as needing to refine their understanding of fractions, an online search would yield around 267 million results. Some of these results introduce the concept of fractions to younger students; some explore notation of fractions more appropriate for the senior years of schooling. Even a young adult, perhaps age 17, does not have the pedagogical knowledge to understand which of these millions of resources best meet their needs. In seeking resources for students that can teach new concepts, there are a few factors to consider:

1. Where is the resource from and which education system does it address?
2. Does it provide direct instruction on crucial concepts, or does it provide repetition to deepen learning?
3. Finally, does it make sense of the mathematical concept that you as the teacher have identified as necessary for this student or students?

In answering these questions, you are more likely to find appropriate resources to support your students. Technology may never completely replace the teacher; careful consideration and curation can remove some of the hurdles to providing the personalised learning experiences that are demanded by today's curriculum documents.

TECHNOLOGY AS A TEACHERS AIDE IN THE CLASSROOM

In a similar and connected way, technology can also be framed as a teachers aide or assistant in the classroom. This entails the use of technology to reinforce previously learned concepts or to provide acceleration or revision experiences for students. Using technology as an aid in the classroom, we are positioning ourselves as holding the mathematical knowledge required by the students.

In some education systems, for example, in the UK, it is normal for teachers to be supported in their classrooms by an additional adult. This support person typically assists with administration, teaching small groups of children and preparing resources. If we frame technology in the same way, we see that it can offer our classrooms breathing space between teacher-directed instruction and independent student learning.

As an aid in the classroom, computers' technology and digital resources become a space that students can use to revisit, explore or extend their learning. Using technology in this way sees the teacher maintaining hold of mathematical knowledge. This includes being the main centre of mathematical understanding and holding all of the answers to student questions and confusions.

This way of framing technology in the classroom appears to be the most popular way of putting technology to work in today's classrooms. This, of course, makes sense. As teachers have traditionally held the key to the knowledge that one learns in their classrooms, changes to how others and technology might impact on that process can be seen as requiring faith in technology resources and so potentially tricky. It asks us to question what our role is in the classroom and how we can best use our expertise. We have invaluable knowledge of our students, their backgrounds in the context of the school and our professional pedagogical understanding.

As we noted before, there is nothing inherently good or bad about using technology in this way. Instead, this section asks that you reflect on how you are positioning technology in the classroom so that you might make clear decisions about the way that you teach and your students learn.

You might ask yourself these questions when considering using technology as a side support to student learning;

1. How are the technology resources directly supporting my teaching and/or my students' learning?
2. Have I chosen the most effective technology resource to achieve this goal?

3. Using my professional pedagogical knowledge, have I made careful decisions about the balance between what the technology resource is teaching my students and what I am teaching my students?

As you reflect on these questions, be sure also to consider the other ways in which technology can be framed in the classroom. Learning mathematics can be complicated; indeed it is a language in its own right!

In learning this new language, there are many concepts to be explored and discovered. How you make use of technology will influence how your students understand this language. Taking the language metaphor further, will you provide the grammar, syntax and vocabulary while the technology offers experiences in creating phrases and conversations?

TECHNOLOGY AS A PROBLEM-SOLVING SPACE

When we consider technology as a space to solve problems, we want students to apply their mathematical knowledge and demonstrate their ability to be numerate. As we explored in the introduction to this chapter, numeracy takes mathematical knowledge into problems and specific contexts (Goos and Bennison, 2008).

In many instances, mathematics teachers have always used problem-solving in their classrooms. However, the idea of mathematical problem-solving is not, in this case, the same as numeracy problem-solving. Let's consider two examples:

*   A mathematical problem: asking students to demonstrate their understanding of a particular algorithm by solving a specific mathematics question.
*   A numeracy problem: takes an algorithm and embeds it in a real-world context such as shopping, home renovating or outdoor pursuits. The students then find an answer to the contextual problem. In doing so, they will, of course, explore the mathematical components of the problem, but they will also be asked to make sense of the context and its impact on their mathematical calculations.

For our purposes, we see technology problem-solving as referring to a numeracy approach to problem-solving. The reason we use with technology for this type of learning is that it provides a broad range of contexts, data and tools to enable students to engage in areas that appeal to them.

An example might be asking students to develop plans to market a simple product. They could be asked to research the market, identify price points and gain statistical data about a potential customer base. The mathematical concepts used here will include statistics, percentages and fractions, and cost versus sale price comparisons. Having provided access to online resources for students to address these areas, we can also use technology to test their theories.

To further use technology as a problem-solving space, students could create a website for their product, stating, of course, that this is an exercise for learning and not a real product.

This website could now provide a space for the school community family and friends to give feedback on the chosen product and the students' marketing approach. Students take on this feedback, refine their product details and prices, and begin to analyse data from their 'sales'.

This website, then, has become a space for them to demonstrate their numeracy and mathematical skills, and to problem-solve in a real-world context with real data.

Before we had access to the Internet and technology resources in our classrooms, we may have attempted a similar activity via in-person feedback through the school. The benefit of technology is that it provides an external audience and an online space that can be easily updated, modified and adapted as students engage with their audience.

When considering using technology in your maths classroom as a problem-solving space, you might consider these questions:

- Will students be demonstrating mathematical skills and numeracy skills in this activity?
- How will technology provide a problem-solving space for my students?
- What is the context for student learning in this activity, and how will technology enhance students' contributions to that context?

CHALLENGES AND CONTROVERSIES IN TECHNOLOGY-ENABLED MATHS LEARNING

CHOICE OVERWHELM

A potential challenge for using technology in the classroom is that the range of resources, tools and hardware continue to grow at an alarming rate. The technology a child uses in pre-school will likely be significantly out of date by the time that same child finishes primary school. Rapid change requires careful planning, particularly when we are focused on supporting student learning.

Instead of attaching ourselves to one piece of technology, we could instead unpack the pedagogical opportunities the resources offers. We can then map these opportunities to other resources.

1. Does this new website offer ways for children to create their own maths problems?
2. Do I want a tool that facilitates repetitive learning tasks for students, and does this resource offer that?
3. If I want students to model their learning, is the resource sufficiently open?

In reflecting on these and similar questions, we are moving beyond the tool itself and instead re-focusing on student learning. We might have discovered a fun-looking app that our students would enjoy, but this alone cannot ensure they learn new skills (Schuetz et al., 2018).

An example of this might be the use of a spreadsheet application, such as Microsoft Excel, in the classroom. This is a much-used tool in secondary schools and increasingly with younger students. In particular, Excel appears to enable students to work data in more in-depth ways than with pen and paper. Students can create graphs, calculate statistics and present their work in several ways. These then are the learning outcomes – graphs, statistics, presenting data; what is lacking here is an understanding of the pedagogical facilities of the tool. For example, Excel provides calculations that are 'correct'. If the answer is unexpected, we know to see if the students' logic is at fault.

Pedagogical skills (creating, interpreting and making meaning from data) are a key factor in choosing digital resources. They should be your guide when looking at new, fun, flashy apps or resources.

MISSING KEY CONCEPTS

In the classroom, we often need to cater to a range of abilities and skills in our students. As some students are ready to move to a more complex definition of a maths concept, others may need further reinforcement of concepts. A challenge lies in mapping students' learning needs to technology offerings. If a child needs to reinforce concepts of multiplication, are they sufficiently able to engage with an online program that offers rote and drill? If students are independent learners in the area of geometry, should they spend time completing single-answer questions online?

In addition to various ability levels, we also need to support students who are progressing well, although with some missing concepts (Murphy, 2016). This 'gap-filling' is an essential part of learning in schools and something that can be overlooked. For example, if a student understands how to calculate the circumference of a circle but struggles to make sense of algorithms, there may be a mismatch in their achievement. They may be able to tell you the process but not the final answer.

In working with students that need different types of support, consider exploring how you use technology.

1. Are students asked to work independently or in groups?
2. Do they share devices or work collaboratively online through cloud-based software (such as Google Drive)?
3. Is this an activity that should be completed alone, or with a peer for mutual support?

Different ways of using the technology can lead, of course, to different outcomes. To focus on group work in the online space, we can use version tracking to understand which team contributed to which section. We might record login times to see when the work is being completed. Perhaps we strategically arrange learning groups around a specific concept, which is worked on as a group and then alone.

As teachers, we will also have a wide range of learning needs in our classroom. Nonetheless, there are ways that technology can support learners and teachers in identifying and addressing those needs.

TECHNOLOGY SKILLS FOR TEACHERS

A significant challenge for schools is that we have today a workforce of mathematics teachers for whom digital technology teaching is a new demand on their skills. These experienced teachers have often developed strategies and ideas for using technology in the classroom despite not having had formal training during their initial teacher education programmes. In Australia, for example, '30% of teachers … are aged 50 and above … This means that Australia will have to renew three out of ten members of its teaching workforce over the next decade or so' (Schwabe, 2018). This suggests that many of these teachers undertook the teaching qualification long before today's technologies were available. Indeed, it has been noted that the kinds of support we offer teachers in schools to use technology effectively varies enormously between schools, states and countries and in some cases is not provided at all.

Indeed, 'technology is often assimilated in the [maths] classroom without a comprehensive understanding of its ability to enhance student learning' (Higgins et al., 2019). This is not an indictment on experienced teachers in our classrooms; we should admire their tenacity and life-long learning strategies that keep them engaging with technology. It does, however, challenge us to consider how best to support teachers in schools to be effective users of technologies for maths learning.

PERCEPTIONS OF TECHNOLOGY IN MATHS

A final consideration of technology use in the maths classroom is the perspective of the broader community. There appears to be a general assumption that if we use a computer to complete a maths task, then it must be correct: 'Within the general public, it is a common myth that the computer is always right – a perception of its "mathematical fidelity"' (Hoyles and Lagrange, 2010, p. 7). This is a challenge as it is, of course, the human interacting with the computer that generates outputs. A computer can create data; it cannot create information.

Hoyles and Lagrange (2010) go on to claim that mathematics has been separated from the rest of a traditional curriculum and is only for special people for whom mathematics comes easily. They conclude by arguing that technology can minimise this challenge by providing contexts and learning activities at a range of different levels.

In contrast, there is also a call from some quarters to re-consider rote learning in maths (Lai and Murray, 2012). There are several arguments for this, including from cognitive load theorists who see an instant recall of basic facts as freeing the brain up for more complex processes (Booth et al., 2017).

As you may have noticed in this book, however, there is no point at which we place one learning strategy over another. We are seeking a considered approach to learning that sees technology as a tool in your kit to support student learning. In seeking to make the best choices for our students learning, we need to consider how we explain and talk about our use of technology in the classrooms. Do our students know how we chose digital activities for them? Do they use technology in a range of ways? Do they question the output from computers or can they interrogate answers? These are the skills that our students need, and in using technology through their maths learning, they can demonstrate their growth.

CRITICAL CONCEPTS FOR TECHNOLOGY IN MATHS LEARNING

In this section, we will briefly explore two innovative ways to use technology in your maths classrooms. These strategies are relatively new and therefore are still evolving. We do have evidence that these approaches can enhance learning; however, you may have to think carefully about whether they are appropriate for your setting.

GAMIFICATION

Gamification refers to using aspects of game-play to frame learning experiences. This might include developing competition between players or teams, encouraging strategy or game design to engage learners in the process and demonstrate skills at the same time. Gamification is a fast-growing strategy used across a wide range of industries; for example, 'The US armed-forces now spends more money on recruitment games than any other marketing platform' (Chou, 2019, p. 10).

A key point is a distinction between game-playing and gamification. Many teachers already use game-play in their teaching, perhaps particularly in the younger years. Teachers might lead a game that is purely for fun or play a game that has some educational element to it. For example, a ball throwing game that requires participants to recite the next times tables answer as they throw the ball, or even a quick game of chasey in the playground. These activities often include all the features of a traditional, formal game: scoring, tactics, right/wrong answers, prizes or 'winners' (Kickmeier-Rust et al., 2014).

Gamification, however, is not the same. An online game that requires the use of geometry is a game. An online activity that uses aspects of game design is gamification. To explain further, gamification is taking the elements of online games that engage children in their learning and applying them in other contexts. There is a psychological aspect to gamification that is explained by Al-Azawi et al. (2016, p. 133): 'On a basic level, gamification techniques tap into and influence peoples natural desires for competition, achievement, recognition and self-expression. Gamification appears to be making a leap from game-play to the workplace at a great pace.'

All this suggests that when using technologies in your maths classroom, you should consider how to gamify learning. Technology provides ways to do this that are interactive and ensure all learners can identify their learning progress. You might give badges for achievements rather than scores or marks; you could engage students in teams, identify more transparent learning milestones and present challenges to demonstrate learning. Several online platforms enable gamification in your classrooms. Search online to find the ones most relevant to your context.

Beyond these additions to what you are already doing in your classroom, Chou (2019) presents an argument for teachers to consider the term 'Human-Centred Design' (p. 9). He points out that adding badges and competition are ways to make learning more fun, and this appears to have been the recent focus of gamification in classrooms. There is more, however, that we can learn from game-play. Gamification can enable teachers to:

1. Provide more frequent and useful feedback to students
2. Provide multiple entries and exit points to meet every student's learning needs
3. Offer learning opportunities that are engaging for individuals and groups (Chou, 2019).

MATHS TRAILS

A second pedagogical approach for using technology for maths learning is Maths Trails. Maths Trails have been around for more than four decades and traditionally are used by creating 'stations' for learning at different physical spaces in a pre-determined environment (Gurjanow et al., 2019). This might be the school grounds, a local park or on an excursion to a farm or museum. In today's digital age there are immense opportunities to rethink Maths Trails and that draw on existing research evidence that technology can enable interactive and creative ways to explore the connection of mathematical concepts and real-work contexts. Researchers such as Gurjanow et al. (2019) and Barbosa and Isabel (2016) continue to demonstrate that Maths Trails have relevance in today's schools. The application of technology also has developed some evidence to suggest we make use of this learning strategy through technology (Fesakis et al., 2018).

In our classrooms, this means we need to consider how, when and where our learning might best take place. For younger students, a trip to the local park to explore different shapes might be enhanced by mobile devices that can take pictures and annotate them to share back in the classroom.

For older students, an exploration of learning stations within the maths classroom might be developed to include QR codes that, once scanned, reveal videos or interactive quizzes about the concept under review. These technology-enabled learning stations could remain in situ during a unit of learning to enable students to engage and revise concepts as necessary.

To go further, classrooms could become virtual reality-enabled. This involves creating models or diagrams that demonstrate maths concepts in action. For example, imagine 'solving problems involving gradients of parallel and perpendicular lines' (Victorian Curriculum and Assessment Authority, 2015) by engaging with a VR model of the Eiffel Tower or exploring perpendicular lines of plant life through a VR model of a leaf or root system.

EXAMPLES OF PRACTICE

In this section, we explore what technology in the maths classroom might look like. Examples include lessons where learning has been completely redefined and some where technology adds to or enhances existing pedagogies. In each example, you will note that the context of the teaching and the learner inform how technology is used. As we have explored in earlier chapters, it is essential to make sense of what will work for your students in your setting when you plan for technology-enhanced learning in the maths classroom.

MATHS AND TECHNOLOGY IN THE EARLY CHILDHOOD SETTING

Before technology in the maths classroom, students in MK's classroom explored geometry ideas such as shapes and measurement using informal units. MK asked them to work out how many blocks it took to measure the length of the table and then compare it to the measures of their friends. In this way, the children began to see that measurement needs to be accurate and that if we use different blocks, we get different answers.

MK follows up this lesson with an activity on the iPads. The children open an app that lets you record your voice while also recording your gestures on the screen. In small groups with MK, the students take turns explaining how to measure using blocks. They move the virtual blocks on the screen and line them up. As they make connections between the blocks and concepts of length and informal units, MK is recording their thinking for her to review later. This will inform her planning and enable her to give precise feedback to the students. The ability to rewatch and review the children's thinking is something that MK relies on the iPads for, and was not possible before the introduction of technology into her early childhood setting.

MATHS AND TECHNOLOGY IN THE PRIMARY SCHOOL SETTING

In Year 5, Seb and his friends are learning about percentages and fractions and how they can help us make sense of large amounts of data. Seb is exploring data from a local football competition and trying to decide which team has been more successful over the past 5 years. He is using total points scored to evaluate each team.

His friend Gabi is similarly identifying the least effective player in each team in terms of points scored. The teacher has provided links to an online database that contains lots of data about each team, player and season they will explore.

The task, then, is for Seb and Gabi to make decisions about which data is useful and why. Using online visualisation tools such as infographics and dynamic charts, Seb can extract the data he needs and creates a visualisation that compares the teams' successes. The visualisation, unfortunately, shows that each team is about the same in terms of total points scored. Seb knows that one team won more games than the others, so how can this be?

Gabi shows Seb her work. She has discovered that while one team did win the competition, in the end, it was a very close season. She creates a cluster diagram to show Seb that each team has a similar number of less effective players which has led to only a slight difference in final points over the season. This might account for why the team comparison did not show a clear frontrunner. Seb uses technology to explore this point further and reflects that he used 'points scored' as the key factor in success. However, many teams only won by one or two points meaning that it was a narrow win. Consequently, when the data was displayed to show how many points teams had won by, it came out as similar. He has a much clearer insight into the data and can make informed claims about what it might mean.

This type of manipulation of large data sets is not possible in the offline world. Creating charts, adding and removing variables and converting data into a range of visualisations at the click of a button are new affordances of technology. Gabi and Seb are certainly learning more about how to read data and extract information than if they surveyed eye colour or shoe size in their classroom. In this way, technology in the maths classroom is supporting students to engage in activities that would otherwise be beyond their abilities.

MATHS AND TECHNOLOGY IN THE SECONDARY SCHOOL SETTING

In Year 9, students in Miray's maths class are exploring numerical data sets and using descriptive statistics. Miray has asked all the students to engage with an online data set that presents information about numeracy levels in countries around the world. This data is from a large global organisation, and the data is free to use. Miray has assigned groups of two students to each of 12 countries. They are told they need to develop a case on behalf of their adopted country for increased numeracy funding. Despite some of the countries already having very high numeracy levels across their populations, Miray asks the class to use descriptive statistics to improve their chances of winning the large funding amount.

Riku is working with her partner on Canada, which appears to have quite a high numeracy rate. This could be tricky! First, they extract the data for their country from the online resource and start to explore what it might tell them. They begin by using the online spreadsheet to calculate the mean (average) numeracy rate over the past 10 years. The data is impressive, with a high percentage of citizens with numeracy skills. Next, they calculate the median of the data to understand how any outliers might be impacting on the mean numeracy rate. It is a lower number but still relatively high. While studying the median data, Riku suddenly notices that there is a cluster of data points at the lower end of the numeracy scale. With her partner, she removes the other data and concentrates on this lower end cluster. What is going on here? Who belongs to this cluster of lower numeracy levels and why?

From here, Riku and her partner realise that the data is telling a few different stories. On the whole, the numeracy levels are high, but when small sub-sets are analysed there is a big gap between some geographic locations in Canada. It appears you are likely to be more numerate if you live in or near a big city! Rural and regional centres report lower numeracy scores. This forms the basis of their presentation, and eventually they argue that the disparity in numeracy levels between urban and rural communities is broad and growing, and therefore they should receive the funding.

Technology here has enabled Miray and her students to engage with real data and to create and re-create diagrams and charts that meet their needs. This lesson was not focused on drawing graphs or creating tables; instead, the learning outcome was focused on comparing data displays and using descriptive statistics. Technology, then, enabled the students to engage with the data itself, rather than conventions of drawing and labelling. With digital technologies, Riku was able to add, subtract and re-create charts and graphs to answer questions as they arose.

BACK TO THE CLASSROOM

The teacher reflects on the way that she wants to use technology and decides that a small group activity using the iPads could be helpful. At the moment, building the three-digit numbers is taking a long time as the group finds enough hundreds, tens and ones to create the model.

Instead, the students will use a computer simulator that will represent the numbers in virtual blocks on the screen. This way, the students will be able to explore more and more complex examples during the lesson.

Having found an online simulator to use, she begins the next class with a review of the main mathematical concepts of place value.

Her small group who struggled yesterday then move to a quiet space to work with their partner. They open the simulator and then roll the dice on the floor. They need to make 986. On the screen, they drag virtual blocks of hundreds, tens and ones to the table until they think they have the right amount. Now the computer will check their work. Oh, dear, it was wrong. They have again confused the tens and ones columns! The simulator begins a short animation that shows them how to move the blocks on the screen to the correct spot and then asks them to retry the task. The students are pleased to be able to quickly correct their work as they go and to be more independent in their learning. At the end of the lesson, the teacher comes by to see how they are progressing. She overhears a conversation about which column is tens and ones and which is always hundreds. She is pleased to hear the mathematical language being used and, as she watches, notices that their answers are more often correct on the first try! A win for this lesson. Of course, this one learning experience will not have consolidated their understanding. Still, she knows that their learning is progressing and technology has enabled her students to have a motivating and engaging learning experience!

CONCLUSION

In this chapter, we have explored what it means to use technology in today's mathematics classroom. We reflected on traditional maths classrooms and where technology might replace, enhance or redefine the learning experiences of our students. We then made sense of what we mean by technology-enabled maths learning and discussed several ways to plan and use technology for maths learning.

Some challenges remain around the use of technology in the maths classroom, and we raised these as areas to consider when we work in schools and other education settings. Your teaching context was noted several times as highly influential in how technology is used for learning, and we explored ways to make decisions about learning and teaching. Several relatively new concepts for technology use in the maths classroom were examined and, connected to these, we offered some evidence-based pedagogical ideas for you to consider.

Finally, we reflected on what learning might look like in early childhood, primary and secondary schools and considered three examples. Each of these provided an insight into how technology might be positioned in the classroom: as a teacher replacement, as a teachers' aide or as a problem-solving space.

This chapter's focus on mathematics learning has informed the use of technology, as will the following chapters. Each learning area has both similar and unique pedagogical strategies, and technology can be used to add to, enhance or redefine learning in specific ways. As we conclude our discussion of mathematics and numeracy teaching with technology, you are invited to explore these additional resources.

FURTHER READING

Discover how technology can be used in the maths classroom:

Bray, A. & Tangney, B. (2017). Technology usage in mathematics education research: A systematic review of recent trends. *Computers & Education, 114*, 255–273.

Explore how you can develop your knowledge and skills to effectively use technology in your maths classroom:

Driskell, S. O., Bush, S. B., Ronau, R. N., Niess, M. L., Rakes, C. R. & Pugalee, D. K. (2018). Mathematics education technology professional development: Changes over several decades. In *Teacher Training and Professional Development: Concepts, Methodologies, Tools, and Applications* (pp. 115–144). Hershey, PA: IGI Global.

Investigate how games-based learning can enhance your teaching and learning practices:

Hainey, T., Connolly, T. M., Boyle, E. A., Wilson, A. & Razak, A. (2016). A systematic literature review of games-based learning empirical evidence in primary education. *Computers & Education, 102,* 202–223.

REFERENCES

Al-Azawi, R., Al-Faliti, F. & Al-Blushi, M. (2016). Educational gamification vs. game-based learning: Comparative study. *International Journal of Innovation, Management and Technology, 7*(4), 132–136.

Barbosa, A. & Isabel, V. (2016). Math Trails: Meaningful mathematics outside the classroom with pre-service teachers. *Journal of the European Teacher Education Network, 11,* 63–72.

Booth, J. L., McGinn, K. M., Barbieri, C., Begolli, K. N., Chang, B., Miller-Cotto, D., Young, L. K., & Davenport, J. L. (2017). Evidence for cognitive science principles that impact learning in mathematics. In D. Geary, D. Berch, R. Ochsendorf & K. Mann Koepke (eds), *Acquisition of Complex Arithmetic Skills and Higher-Order Mathematics Concepts* (pp. 297–325). Oxford: Elsevier.

Chou, Y. (2019). *Actionable Gamification: Beyond Points, Badges, and Leaderboards.* Birmingham: Packt Publishing Ltd.

Fesakis, G., Karta, P. & Kozas, K. (2018). Designing Math Trails for enhanced by mobile learning realistic mathematics education in primary education. *International Journal of Engineering Pedagogy (IJEP), 8,* 49. doi:10.3991/ijep.v8i2.8131

Goos, M. & Bennison, A. (2008). Surveying the technology landscape: Teachers' use of technology in secondary mathematics classrooms. *Mathematics Education Research Journal, 20*(3), 102–130. doi:10.1007/BF03217532

Gurjanow, I., Oliveira, M., Zender, J., Santos, P. A. & Ludwig, M. (2019). Mathematics Trails: Shallow and deep gamification. *International Journal of Serious Games, 6*(3), 65–79.

Higgins, K., Huscroft-D'Angelo, J. & Crawford, L. (2019). Effects of technology in mathematics on achievement, motivation, and attitude: A meta-analysis. *Journal of Educational Computing Research, 57*(2), 283–319. doi:10.1177/0735633117748416

Hoyles, C., & Lagrange, J.-B. (eds) (2010). *Mathematics Education and Technology-Rethinking the Terrain: The 17th ICMI Study.* Springer US. https://doi.org/10.1007/978-1-4419-0146-0

Kickmeier-Rust, M. D., Hillemann, E.-C. & Albert, D. (2014). Gamification and smart feedback: Experiences with a primary school level math app. *International Journal of Game-Based Learning (IJGBL).* Retrieved from www.igi-global.com/article/gamification-and-smart-feedback/117698 (accessed 12 July 2021).

Lai, M. Y., & Murray, S. (2012). Teaching with procedural variation: A Chinese way of promoting deep understanding of mathematics. *International Journal for Mathematics Teaching and Learning,* 1–25.

Li, Y., Silver, E.A. & Li, S. (2014). *Transforming Mathematics Instruction: Multiple Approaches and Practices.* Cham: Springer International Publishing, Retrieved from https://books.google.com.au/books?id=DGv1AwAAQBAJ (accessed 12 July 2021).

Murphy, D. (2016). A literature review: The effect of implementing technology in a high school mathematics classroom. *International Journal of Research in Education and Science, 2*(2), 295. https://doi.org/10.21890/ijres.98946

Ogden, T. & Pierce, E. (2019). The impact of personalised learning on learner agency, communication, and critical thinking in a fourth and sixth grade math class (MA dissertation), St Catherine University, St Paul, MN.

Schuetz, R. L., Biancarosa, G., & Goode, J. (2018). Is technology the answer? Investigating students' engagement in math. *Journal of Research on Technology in Education, 50*(4), 318–332. https://doi.org/10.1080/15391523.2018.1490937

Schwabe, M. (2018). *Volume I: Teachers and School Leaders as Lifelong Learners*. Retrieved from www.oecd.org/education/talis/TALIS2018_CN_AUS.pdf (accessed 12 July 2021).

Victorian Curriculum and Assessment Authority. (2015). *Mathematics—Curriculum—Victorian Curriculum*. https://victoriancurriculum.vcaa.vic.edu.au/mathematics/curriculum/f-10#level=10 (accessed 21 July 2021).

Walkington, C. & Hayata, C. A. (2017). Designing learning personalised to students' interests: Balancing rich experiences with mathematical goals. *ZDM, 49*(4), 519–530.

8

INTEGRATED
STEM LEARNING

IN THIS CHAPTER YOU WILL LEARN:

- How to use technology to support STEM thinking skills
- How to create learning experiences that draw on the affordances of technologies
- How technology can 'host' the STEM learning or 'drive' the STEM learning in your classroom.

INTRODUCTION

The term STEM learning has been promoted since 2001, when the National Science Foundation identified a need to name more clearly the skills that today's students will need to engage in the changing economy (Hallinen, 2020). As many countries experience a shift from product-based to knowledge-based economies, the ability to combine skills and content knowledge in different settings has become increasingly important for everyone, not least our young citizens:

> Knowledge Society is a term to describe societies which are economically and culturally characterised by a high degree of dependency on their potentials to create scientific and technological knowledge. (Treptow, 2020)

While science is often seen as the major component of STEM, it should be remembered that each of the four disciplines of science, technology, engineering and maths have a necessary place in today's schools. Indeed, a number of variations of STEM have emerged with varying foci. STEAM presents a way to bring the Arts into learning. A 2020 definition of STEAM suggests that 'STEM subjects enriched with Arts (STEAM) are assumed to enhance science lessons and make them more attractive' (Conradty and Bogner, 2019, p. 284).

Rather than enhancing science lessons, however, STEMM brings a fifth partner to the original STEM quartet. The final 'M' refers to the inclusion of Medicine. As a professional field that requires ongoing learning and accredited by professional associations and boards, medicine has been seen to have many similarities to the original STEM fields. Medicine has been impacted by the rapid growth of technology and relies heavily on advancements in science, engineering and mathematics to ensure cutting edge healthcare is available. In this way, STEMM provides a cohesive group of skills and competencies that include medicine:

> When grouped with (M)edicine, the inextricably linked STEM(M) fields form an array of disciplines that impact people's lives in myriad, profound ways each day. (Parappilly et al., 2019, p. 2)

While STEAM and STEMM are clearly important areas of learning, in this chapter we will focus on the four disciplines referred to in STEM. We will consider STEM to be a noun in its own right, rather than a simple acronym. The rationale for this approach is that integrated STEM learning has been shown to offer opportunities to learn skills for future employment and the good of the country (Office of Chief Scientist, 2016). Instead of teaching a science lesson, followed by a maths lesson and calling this STEM teaching, we instead are using technology in STEM to create something that is bigger than the sum of its parts. The interconnected nature of STEM disciplines are best represented in certain pedagogical approaches, including problem-based and team-based learning. The focus on problem-solving is an oft-referred to competency for today's learners. A brief reflection on professionals working in any of the STEM fields proves that problem-solving is a core part of an expert's task. As an engineer, you might need to solve problems of weight distribution or friction, for example. A mathematician must solve problems that have both abstract and practical applications. Ensuring that solutions are reproducible is often an outcome of mathematical problem-solving, particularly in the growing fields of computer programming and database development. Similarly, scientists and health workers/researchers are faced with problems that often have several possible solutions. Developing skills and experiences in how we approach and interpret problems means we can then go on to design and test solutions. As teachers, we are also asked to develop future-ready students within our classrooms; indeed Australian school education is positioned as impacting on the entire country's wellbeing: 'It is critical that qualifications at all levels prepare students for the breadth of roles and industries they might pursue' (Office of the Chief Scientist, 2016).

Technology is increasingly in demand as a tool for learning and doing in many industries. However, technology has not always been the focus of STEM learning in schools. At times, STEM has been used as a synonym for science learning, a confusion we will explore later in this chapter. In this chapter, we will argue that the 'T' in STEM is integral to developing the competencies that integrated STEM promises.

This chapter will explore key concepts that inform how STEM is addressed in schools and some of the challenges that you may face when bringing technology into existing STEM or science programmes. We will offer evidence-based concepts that you can use in your teaching practice and suggest practical examples from the classroom.

IN THE CLASSROOM TODAY

Primary school student Rami is excited that there will be a new subject at school this term: STEM. Rami isn't sure what this means, but the teacher said that the class would be thinking, making and doing, which sounds like fun! As the student enters the classroom he sees empty boxes, laptop computers, bowls of water, colouring pencils, measuring tapes and, excitingly, iPads on the tables. 'What is happening here?' Rami wonders?

The teacher, MK, welcomes everyone and asks them to sit at a table. She explains that today they need to begin solving a problem. The school principal has arranged for some architects to come next week to make plans for a new building. The problem, however, is that it means the school will lose most of its parking spaces for staff. Today's task is to work on a design for new car parking at the school. They will need to make a plan of the school grounds and draw in the new car park. Next, they will be using the resources in the classroom to make a model of their plans.

As the Year 4 class move into groups, Rami has a question. He asks MK whether he can work on a computer. He explains he has been learning how to make 3D models using some free software. MK hesitates. She is not sure that working online for this activity is the learning she had in mind. Is there a way to incorporate the hands-on creating, team work and design using only technology? MK remembers that she has iPads available for this lesson. She decides to hand out one iPad to each child. Then she can monitor what the students do and if they are getting the learning experiences she hoped for.

As she hands out the iPads, MK realises that she doesn't have a clear idea of what learning is going to take place today. What should she ask them to do? How could the iPads be used? After today's lesson she will need to do some more thinking.

TECHNOLOGY IN STEM: HISTORY

DEFINING STEM

As STEM education grows in profile nationally and internationally, it has become clear that teachers need specific skills and knowledge to teach STEM in the classroom (Prinsley and

Johnston, 2015). Research tells us that even from primary school, students can benefit from learning with and through STEM activities. Indeed, there are foundational skills that should be taught as early as the first year of schooling (Prinsley and Johnston, 2015).

In Australia, a major reason there is a drive to increase and improve STEM teaching is that fewer and fewer students are entering STEM in higher education. In turn, this means less qualified adults entering the workforce (Department of Education, 2020).

Beyond the focus on developing workplace skills, the Australian government has also noted that STEM learning helps children develop skills important to becoming involved citizens:

> The Australian Government regards high-quality science, technology, engineering and mathematics (STEM) education as critically important for our current and future productivity, as well as for informed personal decision making and effective community, national and global citizenship. (Department of Education, Skills & Employment, 2020)

Integrated STEM is a specific way to think about how the four disciplines work together. To implement an integrated STEM programme we need to consider the overlaps between each of the disciplines. We should acknowledge, of course, that some STEM activities will privilege certain disciplines over others. In the coming sections of this chapter, we will explore what this might look like and how we as teachers can decide how, when and where we engage with science, technology, engineering or mathematics.

STEM THINKING

The idea of STEM as a noun that represents its own content area is one that has been contested. The acronym S.T.E.M. was initially used to bring four learning areas together. The acronym has, however, developed beyond its constituent parts to refer to a new area of learning, one that asks learners to use all four learning areas to understand the world and solve problems.

There are aspects of learning and thinking that have been identified as common across the four disciplines. One list of these competencies includes: problem-solving, creativity, critical analysis, teamwork, independent thinking, initiative, communication and digital literacy (Department of Education, 2020).

Each of these skills can be taught but need to be embedded in contextual learning to be experienced. Technology can offer a space to explore ideas such as creativity, initiative and problem-solving. Consider the use of a collaborative online whiteboard (Blannin, 2020). Students can add their ideas, draw lines to connect concepts, remove and re-imagine their designs and suggest solutions. They can achieve this in a collaborative space, where multimedia and web links offer direct connections to resources and in a way that gives every student the same access and same ability to contribute. In the offline classroom we might see this task completed on large sheets of paper. This clearly also offers collaboration but discon-nects the designing and thinking from digital resources that are often critical to the task itself. Working on one sheet of paper in a group can also mean that one or two members hold the pens – other group members may then become bystanders with less direct contributions than the scribes of the group.

STEM thinking asks us as teachers to consider new learning experiences. Beyond teaching maths, and science, STEM thinking brings together the shared thinking skills that are needed in all four STEM disciplines. This means we need to reflect carefully on the ways that learn-ing is structured. Student-centred learning that engages students in creation, implementation and reflection is one frame through which to evaluate what we do in our classrooms.

DIFFERENT WAYS OF UNDERSTANDING STEM

A challenge of STEM teaching is that there is no single definition of what this term means. Indeed, it has been said that 'One of the problematic issues for researchers and curriculum developers lies in the different interpretations of STEM education and STEM integration' (English, 2016).

Is STEM relevant only to industry and adult professions? In contrast, is STEM something we only teach in schools?

As we have seen in this chapter, STEM is essential for the future, both in schools and in the wider workforce. This is an ongoing issue in schools. Imagine a conversation between teachers in a school. The English teacher refers to STEM learning as using laptops for researching a report. Surely this addresses the 'T' in STEM? The mathematics teacher replies that she, too, teaches STEM when she includes maths problems and asks students to solve them. As you now know, STEM is neither of these. Indeed, STEM education should be understood as a pedagogical approach that ties together four disciplines of learning to enable learners to develop and demonstrate creativity, critical analysis and problem-solving skills.

These thinking skills are crucial to successful STEM learning and should be a part of all STEM teaching. Technology, then, is a means and an end to STEM learning. Technology is not only the tool that supports students to solve problems. It can also be the main learn-ing outcome of the activity. Technology skills include the ability to use, understand and develop solutions to complex problems. Designing a computer network for a remote com-munity, exploring how artificial intelligence might better meet the needs of aged care residents or exploring space through virtual reality and robotics – all of these put tech-nologies at the heart of STEM learning. In each of these examples, there are technological skills to learn. In developing an understanding of how technologies work and their poten-tial impact on the world, students are drawn to demonstrate STEM knowledge and skills. Using artificial intelligence in aged care settings requires students to explore problems, design creative solutions and have a strong understanding of the possibilities of technology. This is STEM learning.

STEM IS NOT SCIENCE TEACHING

A further challenge is to understand and define where STEM learning occurs in schools. In some cases, STEM teaching in schools has become a synonym for 'science' teaching alone. As teachers and school leaders engage with the ideas of STEM it can be hard to see where STEM fits within the existing curriculum. With an often overcrowded curriculum, it can be difficult to make room for what can be seen as a 'new' learning area. Indeed, in many schools STEM has become the job of science teachers. This is, naturally, challenging for science teachers as they struggle to balance their existing curriculum demands and the new ideas of STEM teaching and learning.

A more robust and sustainable way of approaching STEM teaching in schools is to re-think what is already happening. When teachers of different disciplines come together, the load is shared and real changes in teaching practice can occur. Consider a team of teachers from science, maths, technologies and social studies. Each teacher brings unique and necessary skills for solving complex problems with creative and critical thinking. A term- or semester-long programme that engages students in all four disciplines has a much higher chance of successful STEM learning than if each teacher took on board STEM in their own classrooms.

In some schools, specially designed STEM learning buildings offer a physical location for this interdisciplinary learning to occur. Imagine a large open space that provides science equipment, a range of technologies, a research and reference centre and a mathematics lab. Here, students access discipline specific knowledge and move between different learning areas, within one space. For example, while working on a design for a new Mars robot, the student realises that they need to understand the major challenges of vehicular movement in a different atmosphere. The science teachers' knowledge is paramount here. Having understood gravity, atmosphere and climatic conditions, the student must now engage with friction and forces to calculate the size of the wheels. This leads them to the mathematics teacher who can lead them to understand equations and algorithms to find solutions. Finally, the technologies and social studies teachers support learners to make decisions about who, what and how the robot is controlled. This might include developing an understanding of the human need for society and social interaction, the technological limitations of remote control devices or the benefits and challenges of voice-controlled versus programmed robots.

This example provides clear evidence that STEM cannot be taught by science teachers alone. For successful STEM learning in schools, a team approach to planning and teaching is needed. These teams might be flexible with members joining and leaving as needed, based on the focus of the STEM programme. However, a team of teachers, each with unique pedagogical and content knowledge of a field, are more likely to engender true STEM learning. Consider the poor science teacher, who in some cases faces a doubling of curriculum outcomes that need to be addressed. A team approach may be less comfortable for some teachers – however, the teaching of STEM requires it.

SCHOOL ENGAGEMENT

To conclude this section, we must also consider the practical challenges faced by teachers in schools. Change in schools, as in many organisations, is most sustainable when leaders are involved in, and committed to, the change process. It has been noted that, 'creating a school culture and environment that supports an integrated STEM approach to teaching and learning can be costly and time-consuming' (Thibaut et al., 2018, p. 2).

Despite having good intentions of teaching STEM, some school systems are not accommodating. School leaders need to value STEM learning, and the technologies that go with it, if STEM teaching is to be successful. This might mean rethinking the school's timetable or planning schedules, providing extra time and resources for teachers to work together to develop a new way of teaching or even engaging outside professionals to provide advice on how STEM brings together science, technologies, mathematics and engineering in the real world.

This requires time, energy and money in often already-stretched programmes. What is sometimes required in these situations is for teachers at the grass roots level to begin trialling new pedagogies and technologies. In this way, the teachers generate evidence and interest in change relevant to their unique school context. Alongside these teachers, of course, must be a school leadership team that prioritises new ideas, the trialling of new pedagogies and supports the possibility that ideas and trials will fail.

Every school and school leadership team is different and works within a unique community of learners, families and teachers. As teachers of technologies in schools, your role is to demonstrate that STEM learning is not only science teaching, it is not only teaching four distinct disciplines and it is not only using technology to teach other subjects. Your role is to show how STEM teaching brings together a range of thinking skills to enable students to understand, investigate and solve complex, interdisciplinary problems. With a generation or two of learners equipped with these experiences and knowledge, we are perhaps closer to solving global problems such as climate change, poverty and population growth. As a teacher of technologies and STEM you have a chance to impact these challenges.

KEY CONCEPTS FOR TECHNOLOGY IN STEM LEARNING

PROBLEM-SOLVING AS LEARNING

In this section, we will explore two key concepts in STEM learning. First, we will look at problem-solving as a pedagogical strategy and a learning outcome. This means problem-solving can be a 'way' to teach as well as a 'thing' to teach. Technologies are critical to the success of STEM teaching; without them the type, depth and complexity of problems that students can work with is severely limited.

We also need a clear definition of problem-solving. We will use the definition created by the OECD in 2013:

> Problem-solving competency is an individual's capacity to engage in cognitive processing to understand and resolve problem situations where a method of solution is not immediately obvious. It includes the willingness to engage with such situations in order to achieve one's potential as a constructive and reflective citizen. (OECD, 2013, p. 122)

Problem-solving for our purposes, then, sees learners bring together a number of thinking skills to find solutions that are not obvious at first glance. Significantly, a strong problem-solving ability also means that students demonstrate a 'willingness' to engage with, and solve, problems.

Ensuring that our students are, therefore, able to apply their technologies' knowledge is critical to successful learning. Unlike in other subjects we aren't asking students to memorise facts or dates or numbers. Instead we are asking them to take a broader perspective on their learning and make informed decisions about when, how and where technology might help solve a problem. In this way, our learners use technology as both a learning area and a tool for problem-solving, creating effective designs and even imagining future situations.

Today's learners are not passive receivers of information. If you ask most 12-year-olds how they learned something, often they will say they found an online video or tutorial. They often know how to do this before they reach your classroom. Even early childhood learners know that answers to questions can be found on 'mum's phone'. We call these questions a 'google-able' problem.

For example, you can find the answer to 'What is the capital of France?' by searching online. If we ask, 'Why is Paris the capital of France?', however, students will have to read a number of sources, make informed decisions and then come to a conclusion. This is a 'non-google-able' question. It is this type of open-ended problem that technologies and STEM learning can address.

In addition, it is important when working with older children that problem-solving is not something we offer fully formed to our students. We need to ask them to investigate a situation, identify issues and decide how to proceed. Our role is to create situations in which our students can discover problems that they can solve.

When teachers provide learning in this way, research tells us that our relationship with students benefits too, making our job more rewarding and perhaps less stressful, as Morrison et al. noted when they explored a STEM problem-solving programme at one school:

> The teachers' support was personal and caring, they challenged students and provided responsive guidance and advice, responding directly to students' interests while retaining high standards and expectations. (Morrison et al., 2020, p. 2)

We have discussed how we might teach problem-solving skills that bring together technologies and STEM learning; however, it is important to remind ourselves that education can have a broader purpose – the preparation of individuals who are ready and able to contribute to our societies. Today's students are tomorrow's leaders, and as such we are tasked to ensure that they have the relevant experiences and expertise to contribute to leading and growing our societies. As Oleson has noted:

> employers are clamouring for workers who not only have technical expertise in a particular area such as STEM, but also those who can use their technical knowledge to engage in abstract reasoning, problem-solving, and troubleshooting. (Oleson et al., 2014, p. 23)

COLLABORATIVE LEARNING WITH TECHNOLOGY

To solve complex problems we often need more than one brain. Collaboration is an integral part of both STEM and creating technological solutions. In every STEM learning experience there are likely to be numerous types of knowledge, skills and expertise required. As skills develop, change and disappear, we can not, as one human being, maintain currency with everything going on. We need a team.

Collaborative thinking and logic are two benefits of collaborative learning, although many others exist. Consider the idea of collaborative logic. One person's logical conclusion is based on their understanding and prior experiences. If that conclusion is brought to a group and discussed, other experiences become part of the logical solution. When using technology to create or design a solution to a large problem, for example flooding in a rural city, we need to develop a set of assumptions to work from. Technology can work in the same way. When coding computers we create 'if this ... then that ...' scenarios. These are based on assumptions that one thing follows another, such as flooding following high levels of rainfall. Collaborative logic enables us to interrogate these assumptions and develop a more complex, accurate understanding of the situation. In the example above, collaborative logic could lead us to understand that high levels of rainfall, in addition to a long dry summer, impacts on the potential for flooding. Hot summers dry out the land, which can become compacted, making it harder for the rainfall to penetrate, leading to flooding.

Leading collaborative learning in schools can be a challenge. There are likely timetable, resource and room allocation challenges. These structural barriers can limit how and how well students are able to collaborate during STEM and technology learning. These challenges can be overcome, however, with support from school leaders and teachers (Margot and Kettler, 2019).

Technology in STEM offers many benefits, as we have discussed; however, it is important to note that technology can enable effective collaboration by providing online spaces for sharing, discussing and creating. These spaces, such as a cloud platform or shared website, offer a level playing field for students. Contributions to the work are easily recorded and evaluated, encouraging equal contributions and clear authorship. Indeed, some research suggests that using technology to ensure that all students contribute to a task is seen as a clear benefit of technology in STEM learning. Students appreciate the transparency and opportunities to contribute (or not) (Bolatli and Korucu, 2018).

Problem-solving abilities and collaborative learning practices are key strategies for designing and implementing STEM learning. Using technology as both a teaching approach and learning area is integral to ensuring our students develop the crucial thinking skills that will enable them to become successful, contributing citizens in our societies.

EXAMPLES OF PRACTICE

In this section we explore technology learning in a STEM programme. There are, of course, numerous approaches to teaching technology and STEM. In the examples shared here, we have included lessons where learners demonstrate the problem-solving and collaborative skills we discussed in the previous section. In each example you will note that the context of the learning and the learner informs how technology is used. Each school and classroom is unique and as such it is your role as the teacher to ensure that teaching and learning are appropriate for the learners in your care.

STEM AND TECHNOLOGY IN THE EARLY CHILDHOOD SETTING

In MKs classroom, the group has finished a shared reading activity of a traditional European fairy tale. They have heard about Rapunzel and her long hair. Being locked up in a tower, Rapunzel is seeking a way to escape. There is no one around to help, so what might she do? MK asks the children to work with a classroom helper in groups of three or four. Each group will have an iPad. In their groups, the classroom helper will guide the conversation. How will Rapunzel escape? As ideas come from the students, the adult helper begins to draw a design. Next, students add to the drawing and begin to discuss how Rapunzel might escape. The iPad provides a central focus for the discussion and also offers a way to delete, move and modify components of the escape plan. This would be hard to achieve on a piece of paper.

By the end of the class, each group has a proposed solution. MK calls on Laars' group to share their design. Connecting the iPad to the screen, everyone can see what the group has come up with and MK guides some feedback on their work. One student comments, I don't think Rapunzel would have a rope in her room so I don't think you can use that. Another adds, I think that your idea for climbing down the tree is fun. But is the tree really strong? MK asks, what is the tower made of? Is it flat or is the tower made of bricks you could step on and climb down. The lesson ends with each group sharing their ideas. After the lesson, MK will go through the designs and the notes she made on the discussion. What STEM ideas did students present today? What might they need to work on next? Perhaps the idea of height and distance would be useful next, or maybe, as one group suggested, MK should build some wings and fly free! In choosing the next steps, MK can frame their students' learning in STEM and maintain a focus on creativity, sharing and collaboration.

STEM AND TECHNOLOGY IN THE PRIMARY SCHOOL SETTING

Gabi is beginning a Year 3 problem-solving activity this week. Each afternoon, they are spending time working in small groups or pairs to solve a problem that students found in the playground. After heavy rain last week, the Years 3 and 4 area of the playground is flooded. The students thought this was fantastic! They could splash, run and play in the water; of course getting very wet and messy in the process. Gabi noticed that some students were also stood in the middle of the flooded area and floating small 'boats' of twigs and leaves. In the classroom, Gabi asked the students what was happening. The answers ranged from sailing and racing boats, to 'trying to float big bits of mud'. Excellent, thought Gabi. That is a great STEM lesson.

Gabi asked the students who were sailing, racing and floating in the flooded playground to explain to the group what they were doing. Their classmates enthusiastically asked what worked and what didn't.

From here, Gabi introduces a 3D modelling software called Google Sketch Up. She demonstrates how to create a design using basic 3D shapes. The class next work in their small groups to design a perfect floatation design for the flood water – which they will re-create in a sink in the classroom! The 3D software enables students to look at their designs from all angles. From the bottom they can check if there are any potential leaks, from above they can estimate if the boat will balance, from the side they can make informed choices about how high and stable the sides might be. After designing their prototype boat, students send a copy of their designs to another group who provide feedback and suggestions for improvement. The final stage of this three-week activity will be to print the boats using the 3D printer. From here, each group will be able to test their designs, and perhaps save their boat for the next rainy day.

Each week, Gabi reviews the groups' activity and plans for a specific content area to teach. In week two, with most designs ready for peer feedback, she notes that some principles of maths (volume and area) are lacking. These become part of the maths teaching this week. She also notes that some groups are struggling with the design process and using the app. She plans to run short 'workshops' on the software for any groups who choose to attend. In evaluating this task at the end of the three weeks, Gabi identifies aspects of the technology, science and maths curriculum. She also is able to evaluate students on their general capabilities of collaboration, creativity and problem-solving. Not bad for a rainy day, she thinks.

STEM AND TECHNOLOGY IN THE SECONDARY SCHOOL SETTING

Riku is a student in Miray's Year 9 maths class. Today the class are learning about problem-solving in maths and how the teacher isn't the only expert in the room! Miray explains that in the world beyond school, many professions, including STEM and mathematics in particular, require people to be able to work together to solve complex problems. So, collaborative problem-solving is an important part of their learning at school. Miray invites the students to share areas of the curriculum that they feel confident in. How could they share this information with each other easily?

Riku, who is a keen programmer, suggests making a website that they could update with their status in real time. Others agree this would be excellent and really helpful in the classroom. Several students, however, are worried that another website in their classroom would just be distracting – and isn't it hard to build a website?

Miray has another idea. She attended a workshop last term on STEM teaching and wearable technology. She understands that as a maths teacher STEM is her responsibility to teach and that as a teacher she also needs to address the learning outcomes of the Technologies curriculum. At this school, each student has purchased a micro-bit minicomputer at the beginning of the year. These are quite cheap but very powerful computers. Miray knows that not many teachers have used them yet. Perhaps there is a way to bring this technology into her classroom?

For the next lesson, Miray has prepared some resources: several spare micro-bits, pieces of fabric, needles and thread, LED lights, cables and crocodile clips, tape, glue and scissors. She shows the students a bracelet she has made using the micro-bit. On her wrist is a green felt strip with holes cut for five flashing LED lights. Tucked into the band is the micro-bit which, she explains, she has programmed to be touch sensitive. Each time she taps the bracelet, another light illuminates. Perhaps, she suggests, this could solve our problem about collaborative problem-solving?

Riku calls out, each light (1–5) could represent how confident we are feeling in our maths class. Others agree and begin to get excited. Some students at the back mumble, I'm not wearing a bracelet! One student suggests that the device didn't need to be a bracelet though; it could be a badge, a bookmark, a keychain or a simple button on the table. As long as it was visible to others, it would work. This seems to appease the reluctant bracelet-wearers and the class begins to chat loudly.

Before we begin, says Miray, we need to consider the coding we use. It would need to be the same so that we are all sending the correct signals: 1 light = 'I need help', 5 = 'I'm an expert at this'. Riku volunteers to lead the coding for the class. He steps to the front of the room, opens up the micro-bit website and shows everyone how to code a simple sequence and send it to the micro-bit. Miray smiles – this is meeting several of the curriculum outcomes she had planned for this year: designing and using algorithms, testing and evaluating solutions and designing technology-enabled solutions in mathematics. She also had planned to work on peer feedback and creativity. This task seems to tick many boxes.

After today's lesson, Miray decides that these devices, and the data they are collecting, could be another way to use technology and STEM practices in her teaching. She will work with the computer science teacher to understand how to collect data from each of the micro-bit devices (she is told it's not that hard). Then this data can be the basis of her teaching of statistics next term.

Riku is excited: he got to teach in today's lesson! His passion for coding was accepted enthusiastically by his peers and he hadn't realised maths class could be so fun. He thinks there must be some maths in coding but he isn't sure where or how; perhaps he'll ask Miray next lesson. His classmates have already been emailing him with the codes they have written and to ask for help. He might need to get some of his friends to help with this, he thinks.

BACK TO THE CLASSROOM

Our primary school teacher, MK, has reflected on her use of iPads in yesterday's lesson and decided that technology could help this STEM project. For the next class, she plans to put students into groups where one student has more skills in using the iPad and one has skills in problem-solving. These groups should be better balanced, she thinks.

To begin the next lesson, MK leads the students outside and asks them, in their groups, to take photographs of the car park. What works well in this car park? What are the possible challenges? Are there trees in the way? Low roofs? Lots of noise? Having taken these photos the class heads back inside.

MK asks each group to annotate their photos, using a free annotation app, to show the positives and negatives of the current car park. After a little while, MK brings the class back together and each group shares one positive and one negative that they identified. MK curates a running list of these ideas and after every group has shared she displays her list on the screen. Together they work through the ideas, mapping them to a Positive, Negative, Interesting chart that MK quickly drew up. She guides the discussion to identify the possibilities in the negatives (turning them into 'interesting' ideas on the chart). She asks, what needs to be considered now? How might your design ideas change?

Drawing on their real-world photos, analysis and class discussions, the students now head back to their groups and begin their 3D designs. They add labels, questions and comments to their design and use the photos as references for their work.

After the class, MK reviews the designs so far. She is pleased to see that there is a lot more detail than after the first lesson. Students have commented on the location and access to the car park, the number of spaces, the size of the spaces compared to the size of the cars and so on.

These 3D models will be completed in the next lesson, thinks MK. She's sure she saw a 3D printer in the science lab. I wonder how easy it would be to print out the students' designs, she thinks. It would provide a tangible output of their learning and perhaps provide some further motivation to ensure the designs are detailed and clear. She resolves to email the science teacher tomorrow.

CONCLUSION

In this chapter we explored what we mean by STEM and how technology is an equal member of the four STEM disciplines. We discussed that STEM today can be considered a noun all on its own, and is not only a shorthand way of identifying science, technology, engineering and mathematics. We investigated that STEM should be an integrated way of learning through design, creativity and problem-solving.

Next we considered the possible barriers to using technology and STEM in your classroom and discussed some ways to overcome these challenges. In particular, we suggested that we need a clear definition of what we mean by STEM teaching and learning so that everyone understands the integrated approach we are seeking. We also reflected on the role of science teachers in STEM and how in some schools STEM is used as a synonym for science. Considering that science is only one of four learning areas in STEM, we suggested considering how your school and teachers might best position STEM in the curriculum. This included modelling new pedagogies and ways to teach technologies in STEM, seeking out like-minded colleagues and providing evidence for change to school leaders. Hopefully, these suggestions provide a starting point for your teaching in schools.

We identified that technology curriculum documents and STEM learning often include a range of thinking and social skills including problem-solving, collaboration and creativity. We presented examples of why these are important and how we might specifically teach and evaluate thinking skills in our teaching.

To conclude, STEM education, including technologies teaching, is increasing in prominence in policy and practice in schools around the world. This chapter has sought to position the T in STEM as not only referring to using physical devices and networks to teach maths and science. In addition, the T in STEM should lead us to teach integrated thinking skills and design technology-enabled solutions to complex problems. Without these skills, our students will have limited abilities to use technologies effectively and efficiently in their life and careers after school.

FURTHER READING

Discover how 3D technologies can be connected to computational thinking in STEM learning:

Angelopoulos, P., Balatsoukas, A. & Nistor, A. (2020). The use of 3D technologies to support Computational Thinking in STEM education. In M. Kalogiannakis & S. Papadakis (Eds.), *Handbook of Research on Tools for Teaching Computational Thinking in P-12 Education* (pp. 421–455). Hershey, PA: IGI Global.

Explore how technology supports earth science teaching in primary schools:

Bogusevschi, D., Muntean, C. H. & Muntean, G.-M. (2019). Earth Course: Knowledge acquisition in technology enhanced learning STEM education in primary school. In J. Theo Bastiaens (ed.), *Proceedings of EdMedia + Innovate Learning* **(pp. 1261–1270). Amsterdam, Netherlands: Association for the Advancement of Computing in Education (AACE).**

Investigate the use of robots as technology and engineering tools for learning:

Çetin, M. & Demircan, H. Ö. (2020). Empowering technology and engineering for STEM education through programming robots: A systematic literature review. *Early Child Development and Care,* **190(9), 1323–1335.**

REFERENCES

Blannin, J. (2020) Use of digital media boards in primary schools. In A. Tatnall (ed.), *Encyclopedia of Education and Information Technologies*. Cham, Switzerland: Springer.

Bolatli, Z. & Korucu, A. T. (2018). Secondary school students' feedback on course processing and collaborative learning with Web 2.0 tools-supported STEM activities. *Bartın Üniversitesi Eğitim Fakültesi Dergisi*, 7(2), 456–478. doi:10.14686/buefad.358488

Conradty, C., & Bogner, F. X. (2019). From STEM to STEAM: Cracking the code? How creativity & motivation interacts with inquiry-based learning. *Creativity Research Journal*, 31(3), 284–295.

Department of Education, Government of Western Australia (2020) *What is STEM?* Retrieved from www.education.wa.edu.au/what-is-stem (accessed 12 July 2021).

Department of Education, Skills & Employment, Australian Government (2020). *Support for Science, Technology, Engineering and Mathematics (STEM)*. Retrieved from www.education.gov.au/support-science-technology-engineering-and-mathematics (accessed 12 July 2021).

English, L. D. (2016). STEM education K-12: Perspectives on integration. *International Journal of STEM Education*, 3(1), 3. doi:10.1186/s40594-016-0036-1

Freeman, B., Marginson, S. & Tytler, R. (2019). An international view of STEM education. In B. Freeman, S. Marginson & R. Tytler (eds.), *STEM Education 2.0* (pp. 350–363). Leiden: Brill Publishing. doi:10.1163/9789004405400_019

Hallinen, J. (2020). STEM: Description, development, & facts. *Britannica*. Retrieved from: www.britannica.com/topic/STEM-education (accessed 12 July 2021).

Margot, K. C. & Kettler, T. (2019). Teachers' perception of STEM integration and education: A systematic literature review. *International Journal of STEM Education*, 6(1), 2.

Morrison, J., Frost, J., Gotch, C., McDuffie, A. R., Austin, B., & French, B. (2020). Teachers' role in students' learning at a project-based STEM high school: Implications for teacher education. *International Journal of Science and Mathematics Education*, 1–21.

OECD (2013). *PISA 2012 Assessment and Analytical Framework: Mathematics, Reading, Science, Problem Solving and Financial Literacy*, OECD. doi:10.1787/9789264190511-en

Office of the Chief Scientist (2016). *2016 Australia's STEM Workforce Report*. Retrieved from www. chiefscientist.gov.au/2016/03/report-australias-stem-workforce (accessed 12 July 2021).

Parappilly, M., Woodman, R. J., & Randhawa, S. (2019). Feasibility and effectiveness of different models of team-based learning approaches in STEMM-based disciplines. *Research in Science Education*, 1–15.

Thibaut, L., Ceuppens, S., De Loof, H., De Meester, J., Goovaerts, L., Struyf, A., Boeve-de Pauw, J., Dehaene, W., Deprez, J., De Cock, M., Hellinckx, L., Knipprath, H., Langie, G., Struyven, K., Van de Velde, D., Van Petegem, P. & Depaepe, F. (2018). Integrated STEM education: A Systematic review of instructional practices in secondary education. *European Journal of STEM Education*, *3*(1). https://eric.ed.gov/?id=EJ1178347 (accessed 21 July 2021).

Treptow, R. (2020). Knowledge society. *Strategic Transitions for Youth Labour in Europe*. Retrieved from www.style-research.eu/resource-centre/glossary/knowledge-society/ (accessed 12 July 2021).

Office of the Chief Scientist. (2016). *2016 Australia's STEM Workforce Report*. Australia's Chief Scientist. www.chiefscientist.gov.au/2016/03/report-australias-stem-workforce

Oleson, A. K., Hora, M. T. & Benbow, R. J. (2014). *STEM: How a Poorly Defined Acronym Is Shaping Education and Workforce Development Policy in the United States*. WCER Working Paper No. 2014-2, Wisconsin Center for Education Research. Retrieved from https://eric.ed. gov/?id=ED556481 (accessed 12 July 2021).

Prinsley, R. & Johnston, E. (2015). *Transforming STEM Teaching in Australian Primary Schools: Everybody's Business*. Office of the Chief Scientist, Australian Government.

TECHNOLOGY AND THE ARTS

INTRODUCTION

Based on the Australian Curriculum, the arts are composed of dance, drama, media arts, music and visual arts (Australian Curriculum, Assessment and Reporting Authority (ACARA), 2010). No matter the specific discipline, technology is increasingly being used to create artefacts, physically and virtually (Marshall, 2014).

There are many aspects of artistic expression that would be difficult to replicate or translate to the online space. We don't suggest that technology replace traditional media such as painting, dance or music. We do, however, have access to a range of technologies that can enhance the creative endeavours of children and adults. In this chapter, we will explore what technology can offer to the art classroom. Regardless of whether you teach an arts-based subject or a more traditional subject, there are ways that technology devices and software can engage your students in creative and artistic ways.

ART IN TODAY'S SCHOOL

Today's art, music, drama and dance classrooms might look entirely different to what you experienced. Technology in art classrooms offers new pathways into the arts that may not have previously attracted our young people. Consider the student who is a reluctant performer but who can create complex animations and tell her story expressively and uniquely with the aid of a computer. She may enjoy creating music but not the more rigid nature of lessons, rehearsals and performances. A keyboard connected to her computer enables her to be a composer and performer on her terms. Then, social media provides a space for sharing her music and connect her with other learners like herself.

Today, there are many ways to explore art and creativity using technology. There are opportunities for learners to try entirely new types of art practices. One exciting example is the use of technology to create interactive dance pieces, where technology is used to create sound and light patterns that reflect or react to the dancers' movements (Fdili Alaoui, 2019).

More traditional spaces, such as museums, also provide technology-enhanced ways to engage with their exhibits. From virtual tours and holographic tour leaders to interactive experiences, technology is offering a way for visitors to move from being passive observers to a more 'constructive–expressive' experience (Panciroli et al., 2017, p. 913).

Since the 1970s, making music visible has been at the forefront of technology development. Music creates an auditory landscape, and researchers and musicians have been seeking a way to engage our other senses in the experience. A medical condition known as synaesthesia means that when music is heard the individual's brain engages not only the hearing part of the brain but also other senses. For some people, this means they can 'see' music (Carpenter, 2021). Technological advances mean that this unique skill may now be shared. Working with cognitive scientists, computer developers, and people with synaesthesia sees new types of creative expression and science come together (Watkins, 2018).

In the future, we may see an entirely new world of artistic expression. Perhaps augmented reality and virtual reality will immerse us in the landscapes of Monet; a wristband might give instant feedback to the conductor who modifies tempo or intensity based on the reactions of the audience. Perhaps artificial intelligence will learn what music, art and theatre we like and provide a soothing environment as we arrive home from work (Faraboschi et al., 2019). As technology becomes more portable, powerful and user-friendly, there is no limit to what we might experience in our lifetimes.

A teacher's role is to ensure that your learners are ready for this future and enable their creativity throughout their lives. As Maslow theorised (1962), for humans to reach their full potential, we need to meet our basic needs (food, growth, love, etc.) and then strive to become self-actualised. This refers to the idea we should learn and grow throughout our lives. The specific form that these needs will take will, of course, vary significantly from person to person:

In one individual it may take the form of the desire to be an ideal mother, in another it may be expressed athletically, and in still another, it may be expressed in painting pictures or inventions. (Maslow, 1943, pp. 382–383)

However, without the experience of being creative, our students are limited in how they express themselves in the future. The arts are an essential part of being human, and technology is making the arts more accessible in more ways.

IN THE CLASSROOM TODAY

In Gabi's Year 2 classroom, her group of 6- and 7-year-olds are exploring ideas of shape, lines and form in art. The students have created artworks using only lines and then with only shapes. Bringing the idea of form into their work is the next step, and Gabi has planned a short walk around the school grounds.

Tai and his partner take the iPad provided by Gabi and head out to the playground. Gabi explains to the group that they will use the camera on their iPad to take photos that show shapes, lines and forms. They need to find at least three examples and then come back to the classroom.

Gabi sends the students off and follows Tai and his partner as they head over to the large gum tree in the centre of the play area. Tai begins taking photos: of the tree trunk, of his foot, of a leaf on the floor. His partner, however, isn't impressed and begins telling Tai to stop, saying, 'We have to find lines! Let me have a go!'. Tai reluctantly hands over the tablet computer, grumbling, 'Everything is lines, I was taking photos of everything'.

Gabi joins the pair and asks what Tai means. 'You have to have lines to make shapes, and you said a form is a shape that is 3D, like the cube we looked at in maths, so everything is lines!'. Gabi agrees; he is correct, of course, but you can use lines in different ways, and that's what she wants them to consider. 'How might you show me lines by themselves or a 3D form in a photo?'

Tai's eyes light up. 'I could take photos and then draw on them to make my artwork and show you the lines!'.

'Great idea!' says Gabi, thinking to herself, how on earth do we do that?

The lesson continues, and eventually, Gabi is in her room after school, thinking about what Tai said. She had thought her lesson of taking photos was a great idea, but Tai had given her an idea of how to use the technology more creatively. Perhaps there is a way to engage the whole class in identifying lines, shapes and forms and creating their pieces at the same time. Her Year 2 learners were excellent, but they did lack some independence; however, could technology help her provide a collaborative and creative experience?

TECHNOLOGY IN ART

STEAM EDUCATION

In recent decades, the four disciplines of STEM have often been joined with the arts. The resulting acronym of STEAM represents science, technology, engineering, the arts and maths. This strong connection of arts and creativity to science is a new and exciting development. With STEAM, creativity is brought to the forefront. As we saw in Chapter 8, STEM requires thinking about problem-solving and creativity, and so STEAM acknowledges that the arts can significantly contribute to the STEM disciplines.

The arts can enable us to express ideas, emotions and understanding that are not limited by language. Drawing, painting, dance, video-making, composing are powerful tools to share and communicate. Indeed, research suggests that the arts can be used to make it easier to conceptualise complex concepts (Liliawati et al., 2018). We are learning more and more that 'STEAM enhances creativity and thinking skills' (Perignat and Katz-Buonincontro, 2019, p. 32). When we engage students in STEAM projects or learning experiences, we ask them to develop skills in several learning areas. This brings an interdisciplinary and multidisciplinary approach to everything they do (Perignat and Katz-Buonincontro, 2019). Interdisciplinary and multidisciplinary means that skills and knowledge engage several areas of learning at once. An interdisciplinary example might be learning about life cycles and then creating a video animation that shows the life cycle in practice. A multidisciplinary approach might extend this example to learning about the environment and habitats, exploring pollution in a nearby creek and designing community information posters for the school website.

STEAM education, then, provides a way for learners to explore and express their understanding in new ways. STEAM may also have other benefits, including transferring their learning skills into different domains, and developing and using a broader range of thinking skills. As the Australian Council of Educational Research has noted,

> a curriculum that includes some form of creativity and does not make hard sciences the sole focus makes students more well-rounded, develops valuable soft skills, and perhaps more importantly, gives everyone a chance to shine and find their true interests and talents. (ACER for Education, 2019)

One challenge to introducing a STEAM programme in a school is that it can be seen as a fad approach to teaching that will eventually disappear. There are numerous indicators, however, that STEAM and STEM are here to stay. In Australia, for example, the government has created a STE(A)M programme that offers schools, universities and industry incentives for supporting young people to enter the STE(A)M fields. The focus in many countries on developing twenty-first-century skills such as problem-solving, creativity and collaboration also indicates interdisciplinary learning needs to be an essential part of a child's education.

As Taylor (2016, p. 89) has indicated, STEAM is 'not just another curriculum fad but an important response to the pressing need to prepare young people with higher-order abilities to deal positively and productively with 21st-century global challenges'.

Taylor also notes that embedding the arts into STEM education ensures that we maintain a humanistic view of learning. In this context, humanistic means we take into account human values and ethics as we learn. A humanistic view of STEM can 'enrich and expand the scope of STEM education' (Taylor, 2016, p. 92) by bringing creative thought and understanding into a more traditional learning area.

CREATIVE INNOVATION AND DIGITAL ART

In today's classroom, we are charged with teaching a range of skills. We no longer focus entirely on delivering content to students. Instead, we also focus on how we are learning. These are sometimes called soft skills as they can be hard to quantify. When we reflect on art and technology, we can likely grasp the basic concepts of drawing on iPads, sharing a design idea online or creating a video using a smartphone. As a teacher of the twenty-first century, however, we are tasked with drawing out the thinking skills and communication skills that our learners may need in the future. Many, if not all, of these soft skills, are transferable and support learning in other areas. The arts develop a unique set of thinking skills that engage the learner in creating, innovating and communicating. Technology, in addition, provides a new medium for the arts. These new forms of expression offer entry points into creativity for learners who may not see themselves as 'artists' or 'creative'.

From the opposite perspective, there is also a benefit to art practices in engaging in technology. We are starting to see art practices that are entirely digital and use technology to create expressive experiences that would not be possible without technology. In 2020, a conference was held called the 'Mobile Digital Art and Creativity Summit'. At this event, artists who engage with technologies and educations came together virtually to share their art practices. The definition of the event was 'bringing together renowned digital artists who are at the intersection of art, technology and education in a virtual program of workshops' (Mobile Digital Art & Creativity Summit, 2020).

The idea of artists coming together virtually to discuss the impact of technology on their artistic expression is new and exciting. This means that students in our classrooms will increasingly have new forms of art available to them and new technology tools to help them create. In turn, this means that our students need new experiences with technology. We need to move beyond text and static web images and engage with technology as an interactive partner in the creative process. Coding, artificial intelligence and robotics are already beginning to be embedded in the arts. As Faramarzi notes, there is a need to explore the practical impacts of technology on the arts and a need to reflect on how technology shapes what we mean by the arts and creativity:

'As software, algorithms, non-conscious cognitive agents, and cybernetic thinking increasingly shape the world around us, artists need to have a strong grasp of the practical and philosophical implications of this transformation,' Kaganskiy says. 'I'm not saying that every artist needs to learn to code, but they should probably read some media theory and software studies texts, maybe even some posthumanist philosophy'. (Faramarzi, 2019)

CHALLENGES AND CONTROVERSIES

In this section, we will explore some potential challenges that come with using technology in the arts. As you read, consider whether you have experienced these ideas or concepts. What is your reaction to digital creativity and art-making?

IS DIGITAL ART 'REAL' ART?

This question has been asked for many years, although only with the emergence of stylus and tablet computers has it seemed to become a significant concern. One argument says that art should be created at the hands of the artist rather than through the medium of a digital device. On the other hand, you could argue that computers are human-made devices that require significant creativity to develop. As such, the art they create is always mediated by a person.

We should note here that we currently have robots with built-in artificial intelligence that can review an artist's work, draw out themes and concepts and then create entirely new pieces of music, art or theatre. This raises several questions: Who is the creator of this art – the programmer, the artist who influenced the computer or the computer itself? We will likely continue to grapple with the ethical implications of these new technologies. As new devices and software emerge, we have to wonder how our daily lives might be impacted, hopefully for the good of society.

David Hockney is a digital artist who would strongly agree that digital art is 'real' art. He works on iPads and creates a wide range of impressive artworks. He is a visual artist who uses creative apps to draw, paint and sketch. Hockney has held exhibitions worldwide and in many high-profile galleries, including a gallery in Paris. For this exhibition, Hockney (2021) created artwork on a tablet computer. The finished pieces were downloaded onto individual iPads and then hung around the gallery walls. His digital artwork began in 2008 on an iPhone before iPads were available. Using the smaller screen of a smartphone, he created medieval miniatures with exquisite detail. Hockney now lives in Normandy and exhibits in Paris galleries and prints his work to be shared more widely.

When asked if he felt that his digital art-making was different from traditional methods of making art, he said that he saw little difference as he found the creation experiences were very similar and required the same attention to place, context and artistic ideas. He called on doubters to 'Stand in the landscape you love, try and depict your feelings of space, and forget photographic vision, which is distancing us too much from the physical world' (Gural, 2021). In calling us to get out into the world and share what we see, he suggests that we need to focus on our creative expression rather than on the devices, tools or resources we use to express ourselves.

As new media appear, we will likely continue to hear questions about what is real art and what is not. Some examples include iPad artworks, interactive websites, animation, video-making, creating visual essays, creating virtual reality worlds and virtual dance performances.

These are new ways to express yourself, your understanding and your ideas that go beyond text. Consider what you, as a teacher, might learn through new ways of thinking and doing.

VISUAL MUSIC

An exciting example of new types of creativity is the development of visual music. Visual music is a way to engage more than just our ears in music. It provides a way to share the mental models (Senge et al., 2011) that the composer intended. This means that you are being shown what the music seeks to convey when you watch a piece of visual music. This might be in images, but more often, it involves colours, shapes and shifting patterns. Several software packages can react to music in a pre-programmed way to share mood and emotions. The increase in technology comes with some challenges, of course, one of which is the amount of technology now available and the need for artists to refocus on what they are trying to create, whether it is visual art, multi-media, dance, theatre or music:

> Creators of visual music face the challenge of retaining their own artistic impetus amidst an overwhelming choice of instruments, aesthetics, practice, techniques and technologies brought about by the impinging presence of a vast sea of data and tools. (Watkins, 2018, p. 51)

BRINGING TECHNOLOGY TO YOUR CLASSROOM

When bringing technology into the classroom, we have to make a concerted effort to reflect on how we are using technology to support creativity. As Ilić (2019, p. 9) claims, it can be a challenge:

> Acceptance and introduction of ICT in the teaching of art requires from teachers an additional effort to understand and master modern media. It is a process that includes informing about contemporary art, monitoring the development of information and

communication technology and finding ways to apply them purposefully in the educational process at school.

As many teachers will tell you, there are constant changes in education. What we teach and how we teach changes often. As effective users of technology, a bonus is that schools have seen many technological advancements in the past five decades. From cassette recorders to overhead projectors, teachers have a history of embracing technology for education. Many of these technological advancements were challenged at first as not appropriate for education, 'over the years, technology has even created forms of art that did not exist before: are photography and filmmaking not valid forms of artistic expression?' (ACER for Education, 2019).

These new modes of creation still require human interaction and can be seen to supplement and enhance what we do (Souleles, 2017).

Large institutions provide us with compelling examples of technology-enabled art practices, such as the Royal College of Art in London. The RCA has announced plans to expand its curriculum to include science and technology (ACER for Education, 2019) in ways that reflect the types of STEAM learning and digital creativity that we explored earlier in this chapter.

As we conclude this section, we should reflect on the positive benefits of engaging our students in the arts and technology. One study by Wang (2015) identified that learners who used technology to create art were more likely to consider themselves as artists and demonstrated more creativity in other learning experiences:

> Results of this study suggested that through using iPads, students achieved the expected comprehension and performance of artistic skills and knowledge, gained more interest in artistic learning, aroused creative abilities, and generated innovative forms of artistic practices. (Wang, 2015, p. 153)

As a teacher, our role is to ensure our students experience these new ways of creativity and expression.

USING TECHNOLOGY IN THE CLASSROOM

When including technology-enabled arts in the classroom, we need to consider how technology is used. Are we leading students to engage in active, creative activities or more passive tasks that require less creativity? Both active and passive types of tasks have value to the learner. However, a balance is needed so that students engage with making and consuming different art forms in a range of ways. Watching a theatre production is a wonderful experience.

Re-creating a scene in a new setting with animation software adds to the theatre experience and provides ways to create, share and problem-solve.

COLLABORATIVE CREATION

In the classroom, we also need to consider the pedagogy we use with technology and the arts. As we noted above, we can be passive consumers or active creators. Working with others provides a space to explore new ideas, designs and solutions that means we are consuming and creating at the same time.

Collaborative arts projects provide a way to engage students in larger projects that would otherwise be too time-consuming for the classroom. Designing, reflecting on and rethinking our digital creations in a group can help learners be more aware of the communication and collaboration skills they need to develop. This becomes more of an iterative process of designing and redesigning that enables deeper reflection and learning. Working collaboratively to create an art piece, such as a film, a photograph or a painting, brings students together who likely have different perspectives and skills. Creating together enables learners to make informed decisions about their product.

VIRTUAL REALITY

Virtual reality is a growing industry that educators around the world have embraced. Virtual reality (VR) is designed to be an immersive experience for an individual. By wearing special goggles connected to a computer, you can travel to other planets, the bottom of the ocean or even the top of the Eiffel Tower, without leaving the classroom. These VR experiences are also increasingly interactive, with several VR companies now offering tactile sensors. These are devices you hold in your hands or wear on your feet and enable you to feel the virtual spaces physically. You can 'hold' the steering wheel of a virtual race car or 'climb' the steps of the building and receive physical feedback from the device.

As teachers, we understand that VR offers a range of previously inaccessible experiences. As a physics teacher, you can use VR to walk your students through a supernova. An early childhood teacher could help learners retell a story by walking through the forest alongside Little Red Riding Hood. You could even take an African safari together and identify environmental and geographical features.

Engaging in a VR setting is an exciting development for learners as we explore a new type of space. A person in a VR space does not exist entirely in the real world, nor does the person exist entirely in the online world as their body continues to exist and move in the virtual reality space. As we consider bringing these new technologies into the classroom, we need to consider what it means for the learner and their learning. As Kosari and Amoori reflect,

Therefore, in response to the question: 'where is the user?' one could say that even though the user's body is in the real world, as a subject, the user is neither in the real space nor in the virtual space. The user is in a third space made of mental patterns. (Kosari and Amoori, 2018, p. 182)

If you spend time creating and making in a virtual space, where does that artefact of your creativity exist? Who owns it, and can we claim ownership over something that only exists in this new 'third-space' (Kosari and Amoori, 2018) of the classroom? These questions are essential to consider so that we can have discussions with our students about creativity, technology and the online world.

EXAMPLES OF PRACTICE

In this section, we explore what art and technology can look like in three different educational settings. While these learning experiences have been categorised under early childhood, primary and secondary settings, it is always up to you as the teacher to make decisions about how and what you teach in your classroom. You might explore app smashing in early childhood or STEAM sketchbooks in primary classrooms. Be sure to take these examples as possibilities and not necessarily age-based activities.

ART AND TECHNOLOGY IN THE EARLY CHILDHOOD SETTING

MK is working with a group of 4-year-olds today. She is excited to work with the children on their projects. She plans to revisit the walk they completed last week to the nearby park. The children collected some artefacts (twigs, leaves, rocks), and today will be creating environmental art pieces.

As the children arrive, they explore the items they collected that have been spread out on the tables. Calling for their attention, MK asks everyone to look at the big screen. She has attached her iPad and is showing a basic drawing app. MK explains that at each table, there is an iPad and some artefacts. The task is to take photographs of their items and then put them into the drawing app. The parent helpers will support this, but MK knows many of the students can do this themselves.

Once the photos are in the app, the children will work together to create a piece of art. This might involve duplicating pictures of sticks and using them to draw a shape or copying the texture of the leaf and turning it into an animal. The purpose, MK explains, is to use real-world objects to create art, so we need to look at the items very closely and see what patterns, shapes and colours we can see.

By the end of the lesson, each group has some type of artwork ready to share. One group has created a robot out of sticks and leaves. Closer inspection shows that they have rotated the leaves to align the veins. Apparently, this makes the robot rain-proof. They have noted a pattern and used it to add to their artwork. Next time, MK thinks, we will compare the artworks and record the students explaining their creations. Reflection will be helpful for the individual but also for their peers as they listen to what other learners observed and understood from the activity.

ART AND TECHNOLOGY IN THE PRIMARY SCHOOL SETTING

In Year 5, Gabi is preparing to lead a lesson on image manipulation. He has previously worked with the students to identify bias and opinion in written texts. Today they will look at how images can be changed to present specific ideas or emotions.

On the screen, Gabi shares an image of a sophisticated picture book. These books usually include detailed imagery and complex text to tell a story (Callow, 2020). Gabi explains that a sophisticated picture book relies on both the images and the text to understand the story. You can't just read the text or just view the images; you need to engage with both. As a class, they read the first few pages together, exploring the language used and the images provided. What type of drawing is used? What colours are most apparent? What emotion does the text convey? Do the images convey the same emotion or different?

Having explored the pages as examples, Gabi hands out pages from books. These are popular fiction books that many students have read. Every sheet contains one scene from a longer story. Students are asked to create an image to go with the text they have been given using the computers. Referring to the keywords and ideas they wrote together on the board, Gabi reminds the class that their images need to reflect the text and add meaning. They might do this through what objects or characters they choose to include, the colours they use, the relative size of things in the scene or perhaps even the weather in the background.

As they open their computers, the students begin to work in different media. One student is creating a comic frame using clip-art to create her scene. Another student is working with stock photos and manipulating them in photo-editing software. Another student has pulled out her stylus and is drawing her image on her computer screen.

Gabi reflects that over half the class claimed they weren't 'artistic' or 'hated drawing' the last time she attempted this type of activity. This time, technology appeared to have created a space for them to express their ideas in a visual way that was less intimidating and more inclusive.

ART AND TECHNOLOGY IN THE SECONDARY SCHOOL SETTING

In Year 9, Miray is developing a STEAM elective subject for next term. These students have chosen to join this elective as part of their science and innovations programme at the school, and so the work they do will be open-ended and non-traditional. Miray is struggling to understand how she might assess the students' work both during the term and at the end. Searching online for ideas, she comes across the idea of sketchbooks as an assessment tool.

She decides she will develop these types of sketchbooks digitally to record and share their learning as they progress through the term. This will be a valuable artefact to share with other teachers and will also provide a space for students to collate their key resources.

In the first lesson of the term, Miray asks students to consider that STEAM learning is an experience rather than simply a task to complete. To demonstrate, Miray asks everyone to look up 'cornstarch ooze' online. After ten minutes of searching, she asks for explanations of the ooze. She receives a range of answers, most of which draw on the scientific definition of a non-Newtonian fluid (which has the properties of both a solid and a liquid). Building on this definition, Miray asks students to consider how this ooze might be useful or fun or creative and design a use for the ooze in their STEAM sketchbook. This should include at least one video (curated from online), a video created by themselves, images, some text, some audio and one other type of media (infographic, cartoon, animation, etc.). Their designs will be shared in a virtual gallery and will need to be annotated and labelled clearly.

As Miray moves around the room clarifying the task and answering questions, she notes that the digital sketchbooks, hosted on the school's collaborative software, are very flexible. One student is designing a dance to be performed on a stage full of ooze. The performers will disappear under the stage and reappear in the wings as they dance. Another is creating a type of bridge that would be liquid most of the time until someone needs to cross the river. A third student is creating a concept map of ideas and bringing in resources for his future designs. These sketchbooks will be excellent for assessment. Miray reflects that she can use them for mapping each student's learning development as they add more notes, ideas and resources.

BACK TO THE CLASSROOM

In the following lesson for Tai's class, Gabi has set up her room differently. As the students enter the room, they see their names in groups on tables spread around the space. Each table has been set up with a tablet computer, a large sheet of paper, some pens, glue, scissors and some basic instructions on using the classroom printer. Gabi begins the lesson.

In groups, students will be creating a poster. Using all the photos they took in the last lesson, they will be creating a new artwork that shows line, shape and form in the world around us.

Tai looks intrigued as his group of four students opens the folder of photos that Gabi has added to the iPads. There is a photo of his foot. The group begin by outlining on their paper. They agree that they want to create the image of a 'robotic dinosaur' as their poster. This will be fun.

(Continued)

Tai's teammate finds the photo of the foot and says, 'look, we can draw over Tai's foot with this app. It lets us draw on top of photos.' He draws an oval, some small circles and a long rectangle over the photo. 'Let's print it out!' says Tai. The printed image is cut out and added to the large paper on the table. 'Our dinosaur has one foot!', says Tai.

The group continue to look closely at the photos on the iPad and find a few more photos that they can use to show forms and lines and build their robot dinosaur. A photo of a tree trunk, zoomed in and printed several times, becomes the scales of the dinosaur, a photo of a twig is used to give the dinosaur '3D robot antenna', and the bar code on a piece of litter is annotated to show lines and the robot's name.

By the end of the lesson, the groups are all well on their way to creating new artworks that express and represent the world around them using lines, form and shape. Gabi is excited to finalise these unique pieces in the next lesson and explore the creative ways in which the photos were used as inspiration and starting points for their learning.

CONCLUSION

This chapter has explored the arts and creativity and how technology enables new ways of human expression. We also explored the concept of STEAM as a way to bring together essential learning areas (the arts and technology) with twenty-first-century or 'soft' skills (such as communication, collaboration and problem-solving).

Creative expression is an inexorable human right and need. On our planet, humans have created art for most of our history as sentient beings. Indeed, in 2021, archaeologists uncovered a painting of three pigs on a cave wall estimated to be at least 45,500 years old (Cascone, 2021). In Australia, with the oldest continuous culture globally, we have cave drawings dating back at least 30,0000 years (National Museum of Australia, 2021).

The desire to communicate through imagery, music and movement is not new to humans. As teachers, we can engage our learners in creative expression and use technology to reach all our students. We will always need human contact in the arts, but we can offer more ways to share, co-create and experience the arts with technology.

FURTHER READING

Explore the use of augmented reality in a museum setting:

He, Z., Wu, L. & Li, X. R. (2018). When art meets tech: The role of augmented reality in enhancing museum experiences and purchase intentions. *Tourism Management, 68,* 127–139.

Reflect on the use of technologies in music education:

Gorbunova, I. & Hiner, H. (2019, February). Music computer technologies and interactive systems of education in digital age school. In *Proceedings of the International Conference Communicative Strategies of Information Society (CSIS 2018)* **(pp. 124–128). St Petersburg: Atlantis Press.**

Consider the development of STEAM education and its connection to thinking skills:

Perignat, E. & Katz-Buonincontro, J. (2019). STEAM in practice and research: An integrative literature review. *Thinking Skills and Creativity, 31,* **31-43.**

Discover STEAM learning in the early years:

Dejarnette, N. K. (2018). Implementing STEAM in the early childhood classroom. *European Journal of STEM Education, 3*(3), 18.

REFERENCES

ACER for Education (2019). Art Classroom: How technology is changing it. *Acer for Education Magazine*, 21 May. Retrieved from https://acerforeducation.acer.com/learning-skills/art-classroom-how-technology-is-changing-it/ (accessed 12 July 2021).

Australian Curriculum, Assessment and Reporting Authority (ACARA) (2010). *The Arts*. www.australiancurriculum.edu.au/f-10-curriculum/the-arts/ (accessed 21 July 2021).

Callow, J. (2020). Visual and verbal intersections in picture books: Multimodal assessment for middle years students. *Language and Education*, 34(2), 115–134.

Carpenter, S. (2021). *Everyday Fantasia: The World of Synesthesia*. Retrieved from: www.apa.org/monitor/mar01/synesthesia (accessed 12 July 2021).

Cascone, S. (2021). Archaeologists have discovered a pristine 45,000-year-old cave painting of a pig that may be the oldest artwork in the world. *Artnet News*, 14 January. Retrieved from https://news.artnet.com/art-world/indonesia-pig-art-oldest-painting-1937110 (accessed 12 July 2021).

Faraboschi, P., Frachtenberg, E., Laplante, P., Mansfield, K. & Milojicic, D. (2019). Technology predictions: Art, science, and fashion. *IEEE Computer Architecture Letters*, 52(12), 34–38.

Faramarzi, S. (2019, 24 December). Art schools of the future need to teach students to understand technology. How will that change the future of art? *Artnet News*, 24 December. retrieved from https://news.artnet.com/art-world/art-school-tech-adapt-1742802 (accessed 12 July 2021).

Fdili Alaoui, S. (2019). Making an interactive dance piece: Tensions in integrating technology in art. In *Proceedings of the 2019 Designing Interactive Systems Conference* (pp. 1195–1208). doi:10.1145/3322276.3322289

Gural, N. (2021). David Hockney's new works reveal the joy of isolation and embrace of technology. *Forbes*, 19 February. Retrieved from www.forbes.com/sites/natashagural/2021/02/19/david-hockneys-new-works-reveal-joy-of-isolation-and-embrace-of-technology/ (accessed 12 July 2021).

Hockney, D. (2021). *David Hockney*. Retrieved from www.hockney.com/home (accessed 12 July 2021).

Ilić, V. (2019). *Information and Communication Technology in Visual Art Education*. University of Pristina.

Kosari, M. & Amoori, A. (2018). Thirdspace: The trialectics of the real, virtual and blended spaces. *Journal of Cyberspace Studies, 2*(2), 163–185. doi:10.22059/jcss.2018.258274.1019

Liliawati, W., Rusnayati, H., Purwanto & Aristantia, G. (2018). Implementation of STEAM education to improve mastery concept. *IOP Conference Series: Materials Science and Engineering, 288*, 012148. doi:10.1088/1757-899X/288/1/012148

Marshall, M. (2014). Emerging technologies in art education. Master's thesis, Western Michigan University.

Maslow, A. H. (1943). A theory of human motivation. *Psychological Review, 50*(4), 370–396.

Maslow, A. H. (1962). *Toward a Psychology of Being*. Princeton, NJ: D. Van Nostrand Company.

Mobile digital art & creativity summit (2020). Retrieved from www.mdacsummit.org/ (accessed 12 July 2021).

National Museum of Australia (2021). *First Rock Art*. Retrieved from www.nma.gov.au/defining-moments/resources/first-rock-art (accessed 12 July 2021).

Panciroli, C., Russo, V. & Macauda, A. (2017). When technology meets art: Museum paths between real and virtual. *Multidisciplinary Digital Publishing Institute Proceedings, 1*(9), 913.

Perignat, E. & Katz-Buonincontro, J. (2019). STEAM in practice and research: An integrative literature review. *Thinking Skills and Creativity, 31*, 31–43. doi:10.1016/j.tsc.2018.10.002

Senge, P., McCabe, N., Lucas, T., Kleiner, A., Dutton, J. & Smith, B. (2011). *Schools that learn: A fifth discipline fieldbook for educators, parents and everyone who cares about education*. London: Nicholas Brealey Publishing.

Souleles, N. (2017). iPad versus traditional tools in art and design: A complementary association. *British Journal of Educational Technology, 48*(2), 586–597.

Taylor, P. C. (2016). *Why is a STEAM curriculum perspective crucial to the 21st century?* 14th Annual conference of the Australian Council for Educational Research, 7–9 August 2016, Brisbane.

Wang, T. W. (2015). Does iPad technology bolster art teaching and learning? *Visual Inquiry, 4*(3), 153–167. doi:10.1386/vi.4.3.153_1

Watkins, J. (2018). Composing visual music: Visual music practice at the intersection of technology, audio-visual rhythms and human traces. *Body, Space & Technology, 17*(1), 51. doi:10.16995/bst.296

CODING

10

IN THIS CHAPTER YOU WILL LEARN:

- What we mean by computer coding
- How computer coding can be used in the classroom
- The types of thinking that can be enhanced by learning to code.

INTRODUCTION

In this chapter, we will be looking at the rise of computer coding in classrooms around the world. If you were to search online, you would find a range of beginners' guides to learn computer coding. An American not-for-profit organisation, called Hour of Code (https://hourofcode.com), is one of the most popular and prominent websites for beginners in this field. The Hour of Code website provides free video courses in basic coding. From knowing nothing about computer coding, you can program an online character to dance around your screen within an hour. It is essential, of course, to remember that the final product of coding is not necessarily the most important outcome. The process of learning to code, practising a new type of literacy and creating something online offers unique experiences to today's learners.

WHAT DO WE MEAN BY 'CODING'?

Coding is a way of communicating with a computer to achieve some goal. Programming and coding are often used interchangeably, although, in computer science, the terms have different meanings. Coding refers to the act of creating instructions that a computer can 'read' and understand. When you put several codes together, you create a program that achieves some desired outcome. Coding is a part of the larger job of a programmer (Franklin, 2019).

WHY CODING IN THE CLASSROOM?

With changing curriculum demands in several countries around the world, it is crucial to restate that the aim of these documents is rarely to produce a generation of computer programmers. Increasing global and complex challenges, such as climate change, unstable political environments and catastrophic weather events, means a growing need for individuals who can analyse, decompose, reflect on and design solutions. In Australia, the national curriculum documents position coding as necessary for today's students by saying, 'The curriculum is designed so that students will develop and use increasingly sophisticated computational thinking skills, and processes, techniques and digital systems to create solutions to address specific problems, opportunities or needs' (Australian Curriculum, Assessment and Reporting Authority, 2015).

The overall purpose of coding, in most curriculum documents, is not to create a generation of computer programmers. Instead, the purpose of coding in schools is to ensure that our future citizens understand the potential of technology to change lives and address problems. There is no expectation that every child should become a computer technician, programmer, or developer. The inclusion of algorithmic thinking in schools seeks to broaden students' opportunities, not narrow them to the computer science field. Learning to code offers endless possibilities for innovative skills to be developed. These twenty-first-century skills can provide unique learning experiences that teach students how to control technology in our increasingly technology-enhanced world.

IN THE CLASSROOM TODAY

In the early childhood classroom, Tai introduces coding to her group of 4 and 5-year-olds. Using the classroom set of iPads, she has arranged for an app called Scratch Jnr (DevTech Research Group, Tufts University et al., 2021). She had a play with the app at a recent professional learning workshop and thought she'd give it a go. She hopes that her learners will engage with this app as it is brightly coloured, easy to follow and uses images alongside the text on the screen. This should help each child engage and learn.

Tai explains the task: make an animated figure move across the screen. She shows how some of the buttons work and breaks the children into groups of four. Each group has a parent helper who will support them to remain on task. If they finish the first task, Tai asks the children to add a costume to their on-screen character and add a pop-up word balloon. While Tai isn't sure how to do this, she saw another teacher achieve this at the workshop, so hopefully the children or parents will work it out.

Cam is working in a group with three of his friends. His friend's mum is their parent helper, but he seems a little bit confused. No problem. Cam opens the app and begins tapping away. He can drag the cat character across the screen, but he can't see how the coding jigsaw works. He looks over at his friend's iPad and notices she is dragging different jigsaw pieces together and connecting them. Cam tries this, but when he presses 'go', nothing happens. Cam calls out for Tai's help, but she seems very busy and is working with another group.

Tai is indeed feeling busy and overwhelmed. She thought she had the lesson well-planned. However, one group of students is off-task and complaining that their iPad is 'broken'. Another group seems to be drawing on their screen. Not what Tai was anticipating. Cam is calling out that his code doesn't work.

What should I do next time? She thinks. I need to go on a course or spend the weekend figuring out how this coding program works. But then I won't have time for planning, evaluating or replying to all those emails. There must be a way to introduce learners to coding that isn't so stressful and focuses more on the learning outcomes she had planned.

CODING TO LEARN OR LEARNING TO CODE

When we consider teaching coding in our classroom, we need to consider our purpose. Are we coding to learn or learning to code?

Learning to code implies we are teaching the skills of coding directly. We are expressing seeking to develop coding skills such as loops, iteration, calculations, branching, etc. At the end of the lesson, or sequence of lessons, we anticipate that students will have these coding skills.

Coding to learn, however, is more interdisciplinary. We are asking students to create something or achieve some goal by creating a computer program. In the English classroom, we might ask learners to model a character's journey on a map of the world. In science, we might ask them to create an animated solar system model that represents the planets' rotations around the sun. In these examples, coding is a means to an end and a tool to represent their thinking and understanding. To achieve these English or science outcomes, of course, they will need to develop coding skills. The primary outcomes, however, are not digital technology outcomes.

In a pre-technology world, we may have asked students to create a 3D model or diorama to demonstrate their understanding of a novel. To be successful at this task, our learners would need skills in design, construction and model-making, but our focus as teachers would be on their understanding of what they have read. This is similar when we reflect on how we might use coding. Learning to code is not something that happens naturally, of course, and we would need to provide some direct instruction on how to code. In an ideal world, your students would experience a balance of tasks that teach them to code (learning to code) and tasks that engage their coding skills (coding to learn). The critical decision here is to make choices about how you teach coding based on your understanding of your learners, your school context and what you understand as their learning needs.

APPROACHES TO CODING

There are several types of computer programming languages that work in different ways. We next introduce you to two types of coding. As technology develops, we will likely begin to see new ways of controlling computers, such as quantum computing and virtual reality programming spaces (Alexander et al., 2020; Kjaergaard et al., 2020; Soeken et al., 2018). However, the following two examples represent the major types of coding languages and approaches used in schools today.

OBJECT-ORIENTED CODING

Object-oriented coding (OOC) means that each object or item on the screen has unique coding. An object in this context is any aspect of the on-screen environment; this might mean a drawn character, a location on the screen or a video, image or photo.

The easiest way to understand OOC is to consider any online game. In many online games, you play a character who must act, react and achieve some goal within a virtual environment. Each item within the environment is likely coded to act in a certain way. When a door is clicked, it opens. When a specific button is pressed, the character jumps. These actions are controlled by computer programs that are distinct to each object and, as such, are considered to be created using object-oriented coding.

OOC is often a learner's first introduction to coding. Software such as Scratch (https://scratch.mit.edu/) was developed to enable children and young adults to create games and virtual simulations. Many other software companies have also mimicked this approach to coding. Software such as Scratch uses an approach to OOC called 'drag and drop' coding. This refers to the fact that we interact with the software to create coding. Dragging and dropping to create codes is now found in a range of software, most of which are freely available as online, web-based resources and smart device apps (Blannin and Symons, 2019).

To create a program, a learner first selects the object they wish to code. Then, the learner accesses the library of ready-made coding 'blocks' from the on-screen library. Dragging the coding blocks they wish to use into the 'active code' area, they begin to build their program. The student continues to drag these coding 'blocks' into their code. By connecting their chosen blocks, a computer program is developed that can then be 'run'. When they are satisfied, they can then choose another object on the screen and create a separate, unique code for that object. In this way, each object has its own set of instructions.

An example of this might be creating a program that draws a map of a location or space. By connecting a sequence of coding blocks that move their character forwards, backwards, left and right the learner can represent a complex pathway on the screen. When the learner clicks on 'run', the code is executed, and their learning is represented by moving objects on the screen.

TEXT-BASED CODING

Text-based coding uses, as it sounds, standard text conventions to create code. There are an increasing number of text-based languages that our students can use, including the two most popular: Java and Python. Unlike object-oriented coding, text-based coding offers a way to create complex computer actions. Students have more control over the code itself and do not need to rely on ready-made 'blocks' of code.

In Australia, the national curriculum documents now dictate that all learners must experience drag and drop, object-oriented programming and text-based coding languages. Typically, younger students use drag and drop software such as Scratch, and older learners engage with text-based languages such as Python.

Teaching text-based coding can be an exciting way for learners to develop a strong understanding of how computers work and why technology sometimes fails.

As with any language, computer programming languages use sophisticated syntax and grammar rules to enable clear communication (Santos et al., 2020). A text-based language is a way to send commands directly to the computer's processors. We type in our correctly formatted text, and then an intermediary software converts this text into the language of computers – binary numbers. In essence, text-based coding languages provide a more direct connection to the binary base code upon which our computers function.

Drag and drop coding languages, by contrast, can be understood as another layer on top. We drag blocks of code together, which are converted to a text-based language and then translated into the foundational binary code. With this layered representation, we understand that drag and drop coding should not be the only way we teach coding. Research now suggests that students should be exposed to drag and drop and text-based coding to engage learners in coding and provide experiences similar to professional programmers (Moors et al., 2018; Weintrop and Wilensky, 2017).

As you teach coding in your classroom, consider what skills you are developing, how you are using coding and what languages and representations of code are most relevant to your students and your desired learning outcomes.

CLASSROOM CULTURE AND A GROWTH MINDSET

When we first begin teaching computer coding in the classroom, there are a few aspects that can impact the success, or otherwise, of our efforts. One aspect within our control is the culture of our classroom. This can be a significant factor in what and how our students learn (Lundh et al., 2018).

Lundh et al. (2018, p. 1448) concluded that if learners were to engage in coding in the classroom, they are expected to struggle with ideas and explore them in different ways. Play, making mistakes, creativity, and critical thinking are valued. Students have opportunities to collaborate with peers and participate in whole-class discussions to problem solve together and have their thinking and prior learning articulated and challenged.

To consider how we might move ourselves and our students towards seeing coding as a sophisticated learning area, we can draw on the work of Dweck (2017), who proposed that humans hold one of two mindsets, either a growth or fixed mindset.

However, it is important to note that Dweck (2017) does not present these mindsets as binary or inflexible. Instead, her research has identified that individuals hold both fixed and growth mindsets simultaneously, drawing on them depending on the context within which we find ourselves. These fixed and growth mindsets (Dweck, 2017) may determine the risks we will take, the way we understand our abilities and how we confront failure. Dweck explains that:

> People with a fixed mindset believe that their traits are just givens. They have a certain amount of brains and talent, and nothing can change that ... People with a growth mindset, on the other hand, see their qualities as things that can be developed through their dedication and effort. Sure they're happy if they're brainy or talented, but that's just the starting point. (Dweck, 2008)

Mindsets, Dweck contends, are not intended to box a child, or a teacher, into a certain mindset. Instead, individuals demonstrate a fluid mixture of fixed and growth mindsets as they move between contexts: 'we're all a mixture of fixed and growth mindsets ... and we will probably always be' (Dweck, 2015, p. 3).

When we are learning with a growth mindset, we are more likely to take risks and reflect on failures. When we begin teaching computer coding, we will likely face challenges such as our code not working as expected or needing to understand new concepts and language. With a growth mindset (Dweck, 2017), we would look at what isn't working and seek to improve. We would focus on what worked and what we can learn. We would explore new ideas without fear of failure hindering our progress.

In your classroom, you can foster a sense of a growth mindset by modelling what it means to fail and learn from errors. This might mean creating a code and purposefully showing how it doesn't work. You might ask students to create a game using some aspects of programming that you can't create yourself. Enabling students to learn with you and from your failures can be helpful for our learners to see coding (and perhaps all learning) as something that involves trial and error.

To begin with, you might ask students to work with pre-existing programs. An example might be a program in Scratch (https://scratch.mit.edu/) that you have created to take the class attendance each day. As you explain that it is not working, you can ask your learners to find out why. In addressing errors in code, we are engaging in 'debugging'. This involves systematically checking our coding and finding the error. Debugging is a legitimate and highly prized skill for computer programmers (Michaeli and Romeike, 2019). When we address our 'failures' or 'errors' with a straightforward, named task, we are framing our mistakes as something we can solve rather than feeling deflated by our failure.

LEARNING FROM OUR ERRORS

In our classroom, the way we respond to challenges can influence how our learners view their own mistakes. Beyond computer coding, a student's self-efficacy plays a significant role in learning. Self-efficacy was defined by Bandura (1977) and is seen as a significant contributing factor to human action and agency. When we introduce computer coding into the classroom, we may also introduce an entirely new content area or way of learning. There is no clear right or wrong answer to coding; There are often several ways of achieving the same outcome. We need, then, to make sure that we focus on how we are learning and what we learn. One way to do this is to consider one theory of learning, initially developed by Bandura in 1977.

In his social learning theory, Bandura (1977) describes self-efficacy not as a fixed belief in one's abilities but rather as a person's changing cognitive, social, emotional and behavioural responses to situations. A person's belief in their ability to succeed is, according to Bandura (1977), fundamental to being competent or successful at a task. This means that what we believe we can achieve impacts our ability to accomplish that goal. If we feel we can't use the computer to achieve a specific outcome, the likelihood is that we won't.

Understanding that self-efficacy is an important part of our classroom can help us address new technologies, learning areas and curriculum outcomes. When a new technology is introduced to your school, for example, a 3D printer, an interactive screen or a new type of robot, what is your response? Do you accept that your first attempts may be difficult but go ahead anyway? Do you feel deflated when you fail and resolve to avoid the technology in the future?

As a teacher, you are consistently modelling how to learn. The debugging skills we discussed previously are a great example of how technology offers new ways of learning. As we focus on developing a growth mindset and reflecting and learning on our failures, we are also engaging our students in skills for life in the twenty-first century. When we teach and model these skills, we are taking an innovative approach to what it means to learn,

> debugging skills do not only play a major role in the programming domain: debugging is also ubiquitous in our everyday life, and research findings indicate that the explicit teaching of debugging can result in a transfer of debugging skills to a non-programming domain. (Michaeli and Romeike, 2019, p. 2)

ALGORITHMIC THINKING

As our world becomes increasingly digital, it is becoming more apparent that school curriculum documents need to reflect today's society and the types of thinking and learning that are becoming commonplace (Israeli Ministry of Science and Technology, 2013). Curriculum writers worldwide are seeking to engage students in the critical thinking skills that might enable their full engagement in the world of work and life beyond schools.

A computer algorithm is a set of instructions that interact in a sequence to produce the desired outcome. An example is the 'home' button on a mobile tablet or smartphone. When this button is clicked, it triggers a set of algorithms to complete the task, in this case to display the home page on the device's screen. Understanding that logic and sequencing underpin technology and that errors or challenges with technology can be solved through a logical, sequenced approach are skills needed in a wide range of industries (Blannin and Symons, 2019).

One area that is relatively new in mainstream education is a thinking skill called algorithmic thinking. You may have heard the term 'algorithm' in the context of mathematics, and algorithmic thinking is not dissimilar. Algorithmic thinking refers to logical, sequenced processes that together create the desired outcome. A recipe is a simple type of algorithm, as is the 'how-to guide' for building your flat-pack furniture.

Algorithmic thinking is increasingly seen as a critical skill for all students from the beginning of the early years of schooling, even in the early years. As Hromkovic et al. (2017, p. 138) state, 'it is vital that we start with algorithmic thinking early on, and help the students advance towards, ultimately, mastery of the subject'.

Algorithmic thinking with technologies has developed alongside computer programming and the microprocessor over the past five decades. When it comes to computers, this might refer to a series of coded instructions that form a program.

In computer science, algorithmic thinking is made up of four key skills:

- Design thinking (understanding the systems at work)
- Decomposition (breaking large sets of data or problems into logical parts)
- Pattern recognition (identifying similar and different factors within a problem)
- Abstraction (taking a step back from the problem and isolating the themes and central ideas)

Consider the task of designing a bus route to the local art gallery from your school. To achieve this, using algorithmic thinking, students first have to understand the 'rules' of driving on the road (they must stick to roads, follow the rules about which roads are suitable for buses and avoid those that are not suitable). This demonstrates the ideas of decomposition.

Next, learners will need to understand traffic patterns and explore which roads are busiest between the gallery and the school (pattern recognition). Using online mapping software, they can see patterns that emerge at different times of day and use this knowledge to make some basic judgments about the best time of day to leave school and arrive at the gallery (abstraction). Finally, they need to design a route that takes their new knowledge into account, understanding that an excursion to a gallery will occur within the 'system' of a school day (systems thinking). They will need to consider the times of the day they can travel, how long their route will take and how best to maximise their time at the gallery.

Essentially, learners in this example understand the system within which this imaginary school trip takes place. Not unlike how a piece of code fits in part of a more extensive computer program. In schools, it can be easy to believe we already use similar tasks to this example. However, we need to ask how we explicitly teach these skills of algorithmic thinking and use the language of decomposition, systems thinking, pattern recognition and abstraction?

SYSTEMS THINKING

As one of the four thinking skills embedded within algorithmic thinking, systems thinking has been highlighted as a new and potentially challenging skill for learners (Hromkovic et al., 2017). To understand what we mean by systems thinking, consider this scenario. If your printer stops working, do you throw the machine away, assuming the printer is broken, or do you, instead, check the power and computer connections, check the paper supply and the computer software? To understand that a printer only works when the entire system works is to understand systems thinking.

There are different definitions of what we mean by systems thinking, but York et al. (2019, p. 2742) offer an excellent place to start:

> Systems thinking is an holistic approach for examining complex problems and systems that focuses on the interactions among system components and the patterns that emerge from those interactions.

Many aspects of computing require an ability to understand the complex systems within which they are embedded. Systems thinking seeks to understand the interactions of people, places, objects or ideas within a system (Blannin and Symons, 2019). In a school setting, this might be exploring how predators and prey interact in an exosystem or understanding how a Wi-Fi signal reaches your wireless device or creating a digital game.

As you reflect on where coding skills and algorithmic skills might fit in your teaching practice, consider what thinking skills your planning might engender and how you might make those ways of thinking explicit to the learners in your care.

EXAMPLES OF PRACTICE

In this section we present some examples of coding in the classroom. Coding and coding concepts can be taught from the early years until senior secondary school and the following examples offer ideas of what this might look like at each stage. You will note that, in each example, technology and devices are used differently. This might be as the key focus of the lesson or a tool to provide a context for developing certain skills. In your teaching, you will need to determine the appropriate way to position the technology device and coding resources, so that it makes sense for the learner and their learning.

CODING IN THE EARLY CHILDHOOD SETTING

MK is working with 4-year-olds this week and is keen to practise some new skills she learned from the primary school teachers last week. She decides that algorithmic thinking would a great way to begin and so plans a game to play.

In the classroom, the children sit in a large circle and listen to MK explain the game. 'You will play with robots today!', she says, and the children get excited. Pairing the children off, she hands out lanyards to each pair; one lanyard has a label 'robot', and the other is labelled 'controller'. Using a pair of children as an example, MK shows everyone how to play the game. By giving instructions, the controller has to guide the robot to the other side of the classroom, navigating around tables, chairs and other students. The challenge, however, is that the robot can only do exactly what the controller says. MK reminds them that robots can't make any decisions for themselves.

As the game begins, MK works with two students. Aimee is the robot, and Gai is the controller. As Gai gives her first instruction, Aimee says, 'No, that will be too far. It should be only two steps forward.'. MK intervenes and reminds Aimee that Gai is the controller. After a few more attempts, MK is pleased to see that Gai has improved her instructions. Gai takes her time to plan her next instruction and MK notes that Gai paces out distances and estimates the number of steps her 'robot' needs to take before instructing her robot to move.

At the end of the lesson, MK calls the group together. She asks the children to tell her what they think they learned today. Aimee calls out, 'Robots don't have very good brains!'. Another child says, 'Instructions are hard'. Gai notes that, 'You have to do it step by step so that your robot doesn't crash'.

MK is pleased to hear this language and talks about how computers work in the same way. Computers can only do precisely what humans have programmed them to do. They need people to set them up and provide instructions. The conversation continues as the children begin talking about using an iPad at home. They note that when you push the button, then the home page appears. When you click an app, it opens. MK agrees and says this is a bit like their robot game. If you click one thing, then something will happen and should always happen in the same way. MK draws the lesson to a close with a brief reflection on how robots work by understanding instructions and carrying out exactly what they are programmed to do.

After the lesson, MK concludes that the lesson went well. The students have begun to understand the idea of algorithmic thinking, and in the next lesson they will be ready to use symbols to draw a set of instructions.

CODING IN THE PRIMARY SCHOOL SETTING

Rami's class are learning about the traditional narrative writing structure of:

- Introduction
- Facing a problem
- Solving the problem
- A conclusion.

Kai and his fellow Year 4 students have all watched a short, animated film online, and Rami now asks them to create a story that presents the same characters having a different adventure. They will need to follow the narrative structure to present their new story.

Kai and his two classmates have decided to create an animation of their story using software called Scratch. Scratch is a coding software that uses blocks of codes that you connect. Kai enjoys using Scratch because it's easy to check if his code doesn't work. As they begin, the group decides on the setting for the story and upload an image for the background. Next, they bring in the characters they want to use and then decide to code one character each. They work on their computers to program each of the characters. Using the drag and drop jigsaw puzzle pieces, Kai creates a code to make his character run towards the river in the scene. He presses play but realises that his classmate's sheep character is flying. That's not right! Kai works with his friend to update the coding so that the sheep moves along the grass instead. As the lesson concludes, Kai's group has created a short story that presents the introduction and a complex problem the characters have to solve. The coding process has seen the group make plans, test their ideas, create a story outline and interact with each other.

Rami is pleased to see the range of skills that the students have used in this lesson. They have collaborated and successfully developed a piece of work that demonstrates their learning. Rami plans to work with them in the next lesson to understand the sequence of events in a narrative and how their code can reflect that. Coding has helped her learners to practise twenty-first-century skills and develop their literacy understanding too.

CODING IN THE SECONDARY SCHOOL SETTING

In Miray's Year 9 class, the students are working in small groups. Each group is gathered around a laptop. Miray has asked them to find the moon. Initially, the students thought this was an easy task. They could just look out the window. Miray, however, has planned to engage her learners in this problem-solving activity for the next two weeks. This first lesson will ask them to identify and understand the problem itself: how can we locate the moon when the Earth and moon continue to move relative to each other? This science project will also see her learners create hypotheses and test them out using Python coding language. Python is a great tool to use as it is made up of recognisable words and structures that the students can easily follow.

Riku's group has opened a web browser and entered 'Where is the moon'. The results are not as they expected. There is information about the moon's distance from the Earth and the sun, statistics about the path of the moon's orbit and images of the phases of the moon. Their search did not tell them the location of the moon right now.

Miray calls the class to attention and asks them to share their findings. It seems every group has had the same issue as Riku. There are lots of details about the moon but not its current location. Miray explains that, as they have discovered, the precise location of the moon, relative to us on Earth, requires careful calculation. She introduces the class to Python and reminds them of their work using the coding language last term. This week, they will create a Python program to follow the moon's movement and identify its location relative to Earth. Their code will calculate the moon's location and tell them what country or landmass it is currently orbiting.

Riku is intrigued and a little confused. He has used Python before, but this looks complicated. He feels better, however, when Miray explains that they will be using an existing piece of Python code, so they don't need to start from scratch. Their task will be to ensure the code works and provides the location of the moon.

To demonstrate that their code works, Miray asks each group to predict the moon's location precisely three weeks from today, at this exact time.

Riku downloads the Python code from the online classroom space and begins to analyse it with his group. The code looks relatively straightforward, but there are a few calculations he doesn't understand. His group begins to search online for new words such as 'trajectory' and 'eclipse' noted in the code.

As the students work in their groups, Miray is pleased to see their enthusiasm. She knows that this is a challenging problem, but she is confident the students will develop something that works. The process of developing the code and testing it is, she thinks, just as important as the final piece of code. Her students are investigating the cycles and rotations of the moon and pulling the code apart to understand it better. This is much more effective learning than teaching them to locate the moon using a mathematical formula to calculate three-dimensional coordinates, as she did last year. She can overhear two groups discussing the need to locate the moon in space so they are already understanding why we might need three-dimensional coordinates. Miray writes this down in her notes as she moves around the room, offering advice and planning for future lessons. The many discussions of scientific concepts that are occurring around her will form the basis of her teaching next week.

As the lesson draws to a close, Miray introduces the class to an online observatory website and app that plots the moon's path. In the next lesson, she tells them they will use the online observatory to check if their code works. If it doesn't work, their task will be to find out why. If their coding is successful, they will become 'debuggers' for the class and move between the other groups to share their code and how it works.

Riku is excited and notes down the name of the online observatory app. He will have a look at this later in preparation for his next class.

BACK TO THE CLASSROOM

At home that weekend, Tai looks up 'How to teach coding to 5-year-olds'. There are lots of resources, and she scrolls through quickly. It's too much and overwhelming. One article, however, piques her interest: 'How much do you need to know to teach coding?'.

Reading the article, Tai realises this might be less challenging than she thought. The author points out that you don't need to be a computer scientist to teach and use coding in the classroom. As a teacher, Tai brings her knowledge of teaching and learning and her pedagogical skills, which can be enough for a successful lesson.

Relaxing a little, Tai reflects on last week's classroom experience. She was trying to fix the code for each student. She was working to make a 'perfect' code so that each child felt successful. She had overlooked, however, what they had achieved. Instead of focusing on just making the character move, she could have instead asked students to explore the app first and then build on whatever they have learned.

Cam, for example, couldn't get his character to move, but he had coded it to change costumes and had added balloons that flew across the screen. If Tai focused on what they could achieve when left to explore independently, perhaps the students could figure out the more complicated next steps.

Thinking about her class next week, Tai resolves to ask more questions and provide fewer answers. She will resist the urge to fix the coding and instead focus on the lesson's learning outcomes: problem-solving, pattern identification and developing computational thinking skills.

Back in the classroom, Tai explains that they will be working on developing their thinking skills today. 'We are going to use our problem-solving brains to get our projects to work', she declares.

As Cam opens his iPad, he looks at his code from the last lesson. There is a pattern to his coding. He realises that all the blocks are connected except one. As he chats with his neighbour, he notices that this isn't quite right. He connects the blocks and clicks go – it works. Cam excitedly calls out to Tai, 'I spotted a pattern, and it was broken and, when I fixed it, my cat moved across the screen properly!'.

Tai moves to Cam's side and smiles. Cam's program is still not quite doing what she had hoped, but the learning outcomes of problem-solving, pattern identification and developing computational thinking have certainly been met.

As the lesson draws to a close, Tai reflects that she knows a little more about the coding program than she did last lesson, but she still is not an expert. However, today's class ran much more smoothly. Perhaps her pedagogical knowledge and expertise are more important than knowing how to use every button in the software, as the online article suggested.

CONCLUSION

In this chapter, we explored ideas of coding and programming for the classroom. We discussed what coding might look like in the classroom and the different types of coding languages students can use. Algorithmic thinking and systems thinking also provided valuable insights into how learning to code can support our students to become more independent learners.

As we conclude this chapter, we remind ourselves of our initial discussion about coding. When we teach coding in schools, we are not trying to create a generation of computer programmers. Instead, we are hoping that our learners will develop a strong understanding of how computers work, which hopefully provides them with the confidence to use technology, create new products, and solve complex problems. As an essential twenty-first-century literacy, coding offers us a way to control technology and create new devices and software to meet our needs.

FURTHER READING

Explore how educators are engaging indigenous students in remote communities in coding and making:

Soro, A., Wujal Aboriginal Shire Council, Taylor, J. L., Esteban, M. & Brereton, M. (2020). Coding on Country. *Extended Abstracts of the 2020 CHI Conference on Human Factors in Computing Systems*, 1–8.

Learn how some teachers overcame their personal bias against coding and developed exciting classroom experiences:

Menke, J. & Miller, C. (2020). From terrified to comfortable: A fourth-grade teacher's journey into teaching coding. *Education Across Cultures: Proceedings of the 42nd Meeting of the North American Chapter of the International Group for the Psychology of Mathematics Education.*

Consider how you might engage children under 7 in programming and computational thinking skills:

Bers, M. U., Ponte, I., Juelish, K., Viera, A. & Schenker, J. (2020). *Coding as a Playground: Programming and Computational Thinking in the Early Childhood Classroom* (2nd edn). New York: Routledge.

REFERENCES

Alexander, T., Kanazawa, N., Egger, D. J., Capelluto, L., Wood, C. J., Javadi-Abhari, A. & McKay, D. C. (2020). Qiskit pulse: Programming quantum computers through the cloud with pulses. *Quantum Science and Technology, 5*(4), 044006.

Australian Curriculum, Assessment and Reporting Authority. (2015). *Australian Curriculum: Digital Technologies*. Retrieved from: www.australiancurriculum.edu.au/f-10-Curriculum/Technologies/Digital-Technologies/ (accessed 13 July 2021).

Bandura, A. (1977). Self-efficacy: Towards a unifying theory of behavioural change. *Psychological Review, 84*(2), 191–215.

Blannin, J. & Symons, D. (2019). Algorithmic thinking in primary schools. In A. Tatnall (ed.), *Encyclopedia of Education and Information Technologies* (pp. 1–8). Cham: Springer. doi:10.1007/978-3-319-60013-0_128-1

DevTech Research Group at Tufts University, Lifelong Kindergarten Group at the MIT Media Lab & The Playful Invention Company (2021). *ScratchJr: Coding for Young Children*. Retrieved from https://scratchjr.org/ (accessed 13 July 2021).

Dweck, C. S. (2008). *Mindset: The new psychology of success*. New York: Random House Digital, Inc.

Dweck, C. (2015). Carol Dweck revisits the 'Growth Mindset'. *Education Week*, 22 September.

Dweck, C. (2017). *Mindset: Changing the Way you Think to Fulfil your Potential* (updated edn). London: Hachette UK.

Franklin, A. (2019). Coding vs programming for beginners: What is the difference? [Blog] *GoodCore*, 6 August. Retrieved from www.goodcore.co.uk/blog/coding-vs-programming/ (accessed 13 July 2021).

Hromkovic, J., Kohn, T., Komm, D. & Serafin, G. (2017) Algorithmic thinking from the start. *Bulletin of the European Association for Theoretical Computer Science, 121*, 132–139.

Israeli Ministry of Science and Technology (2013) *Science and Technology*. Retrieved from https://mfa.gov.il/mfa/aboutisrael/science/pages/science and technology.aspx (accessed 20 November 2019).

Kjaergaard, M., Schwartz, M. E., Greene, A., Samach, G. O., Bengtsson, A., O'Keeffe, M., McNally, C. M., Braumüller, J., Kim, D. K., Krantz, P. et al. (2020). *Programming a Quantum Computer with Quantum Instructions*. Retrieved from https://arxiv.org/abs/2001.08838 (accessed 13 July 2021).

Lundh, P., Grover, S. & Jackiw, N. (2018). *Concepts Before Coding: The Impact of Classroom Culture and Activity Design on Student Engagement with Computer Science Concepts*. Retrieved from https://repository.isls.org/bitstream/1/671/1/336.pdf (accessed 13 July 2021).

Michaeli, T. & Romeike, R. (2019). Improving debugging skills in the classroom: The effects of teaching a systematic debugging process. *Proceedings of the 14th Workshop in Primary and Secondary Computing Education*, 1–7. doi:10.1145/3361721.3361724

Moors, L., Luxton-Reilly, A. & Denny, P. (2018). Transitioning from block-based to text-based programming languages. *2018 International Conference on Learning and Teaching in Computing and Engineering (LaTICE)*, 57–64. doi:10.1109/LaTICE.2018.000-5

Santos, S., Tedesco, P., Borba, M. & Brito, M. (2020). Innovative approaches in teaching programming: A systematic literature review. *Proceedings of the 12th International Conference on Computer Supported Education*, 205–214. doi:10.5220/0009190502050214

Soeken, M., Haener, T. & Roetteler, M. (2018). Programming quantum computers using design automation. *2018 Design, Automation & Test in Europe Conference & Exhibition (DATE)*, 137–146. Retrieved from https://arxiv.org/abs/1803.01022 (accessed 13 July 2021).

Weintrop, D. & Wilensky, U. (2017). Comparing block-based and text-based programming in high school computer science classrooms. *ACM Transactions on Computing Education (TOCE)*, *18*(1), 1–25.

York, S., Lavi, R., Dori, Y. J. & Orgill, M. (2019). Applications of systems thinking in STEM education. *Journal of Chemical Education*, *96*(12), 2742–2751. doi:10.1021/acs.jchemed.9b00261

11

TEACHING WITH A RANGE
OF DIGITAL DEVICES

IN THIS CHAPTER YOU WILL LEARN:

- Bring-your-own-device programmes in schools
- The potential for bring-your-own-device programmes to enhance learning
- Strategies to ensure your students have access to appropriate and beneficial technologies.

INTRODUCTION

When you were in school, you may have had access to a classroom full of desktop computers. Perhaps it was called a computer lab and included rows of desks and computers lined up and facing the front of the room. This was how technology first appeared in schools. These spaces provided a specialised learning experience that focused on creating documents and presentations and other basic skills.

Today's classrooms can look quite different. In some schools and education centres, there are 'pods' of computers attached to one or two classrooms. These pods are accessible for more ad hoc learning and enable students and teachers to use technology as they see fit, rather than based on a timetable. However, with the rise of mobile technologies, there is an even newer approach to technology use in schools. Tablet computers offer wireless usage (aside from charging stations), and wireless Internet turns every room into a 'computer room'. You might understand the potential of having one device for every child in your classroom, but what might be the reality?

Bring-your-own-device programmes have sprung up worldwide to address the challenges of how we provide a device for every learner. As the name suggests, a bring-your-own-device (BYOD) programme encourages learners to bring any internet-connected device into the classroom. This might be a brand-new laptop or a 10-year-old smartphone. We will discuss the challenges of inequity of access to devices further in this chapter; for now, we are exploring the potential benefits and drivers for BYOD in schools.

When we use our computer device, we can decide how the device works to suit our needs. We might pin specific software to the homepage, save links to helpful websites or change the font size to increase the clarity of the text. This means no device is identical to the others, even if we were to provide a laptop to every child. Personalising our technology can enable,

> provision of learning activities (e.g. through proprietary apps, including educational games); ready access to educational material on the Internet (including videos made by teachers for the purpose, within a broad 'flipped classroom' model); convenience tasks such as taking photos of visual activities, providing spellings, note-taking, distribution of notes, looking up information on the Internet, distributing homework tasks, and so on; facilitation of communications between students for collaborative work, and between students and teachers for feedback, guidance and assessment; sharing of student work in the classroom. (Blikstad-Balas and Davies, 2017, p. 17)

With these benefits in mind, other practical outcomes may support learning. These include ensuring students can access a device at their point of need, rather than waiting or sharing. The teacher can focus on the learning outcomes and potentially spend less time arranging for devices to be available. At a school level, BYOD offers a more straightforward approach to 1:1 computing. When every child has a device (1:1), the school does not usually need to manage devices, insurances, repairs and replacements. For this reason alone, some schools choose to establish a BYOD programme.

Some companies will provide the same device to every child on behalf of the school itself. In this case, the learners' families engage directly with the computer company for purchasing, warranty, insurance and repair enquiries. This can relieve the pressure from school leaders, particularly in smaller schools or educational setting where each member of staff may already wear many different hats. When schools choose to engage an external company for their BYOD programme, there are other benefits, including that every child will have the same device. This means teachers can effectively use the technology for learning, as they are not spending time converting their teaching plans from one platform to another. In addition, there is more equity in access to devices if the school can purchase or co-fund the BYOD programme for families on limited budgets. This can limit the challenges of a divide between those who have the newest, most powerful devices and those who do not.

A BYOD programme enables a learner to bring any device that has Internet connectivity. The widespread rise of smartphones means we see more and more of these devices in our classrooms. The challenges of inequity continue with these programmes unless the school leaders, and you as the classroom teacher, work to mitigate these problems. When one child uses a laptop and another uses a tablet computer, there are different affordances or opportunities for learning. This is not necessarily a bad thing but suggests that we need to be clear in our learning outcomes. Are we teaching typing, for example, or are we teaching retelling a story? Teaching typing would typically involve a keyboard, something that not every student will have. If we focus instead on retelling a story, the smartphone users might create a video using the built-in camera. The laptop users might create a presentation that uses sounds and images from the Internet. From a teaching perspective, both of these activities provide ways to present their learning. In the longer term, there are questions about which skills we prioritise in the classroom and our students learning.

IN THE CLASSROOM TODAY

Sam's humanities class has just begun to study the indigenous history of their local area. She is keen to engage her learners in interactive discovery-based learning rather than specifying readings and setting written tasks. As a relatively new teacher, Sam is keen to improve her teaching and visits her mentor's classroom. In Kai's room, the Year 10 students are creating an animation based on a newspaper headline. This is similar to the lesson Sam taught earlier this year, although her students didn't create digital animations.

As she observes the class, Sam notes several different devices in the room: laptops, tablets, smartphones. Some are older, and some look brand new. Sam wonders how the lesson will go. There seems to be so many devices to manage.

Kai calls the class to attention and explains the activity. They are creating animations based on the newspaper headline they have chosen. The aim is to develop critical thinking around the language used in the media. Kai explains that they can create their animation in any way they choose. There are several pieces of software on the school's website, and they can use any of the other software in the list she provides on the screen.

As students move off to begin their work, Sam asks Kai about the different devices. Kai admits this lesson will be a learning experience. Perhaps the devices will all work; perhaps they won't. Sam is impressed with Kai's willingness to try what seems a risky way to teach.

The students are beginning to face a range of issues. One group has opened up the software on the school website but can't get their microphone to work. Without it, they won't be able to record their voiceovers. Another group has their microphone working

(Continued)

well, but it is deafening. When Sam asks them to turn down the volume, they explain their headphones are broken.

Kai calls the class to attention and asks them to list their challenges so far. Kai has decided that there may be some learning strategies she can draw from these problems. As the students call out their issues, Kai writes them down on the board: no power, need to plug in, camera not working, microphone and headphones not working, student not sharing the device appropriately, students being too silly with voiceovers and noise levels.

Once the list is made, Kai asks the students what they might do about these problems. Silence. The students are focused on the problems, Kai whispers to Sam, not on the other possibilities of the devices.

After waiting for a few more minutes, one student calls out, 'Maybe we could split the room into quiet and noisy areas?'. Kai says, 'Ok, what else?'. Another says, 'We could share these headphones so if that group starts first, we can use them afterwards'. Now there are several ideas: create paper animations and video them later, work on the design now and animations later, create voiceovers in the hallway, design the characters using the big classroom screen, create a plan for what we want to get done today, tomorrow and next week. Kai welcomes every idea and sends the students back to work to implement these changes.

After the class, Sam asks Kai why the learners were asked to find solutions. Isn't it the teacher's job to make sure everything is working? Kai smiles and reminds Sam that teaching problem-solving and critical and creative thinking are also a part of the curriculum. How better to teach these skills than in a context where learners can explore and trial their ideas?

Sam reflects on the lesson. There were still challenges in the classroom after the students had put into practice their great ideas. The learners did, however, seem focused more on the activity than the device. The noise level in the room had settled down, and she had heard several students offering to help their classmates. In her Year 7 class, Sam isn't sure that the students would be able to work independently, but perhaps there are aspects of Kai's approach that would help her use the multiple types of devices in her classroom.

STRUCTURES AND USES OF BRING-YOUR-OWN-DEVICE PROGRAMS

There are currently three main ways that bring-your-own-device (BYOD) programmes are implemented in schools. This section will briefly explore these approaches and reflect on what each offers to our classroom.

1. DEVICE IS SPECIFIED BY THE SCHOOL

The first type of model for BYOD is where the school decides that one or more year levels will have access to a specific device. Often the school provides the device, and the families pay the school. This means that the school manages any problems with the device. It also means that the school can purchase software licences to cover all their devices, and individuals do not need to buy them separately.

In the classroom, this model of BYOD is probably the easiest to integrate into your existing programmes. This is a positive as we can probably continue with our teaching as we have done in the past. It also means we run the risk of missing the opportunities for teacher learning. When every child has the same device, it can be less imperative to individualise the curriculum or move beyond our comfortable, more traditional practices.

The school leaders can cohesively manage their fleet of devices at the school level and may run their own repairs system where the school technicians manage warranty and repair claims. This can be cost-effective and enable the school to loan replacement devices to students when their computers are under repair. This has the potential to avoid increasing any inequity in technology access in the school.

2. CHOOSING FROM A LIST

Some schools prefer to offer a range of options from which families can choose. This might include several different models of laptops or tablet computers and devices at different price points. Offering different options may give families a chance to choose a device for their child that fits within their budget or supplements existing devices at home. In some instances, students have access to high-end technology at home. The family may then decide that they need only invest in the lower-priced school device to meet their child's at-school needs.

As teachers, this model of BYOD can allow us to explore new ways of teaching and learning through different devices. There can be benefits, for example, in a classroom that has access to Apple Mac and Windows computers. Each offers unique benefits such as video editing, 3D printing or music creation. This mix of devices can open doors for students and teachers to explore new ways of thinking and making.

Managing this kind of programme at a school requires technicians or external support staff to be familiar with various devices and operating systems. This approach provides the school with a way to support students who cannot purchase a device or who require a loaned laptop or tablet computer while theirs is under repair.

This model of BYOD requires the school to be fully invested in a more open approach to BYOD that can be more complex to manage and run.

3. BRING ANY DEVICE

Finally, some schools have designed a bring-your-own-device programme that enables students and families to bring to school any device they prefer. This might be a device already used at home by the student, but it could also be a secondhand purchase or brand new device.

This model offers excellent flexibility to families. They can choose to provide whatever device suits their family, their budget and their child. For example, students with different learning needs may prefer to use a tablet computer rather than a laptop or a family with several computers at home could arrange for their child to use one of their older laptops at school. This flexibility is sometimes seen to provide more equity to learners and families as they are not required to purchase a potentially expensive device (Marshall, 2015). However, as we will see in the next section, there are also challenges to the equity that this type of bring-your-own-device programme might bring. Students who bring older devices may suffer from stigma associated with their perceived lower technology access. In contrast, students with newer, more efficient devices may be seen as somehow more technologically literate or talented (Palmer, 2017).

In the classroom, this model of BYOD should enable learners to make more decisions about their learning and what resources they prefer to use, create and share. As a teacher, this can be challenging as we need to rethink the purpose of our teaching. We need to consider whether the devices should inform the learning activities we plan or, instead, whether we should see the device as a conduit for learning and expression. Ultimately, it is up to the teacher to ensure that any technology devices in the classroom are used effectively and efficiently.

FACTORS FOR BYOD SUCCESS

Yeop et al. (2018) investigated the factors that may support successful bring-your-own-device programmes. Their research is of interest as they focused on bring-your-own-device programs in Malaysia. The Malaysian government has identified that technology use and access are now necessary for today's learners. Yeop et al. (2018) identified four factors that support effective bring-your-own-device programme implementation:

- Availability of infrastructure
- Knowledge of health impacts
- Safety control requirements
- The skill level and teacher knowledge (Yeop et al., 2018, p. 315).

As you explore the context for your bring-your-own-device programme, you will need to consider these four factors.

This might mean understanding the infrastructure. Does your teaching space have Wi-Fi access? Is there a password, and can this be shared with students? What are the security settings, and what websites and online resources are blocked (and would need to be opened) or open (and need to be blocked)? Who are the key people who can support your use of technology? Does the school have a technology support person, or a teacher designated to support technology use?

You also need to reflect on how, when and where the devices will be used. A laptop could be used at a desk, on the floor or next to the sink. Which would be the better choice, and how will you communicate this to your students? Health impacts refer to the potential physical and psychological issues that might occur through technology use. Physically, learners should also understand some basic ergonomics (Bettany-Saltikov et al., 2019). Assuming contortionist positions while working on their device may have ongoing effects on children's bodies (Straker et al., 2018). Whether they are using mobile devices or laptop computers, we need to ensure that our learners take care of their bodies. Straker et al. (2018) identified that with the introduction of touch-screen devices, the potential for injury has changed with more mobile, smaller devices.

Worryingly, there also seems to be a divide in healthy and unhealthy use of technology in classrooms based on students' backgrounds:

> Children in more advantaged areas reported patterns of technology use which were more likely to result in better health and development outcomes, suggesting access to technology is only widening the gap between advantaged and disadvantaged children. (Straker et al., 2018, p. 659)

Our role is to acknowledge these challenges and to consider where and how learners are using their devices. It appears essential that we vary how we use technology. Moving from typing on a laptop to clicking on a tablet touch screen enables learners to use different muscles and reduce the possibility of injury (Straker et al., 2010).

Yeop et al. (2018) identified a third factor necessary for a successful bring-your-own-device programme: safety control. Safety control practices suggest we need to consider how to ensure learners are safe online. We need to develop digital citizenship skills and provide ways for students to share any problems they come across. All learners should know what to do if they see or read something unpleasant online. Many schools and early childhood settings have policies in place that inform staff how to manage online issues. There may be rules around supervision of devices or sharing resources. There might be regulations about how you interact online with learners and their families, or perhaps a process to report troubling behaviour. If your educational setting does not have this type of policy, perhaps you could lead its development.

Finally, your skills with technology and knowledge of learning will impact the success of a bring-your-own-device programme in your classroom. Referring to this book is an excellent place to start. In addition, being a teacher is to be a life-long learner. You will need to be brave and open to taking risks. As we explored in Chapter 10, a growth mindset (Dweck, 2017) can lead you to frame problems and challenges as ways of learning rather than a driver to stop experimenting. As you engage with the range of devices in your classroom, you will likely face issues. Your job, however, is to step back and reflect on what went wrong. Was there an issue with infrastructure, cyber-safety or your knowledge? Once you have identified which factor might be lacking, you can develop an improvement plan.

Changes in our practice and our schools is rarely a straightforward process. Moving to a bring-your-own-device programme, or joining a school with one in place, can be an exciting time. We need to consider how our learners might benefit from access to their own devices and be sure to maintain our focus on their learning and not on the devices themselves. Technology is nothing without your expertise, whether there is a bring-your-own-device programme or not.

EQUITY

Not every student in your classroom or your school will have access to a device they can use in the classroom. Your educational leaders may be able to address issues with infrastructure, Wi-Fi access and implement policies for use and safety. The provision of the devices, however, may be beyond the control or finances of the school, 'BYOD does raise issues around equity and the digital divide – for example, what is to be done about those who cannot afford their own devices?' (Maher and Twining, 2017, p. 4).

Your teaching location, context and student backgrounds will likely inform the types of devices brought to school as part of a bring-your-own-device programme: How can we ensure that we do not create further inequity in learning? Access to technology is a crucial challenge for schools, and our role is to creatively develop processes and policies to counter any inequity in access to devices (Palmer, 2017). This might mean raising funds for a school set of devices, securing grants from philanthropic organisations or even collecting used devices from families who might be able to donate.

If we don't consider the potential risks of a bring-your-own-device programme, we risk increasing the divide between students who have access and experiences with technology and those who don't. We need to be sensitive to the differences in our learners' ability to engage in a bring-your-own-device programme. While we have provided some ideas for how this might be achieved (through outside funding or school-owned devices), we must also consider that students who use them might face feelings of difference or inferiority to their peers. As a teacher, we want to ensure that our learners have access to devices and can learn without worries about their sense of status and self.

> As we move forward with the latest technologies, we must keep sight of the crucial issue of digital equity. It is important to consider the availability of loaner equipment and school-owned devices that are accessible to lower-income students in a stigma-free manner. (Consortium for School Networking, 2012, p. 5)

Before we begin a bring-your-own-device programme, there are several considerations. Safety, equity and our skills and knowledge should be the first areas we focus on, rather than on the devices, to ensure quality teaching and learning.

BACK TO THE CLASSROOM

In Sam's class, the Year 7 students are excited by the idea of making an animation. Before they begin their work, Sam explains the learning outcomes for this activity. They are going to demonstrate that they understand the significance of Indigenous history in their local area. They will present their knowledge of Indigenous language, culture and practices, and teach their findings to their classmates.

Sam takes a deep breath. She is going to follow Kai's example and take a risk. She explains that the students can present their learning in any way they like, such as a movie, a graphic design or a game. The students are excited and begin to chat with their friends. Sam is apprehensive but is open to learning from this experience. She explains that each small group of learners will need to negotiate how they will present their learning. In this way, she thinks, I will have some idea of what is happening and how their learning progresses.

The students move into small groups and begin to plan their work. As Sam moves around the room, she engages with students at each table. One group wants to know if they could write a rap song. Sam says that sounds ok but that there might be other cultural associations with rap. She asks them to investigate if it would be appropriate to represent Indigenous history through rap music. Sam thinks that she is not sure about this but will engage with the group later after they have completed some research. In another group, each of the four students has pulled out their smartphones and are talking about which app might help them create a diagram or map. Sam listens quietly and is pleased to hear them using the language of the learning outcomes: significance of the Indigenous history, culture and people. These are key terms for this term, and she is excited to hear them begin discussed.

As the unit of work comes to an end, Sam reflects on what the students have created. The 'showcase of learning' she arranged yesterday was impressive. Kai even said she had learned some new ideas for teaching and learning too. Each group had chosen a unique format for sharing their learning. Sam evaluated humanities learning outcomes and some of the skills she saw in Kai's class: creativity, collaboration and problem-solving. Overall, it has been an exciting project, and one Sam hopes to repeat next term in another topic area. She makes a note to herself. Taking a risk and enabling the learners to make choices has been challenging but very rewarding. The learning appears to have been just as effective. There is no need to make things more challenging by developing one task to suit every device in her classroom. The different devices offer a range of creative options for her learners. Next time she will mix up the groups to expose them to different devices and learning strategies. By being more open to different ways of learning, Sam feels confident she has inspired the students to engage more in the content.

CONCLUSION

Bring-your-own-device programmes are increasingly used in schools and education settings to enable learners to access a wide range of online learning resources. There are benefits to this approach to technology in schools, including enabling learners to experience different types of interfaces, learning tools and strategies for interacting with technology. The challenges include that we must be conscious of enforcing a digital divide between learners in our classrooms and that one teaching strategy (such as animations) may not meet the needs of all our learners and their various devices.

Overall, suppose we focus on the learning and the learner. In that case, bring-your-own-device programmes have great potential to ensure our learners have access to relevant and stimulating education.

FURTHER READING

Explore how BYOD might support different ways to teach literacy and numeracy in the classroom:

Alirezabeigi, S., Masschelein, J. & Decuypere, M. (2020). The agencement of taskification: On new forms of reading and writing in BYOD schools. *Educational Philosophy and Theory*, 52(14), 1514–1525.

Read more about equity and learning with a BYOD programme;

Adams, H. R. (2020). *Intellectual Freedom Issues in School Libraries* ABC-CLIO.

Reflect on parents' engagement in BYOD programmes:

Liao, C. C., Cheng, H. N., Chang, W.-C. & Chan, T.-W. (2017). Supporting parental engagement in a BYOD (bring your own device) school. *Journal of Computers in Education*, 4(2), 107–125.

REFERENCES

Bettany-Saltikov, J., McSherry, R., Schaik, P., Kandasamy, G., Hogg, J., Whittaker, V., Racero, G. A. & Arnell, T. (2019). School-based education programmes for improving knowledge of back health, ergonomics and postural behaviour of school children aged 4–18: A systematic review. *Campbell Systematic Reviews*, 16(1–2). doi:10.1002/cl2.1014

Blikstad-Balas, M. & Davies, C. (2017). Assessing the educational value of one-to-one devices: Have we been asking the right questions? *Oxford Review of Education, 43*(3), 311–331. doi:10.1080/03054985.2017.1305045

Consortium for School Networking. (2012). *Making Progress: Rethinking State and School District Policies Concerning Mobile Technologies and Social Media.* www.cosn.org/sites/default/files/pdf/MakingProgress_Web%20-Final.pdf (accessed 21 July 2021).

Dweck, C. (2017). *Mindset: Changing the Way You Think to Fulfil your Potential* (updated ed.). London: Hachette UK.

Maher, D. & Twining, P. (2017). Bring your own device – a snapshot of two Australian primary schools. *Educational Research, 59*(1), 73–88. doi:10.1080/00131881.2016.1239509

Marshall, G. (2015). BYOD benefits include engagement, relevance, personalisation of learning. [Blog.] *ISTE*, 1 January. Retrieved from www.iste.org/explore/entrsekt/BYOD-benefits-include-engagement%2C-relevance%2C-personalization-of-learning (accessed 13 July 2021).

Palmer, D. S. (2017). A look into the planning processes of bring your own device programs in k-12 schools. PhD dissertation, School of Education, University of Pittsburgh.

Straker, L., Maslen, B., Burgess-Limerick, R., Johnson, P. & Dennerlein, J. (2010). Evidence-based guidelines for the wise use of computers by children: Physical development guidelines. *Ergonomics, 53*(4), 458–477. doi:10.1080/00140130903556344

Straker, L., Harris, C., Joosten, J. & Howie, E. K. (2018). Mobile technology dominates school children's IT use in an advantaged school community and is associated with musculoskeletal and visual symptoms. *Ergonomics, 61*(5), 658–669.

Yeop, Y. H. bin, Ali, Z., Norul, S., Asma, U. & Fariza, W. (2018). BYOD implementation factors in schools: A case study in Malaysia. *International Journal of Advanced Computer Science and Applications, 9*(12). doi:10.14569/IJACSA.2018.091245

NEXT STEPS IN YOUR TECHNOLOGY JOURNEY

In concluding this book, we explore how and why technology can be encouraged in the classroom. As a teacher, you are a leader of learning, regardless of your career stage. This means that you have the potential to share your knowledge and skills with your colleagues and inform their practice. Having explored the use of technology in education, examples of practice and learning theories, you are now ready to lead change through modelling and sharing your practice. How best to support others to engage in effective technology use, however, is a challenging question.

A recent research project (Blannin, 2017) sought to improve the quality and relevance of primary school students' educational experiences by better understanding teachers' decisions to use, or not to use, technologies. In this research, we understood that a teacher is a key contributor to improving student outcomes (Hattie, 2009), and so we focused on the teacher in their classroom.

We sought to understand how teachers decide to use technology because if teachers make more effective use of technologies, student learning experiences and outcomes may improve. A range of research supports this connection (Pow and Fu, 2012), and we wanted to understand why, despite this strong evidence, some teachers don't integrate technology into their teaching. We believe that teachers and leaders might use the insights from this study to enhance the quality and relevance of school students' educational experiences. To this end, a diagram was created (Figure 12.1) that shows the factors that appear to inform whether the teacher will, or will not, use technology. Our data tells us three main factors impact whether teachers use technology in their classroom (Blannin, 2017):

1. An awareness of global changes to how we live, beyond schooling
2. An engaged and supportive school leadership
3. An understanding of the professional digital pedagogies that we need to use for teaching and learning.

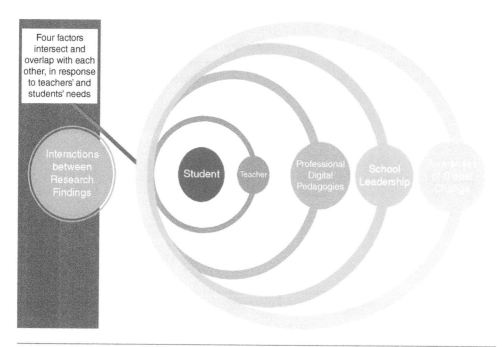

Four factors intersect and overlap with each other, in response to teachers' and students' needs

Figure 12.1 Factors that impact on whether teachers are likely to use technologies in the classroom (Blannin, 2017)

Figure 12.1 represents these factors as a solar system. We use this solar system model to represent the closeness of these factors to each other and their interactions with each other. This provides us with the analogy of orbiting factors within which our student's education sits. As a teacher, we need to understand that these factors can help inform how we use technology in our classroom.

Beginning with the student at the centre, the diagram positions teachers (in orange) as surrounding the student and acting as a conduit for their engagement in the wider world. This suggests that if we focus on the student when we decide how we teach, we may be increasingly motivated to use digital technologies (Blannin, 2017).

The next step out in the solar system diagram, in green, represents the types of learning strategies that teachers might use to learn new skills with technologies. We have labelled these Professional Digital Pedagogies (PDPs). These personal and professional learning strategies are unique to each teacher and might include formal, informal, in situ and off-site learning. This is important for you in your classroom and for how you model learning with and through technology. Traditional professional learning appears to be insufficient for supporting teachers to use technology. We need to consider new learning methods that include reading case studies on blogs, watching videos online, joining social media chat groups, following relevant hashtags or building international partnerships online. These innovative learning strategies are more dynamic and targeted than traditional workshops of after-school training sessions. How might you encourage and model these new ways of developing your skills?

The next orbiting factor, in blue, represents the school leadership. Our school leaders need to provide access to examples of technology careers, industries and higher learning opportunities. School leaders might highlight these global changes by:

- Engaging with technology industry partners to provide examples of skills in practice
- Working with parents and teachers to explore new technologies used at home; for example, artificial intelligence or voice-activated devices
- Supporting teachers to explore emerging, new or industry-based technology resources and devices; for example, geography-focused, location-specific software or augmented reality excursions.

The final factor in this diagram, in turquoise, is teachers' awareness of global changes to the workplace. Teachers and leaders who more readily engage with technologies in the classroom seem to have a deep understanding of the changing nature of the global workforce as a key influence on their choices to use technology (Blannin, 2017). For some teachers, a deeper understanding of how life has changed in workplaces worldwide may inspire them. In turn, this may drive them to ensure that all learners have experiences in new pedagogies and technologies.

In your education setting, this diagram may help you develop support structures for effective technology use. Understanding that awareness of global changes can inspire teachers to engage in new approaches to teaching, for example, means that sharing examples of changing workplace demands in meetings, in emails and with visiting speakers may be helpful strategies.

FACING THE FUTURE OF EDUCATION, SOCIETY AND CHANGE

We are currently living through the most dramatic time of social change in human history. Alongside our family, friends and the global population, we have witnessed changes from pen and paper communications to email, texting and video calls, from weekly cinema viewing to on-demand, Internet-delivered television, and from a single landing on the moon to the recruitment of space tourists and Mars colonists. These achievements stem from the human ability to solve problems creatively and they give us a sense of how humans can interact and grow.

Nearly two decades ago, in 2001, futurist Dr Ray Kurzweil concluded that: 'We won't experience 100 years of progress in the 21st century – it will be more like 20,000 years of progress [at today's rate]' (Kurzwiel, 2001).

Even a short reflection on our daily lives proves that much has changed. Even when we consider major events in human history such as the Renaissance, the development of the printing press or the Industrial Revolution, we still find no precedent, strategies or references for adapting to change at this speed. From online banking, shopping and dating to 3D printing, virtual reality and massive open online courses (MOOCs), being a global citizen today demands new skills and experiences.

Consider this, if you use email, social media, mobile devices, tablet computers, cloud-based storage, wireless Internet, blogs, wikis or digital cameras – you have the last 20 years to thank. Of Kurzweil's 147 predictions since the 1990s, 115 have proven accurate within a year or two, giving him a hit rate of 86 per cent (Diamandis, 2017). With this impressive track record, we are inclined to trust Kurzweil when he says there will be no slowdown in this pace of change.

His predictions in 2015 suggest that we should already be focusing on the next big, emerging technologies. Are you ready for virtual reality and holograms in your home or for accessing your uploaded consciousness and that of your ancestors from cloud computers (Lewis, 2013)? Most of us can agree that the predicted mass decline of disease can only be positive, despite population number concerns (University of Notre Dame, 2019). By 2030, nano-robots will likely be programmed to take over numerous biological functions, effectively eliminating death from common disease. Change and technological growth will remain a constant in society throughout our lifetimes (Price et al., 2017).

For some people, these changes might make us panic. For others, we might be excited about our futuristic planning. As a society, we have no precedent, strategies or references for adapting to change at this speed or on this global scale. In education, in particular, we need to ensure that we provide learning that equips today's humans to become influential citizens. Taking onboard calculated predictions from experienced educators worldwide (Alexander et al., 2019), the classroom of 2040 will look very different.

To conclude this book, let us face a possible future head-on. What does ongoing technological change mean for our children and grandchildren in classrooms of 2040? Potentially, it may look something like this:

As Year 8 teacher Anh enters his English classroom, his Internet-connected glasses flash up a reminder, 'Nick is away today', and the implant under his skin buzzes gently. Anh waves the reminder away by moving his finger in front of his face. He'll update the roll later.

This classroom has no defined teacher space, so Anh moves to the window and taps his implant to connect to the room's Wi-Fi. His glasses provide the weather update, overlaying the view in a mixed reality way – it will be a rainy bike ride home.

As he scans the room, he uses the mixed reality to check that the interactive walls, heating and lighting are all set to his preferences. The door facial recognition

(Continued)

scanner usually identifies him and sets his preferences automatically, but it's always good to check.

The classroom is open with couches and comfortable chairs. On each arm, a small flexible screen is attached. Ahn is glad that he doesn't have to deal with broken device screens anymore. These flexible paper-sized screens are so easy for students to use, connect to and share.

There isn't any maintenance either. A win for the school administration, he knew.

Every wall is covered in interactive wallpaper, with no wires or cables to be seen. Thank goodness for air-harvested power, he thinks.

On one section of the interactive wall, three students are finishing their homework from the last lesson. They add the final drawing (with their finger) and double-tap the wall to submit it.

More students arrive, with the usual noise and boisterous exclamations. Anh calls them to attention, and they settle down.

Some students move to the couches, some to the stools near the interactive walls. Others pick up a digital notebook from the table at the back of the room and find their friends. Ahn looks around the room, scanning faces and taps in the air in front of him to submit the role. Anh begins the lesson.

Each student has worked on an individual project this term, and Anh has accessed analytics from their devices to plan today's lesson.

Three students spent a lot of time on YouTube last lesson. They looked at on-topic videos, but the amount of re-watching and reviewing a particular concept has Ahn concerned. He'll work with those students first.

He directs them to one side of the room and asks them to log in (via secure fingerprint identification). He'll join them in a moment. Four students seem to have finished their project, but they need to be challenged to go deeper.

The virtual assistant in the online word processor sent Ahn an email last night noting that their vocabulary, technical language and sentence structures lacked the complexity expected. Anh has noted this and has a set of questions for this group to answer today.

Ahn looks at the floor, and his heads-up display appears. From the projection, he selects the list of questions he prepared and sends them to the students in front of him. They head off to begin work on their flexible screens.

The rest of the students work on their projects. Ahn spends the rest of the lesson moving between the groups. He shares ideas and examples digitally, and by the end of the lesson, he has a plan for each student for next week. He'll gather today's analytics this afternoon and finalise everything.

As Ahn heads home, he's excited for tomorrow. He has booked the immersive virtual reality lab. The class will be off to Stratford-upon-Avon to watch Shakespeare's *Othello* and then on to a Q&A with Shakespeare himself.

All the technology in this scenario is available now or about to be launched. These are not aspirational tools but existing products that are currently being tested around the world. The challenge, of course, is that these are the technologies we know about. What else might be developed in the next 10, 20 or 30 years? How might they impact on our role as teachers? It is up to us to help our learners engage in a world of technology-enabled workplaces and changes to our daily lives.

How will your students change the world? What might you need to learn next? We don't know – and that's the exciting role of today's teacher – we keep an eye on today, with tomorrow firmly in view.

REFERENCES

Alexander, B., Ashford-Rowe, K., Barajas-Murphy, N., Dobbin, G., Knott, J., McCormack, M., Pomerantz, J., Seilhamer, R. & Weber, N. (2019). *Educause Horizon Report: 2019 Higher Education Edition*. Retrieved from www.learntechlib.org/p/208644/ (accessed 13 July 2021).

Blannin, J., (2017). Accounting for teachers' choices to use, or not to use, Web 2.0 technologies in upper primary school classrooms (PhD dissertation, The University of Melbourne). Retrieved from https://minerva-access.unimelb.edu.au/handle/11343/208015 (accessed 5 July 2021).

Diamandis, P. H. (2017). *86% Accuracy Rate in Tech Predictions*. Retrieved from www.diamandis.com/blog/86-accuracy-rate-in-tech-predictions (accessed 13 July 2021).

Hattie, J. (2009). *Visible Learning: A Synthesis of Over 800 Meta-analyses Relating to Achievement*. Abingdon: Routledge.

Kurzweil, R. (2001). *The Law of Accelerating Returns*. Retrieved from www.kurzweilai.net/the-law-of-accelerating-returns (accessed 13 July 2021).

Lewis, T. (2013). *The Singularity Is Near: Mind Uploading by 2045? | Live Science*. www.livescience.com/37499-immortality-by-2045-conference.html (accessed 21 July 2021).

Pow, J., & Fu, J. (2012). Developing digital literacy through collaborative inquiry learning in the Web 2.0 environment – An exploration of implementing strategy. *Journal of Information Technology Education: Research, 11*, 287–299.

Price, D., Claxton, G., Stevenson, M., Robinson, L., Kidd, D., Hannon, V., Waters, M., Roberts, H., McGill, R. M., Barwell, C., Holt, M., Rees, J., Stewart, H., Knight, J., Roskilly, N. & Jackson, D. (2017). *Education Forward: Moving Schools into the Future*. London: Crux Publishing Ltd.

University of Notre Dame (2019). Can we feed 11 billion people while preventing the spread of infectious disease? *ScienceDaily*. Retrievable from www.sciencedaily.com/releases/2019/07/190702184601.htm (accessed 13 July 2021).

INDEX